T0301429

THE KEYNESIAN REVOLUTION AND ITS ECONOMIC CONSEQUENCES

For John Thompson
who has seen it all before

The Keynesian Revolution and its Economic Consequences

Selected Essays by Peter Clarke

Peter Clarke

Professor of Modern British History,
University of Cambridge, UK

Edward Elgar

Cheltenham, UK • Northampton, MA, USA

Published by
Edward Elgar Publishing Limited
8 Lansdown Place
Cheltenham
Glos GL50 2HU
UK

Edward Elgar Publishing, Inc.
6 Market Street
Northampton
Massachusetts 01060
USA

A catalogue record for this book is available from the British Library

Library of Congress Cataloguing in Publication Data
Clarke, Peter, 1942–
    The Keynesian revolution and its economic consequences: selected essays/by Peter Clarke.
    Includes bibliographical references and index.
    1. Keynes, John Maynard, 1883–1946. 2. Economists—Great Britain—Biography. 3. Keynesian economics. 4. Great Britain—Economic policy. I. Title.
HB103.K47C528   1998
330.15'6—dc21   97–29957
                                                                                   CIP

ISBN 1 85898 590 0

Printed and bound in Great Britain by
Biddles Ltd, Guildford and King's Lynn

Contents

Acknowledgements
and original places of publication

Apart from the footnote changes indicated in this volume by square brackets, the text has been reprinted substantially as it originally stood, though minor infelicities or anachronisms have been silently amended. I have also excised some repetitious material, notably in chapter 1, recapitulating references now accessible elsewhere in this volume.

The publishers wish to thank the following who have kindly given permission for the use of copyright material.

Chapter 1   Cambridge University Press 'The Historical Keynes and the history of Keynesianism', in T.C.W. Blanning and David Cannadine (eds), *History and Biography: Essays in Honour of Derek Beales*, 1996, pp. 203–26.

Chapter 2   Originally published as 'J.M. Keynes, 1883–1946: 'The best of both worlds', in Susan Pedersen and Peter Mandler (eds), *After the Victorians: Essays in Memory of John Clive*, Routledge, 1994, pp. 170–87.

Chapter 3   Oxford University Press for 'The politics of Keynesian economics, 1924–31', in Michael Bentley and John Stevenson (eds), *High and Low Politics in Modern Britain*, 1983, pp. 154–81.

Chapter 4   Previously unpublished.

Chapter 5   Originally published as 'Hobson and Keynes as economic heretics', in Michael Freeden (ed.), *Reappraising J.A. Hobson*, Allen and Unwin, 1990, pp. 100–15.

Chapter 6   *History of Political Economy* for 'Keynes in history', *History of Political Economy*, xxvi (1994), pp. 117–35.

Chapter 7   Woodrow Wilson Center for 'The Treasury's analytical model of the British economy between the wars', in Barry Supple and Mary Furner (eds), *The State and Economic Knowledge*, Cambridge University Press, 1990, pp. 171–207.

Chapter 8   Professor F.B. Smith for 'The twentieth century revolution in government: the case of the British Treasury', in F.B. Smith (ed.), *Ireland, England and Australia: Essays in Honour of Oliver MacDonagh*, Cork University Press, 1990, pp. 159–79.

Chapter 9   Originally published as 'Keynes, Buchanan, and the balanced budget doctrine', in John Maloney (ed.), *Debt and Deficit: An Historical Perspective*, Edward Elgar, 1997.

Chapter 10   Anthony Seldon for 'The Keynesian consensus and its enemies: the argument over macroeconomic policy in Britain since the Second World War', in David Marquand and Anthony Seldon (eds), *The Ideas that Shaped Post-War Britain*, HarperCollins, 1996, pp. 67–87.

Every effort has been made to trace all the copyright holders but if any have been inadvertently overlooked the publishers will be pleased to make the necessary arrangements at the first opportunity.

Footnote citations

All books cited are published in London unless otherwise specified.

All references to Keynes's own published writings are to the excellent Royal Economic Society edition, edited by Donald Moggridge and Austin Robinson, *The Collected Writings of John Maynard Keynes*, 30 vols. (1971–89), cited as *JMK*, with the volume number.

Square brackets indicate substantial additions to a footnote for this edition.

Introduction

1

John Maynard Keynes remains the most influential economist of the twentieth century; but his four major claims to importance are not all strictly economic. Firstly, he was a publicist who presented the classic critique of the Versailles peace settlement at the end of the First World War. Secondly, he emerged as a spokesman for radical changes in British domestic economic policy between the wars. Thirdly, during the Second World War, he exercised an official responsibility for restructuring international financial relations. Fourthly, through his book *The General Theory of Employment, Interest and Money*, he challenged the theoretical assumption that the economy was in principle self-righting, and thereby established 'Keynesianism' as a doctrine of demand management by the state, aimed at maintaining full employment.

The centenary of his birth in 1983 caught his reputation at an awkward moment; and 1986, the fiftieth anniversary of the publication of the *General Theory*, was hardly better. The 1980s were not kind to Keynes's memory, still less to the credibility of his doctrines. The rise of 'Thatcherism' in Britain and of 'Reaganomics' in the USA saw the explicit rejection of a Keynesian approach to economic problems – now denounced as 'the policies that failed before'. Margaret Thatcher claimed from time to time that she was actually the true follower of Keynes, which was a backhanded tribute to the continuing hold of his name. It took Ronald Reagan to put him down with the one-liner that this man Keynes didn't even have a degree in economics.

The man whom I call 'the historical Keynes' ought to be understood in the context of his own times and his own preoccupations, while the subsequent institutionalization of 'Keynesianism' needs to be comprehended as a different, if closely related, historical problem. The essays collected in this volume take up these themes in different ways, and often in considerable detail; but a more general account of the career of the historical Keynes may be the most helpful way to begin.

2

It has often been noted that Keynes was a Cambridge man through and through, born in the city and bred in the university. His father was a philosopher who became a leading administrator in the university; his mother was the first female mayor of the city. Harvey Road, where they lived throughout a remarkably long marriage, has found its very name appropriated as a symbol of the ordered world in which young Maynard, born in 1883, grew up. The precocious boy was sent to Eton and, like many Etonians in those days, went on to King's College, Cambridge, where he read mathematics. In 1905 he gained a First Class degree in Mathematics, Twelfth Wrangler, as the traditional rank order had it – a good but not brilliant result. As an undergraduate he was president of both the Liberal Club and the Cambridge Union Society, with a well-formed aptitude for political controversy, notably on the side of free trade. He was also a member of the select society, known as the 'Apostles', which became the core of the Bloomsbury group – a cultural force whose influence need not be laboured, with two of the foremost novelists of the first half of the twentieth century, Virginia Woolf and E.M. Forster, within its mutually admiring circle. Keynes's close friendship with the writer Lytton Strachey and the painter Duncan Grant, also 'Bloomsberries', was reinforced by their shared homosexuality.

After two years as a civil servant in the India Office, Keynes returned to Cambridge in 1908 to teach economics, with a salary provided by Professor Alfred Marshall, a family friend as well as the leading figure in the British economics profession. It was as Marshall's protégé that Keynes became an economist, though his strictly academic research was still in the field of probability, on which his dissertation won him a Fellowship at King's in 1909. With useful connections like these, Keynes became editor of the *Economic Journal*, the foremost periodical in the discipline, in 1911, as a young university teacher still under thirty. This was to be an important thread of professional continuity in an otherwise extraordinarily diverse career.

During the First World War he entered the Treasury as a civil servant and was soon entrusted with wide responsibility for the external finance of the war. Keynes's attitude to the war was the product of conflicting claims upon him. He was not a pacifist but, like many of his Bloomsbury friends, he asserted a conscientious objection to conscription. Many conscientious objectors faced hardship and even prison for their beliefs; but Keynes was spared such consequences by his privileged position in the Treasury. He went to the Versailles peace conference as the official representative of the Treasury, but he had already manifested signs of unrest because of his liberal outlook. It is not altogether surprising that he resigned in June 1919, dismayed by the heavy scale of reparations demanded from Germany, and determined to expose the Treaty's shortcomings. Within a few months *The Economic Consequences of the Peace* (1919) was ready to be launched upon a tide of already expectant public opinion, which it caught with a remarkably complete measure of success. Keynes revealed, moreover, his striking distinction as a writer, fusing high moral passion and soaring metaphors with hard economic analysis, limpidly expounded. The nub of his case was that reparations implied a transfer of wealth from poverty-stricken Germany in the form of real resources, which Germany could only generate by establishing a degree of economic domination over the rest of Europe for which no one was prepared.

The enthusiastic reception accorded to the book, which made its author a household name in educated circles on both sides of the Atlantic, gave Keynes a platform of which he made full use thereafter. Though keeping his Fellowship at King's, Keynes did not revert to full-time academic teaching and research after the war. He never held a university chair of economics and when people called him 'Professor Keynes' he would jokingly protest that he refused to accept the indignity without the emoluments. Keynes's attitude towards economics – 'An easy subject, at which very few excel!' – was thus somewhat ambivalent. No one was less content to leave economics to the economists.

After the First World War, then, Keynes divided his time between Cambridge and his house in Bloomsbury, where the cultural and business life of London, as well as politics, were open to him. He became a rich man through speculation, worth half a million pounds at the peak in 1936. (This would have to be multiplied by at least twenty in today's values). He married the ballerina Lydia Lopokova in 1925 and they had a happy if childless marriage, sustained by a common interest in the arts, of which Keynes was a great patron. Indeed he was later to play a vital role in enlisting government support for the arts through the formation of the Arts Council of Great Britain.

3

From the time of the First World War onward, Keynes was called on periodically by government for expert advice over economic policy. The arguments in which he became engaged had an inescapable political twist which Keynes did not seek to evade. Indeed in the late 1920s he sought to politicize economic policy by insisting that government must accept responsibility for its adverse economic consequences, especially mass unemployment. In 1925 Keynes found his confidential advice overruled when he argued against an imminent return to the Gold Standard at the traditional parity of $4.86. When the Chancellor of the Exchequer, Winston Churchill, announced Britain's return to Gold, Keynes took the decisive step of openly using the press to make his criticisms public. He argued that, with an inappropriately high parity for sterling, the monetary mechanism would not in fact work smoothly to deflate domestic prices but would provoke unemployment. At this stage, however, Keynes did not doubt the (Marshallian) postulate that a market-clearing equilibrium would be established in the long run.

It is sometimes asserted, and even more often implied, that Keynes was irresponsible. His most famous dictum – 'In the long run we are all dead' – is customarily cited in this sense. What Keynes meant when he proclaimed this in the 1920s was not that the future could be treated with feckless disregard but that it was irresponsible for policy-makers to close their eyes to the immediate impact of their actions by assuming that it would 'all come out in the wash'. He wanted them to appreciate the consequences of big decisions, not to ignore them.

In the 1920s Keynes, in collaboration with another Cambridge economist, Hubert Henderson, became actively involved in Liberal Party politics. Keynes's support for dynamic, optimistic, radical politicians like Lloyd George and Oswald Mosley was rooted in temperamental affinities. 'We need the breath of life', Keynes insisted in the 1929 General Election. 'There is nothing to be afraid of.' Little wonder that he later endorsed the New Deal policies of Franklin Roosevelt, with his message to the American people that they had nothing to fear but fear itself. Keynes was the quintessential exponent of 'can-do' economies.

When the Liberal Party entered the 1929 General Election with a pledge to cut the high level of unemployment to 'normal' proportions, Keynes and Henderson produced their famous pamphlet *Can Lloyd George Do It?* in support. Public works, it suggested, notably a loan-financed scheme of road-building, could stimulate a cumulative process of economic recovery. Essentially this was a plea for a bold state-led initiative, in the confident hope that, with spare capacity available, such a programme would succeed in mobilizing idle resources.

The inconclusive election results, however, suggested that Keynes had failed to persuade 'outside opinion' of the merits of the Liberal proposals, and a minority Labour Government took office from 1929 to 1931. Keynes was now given a chance to influence 'inside opinion' through his concurrent membership of the (Macmillan) Committee on Finance and Industry and the newly instituted Economic Advisory Council (especially the EAC's committee of economists, of which Keynes was chairman).

As well as irresponsibility, a parallel charge often levelled against Keynes is that of inconsistency. There is the well-known jibe, in circulation from as early as 1931, that among five economists you would find six opinions, two of them held by Keynes. His interventions in policy debates over the previous couple of years may have fostered this impression. After all, he had advocated public works in 1929 in his pamphlet *Can Lloyd George Do It?* Yet he published an academic book, *A Treatise on Money* (1930), which stated that cheap money was the real solution. Then again, he outlined no less than seven remedies for unemployment, including both public works and cheap money, in testimony to the Macmillan Committee at the beginning of 1930. And later that year he moved towards the option of tariffs.

Keynes plainly did not always say the same thing. But all these different remedies were congruent, and in fact were based upon a common analysis – that of the *Treatise*. The novelty of the *Treatise* was to repudiate the identity of investment and saving. Instead it talked of Enterprise and Thrift as different processes controlled by different people – albeit processes that were in theory brought into equilibrium by the adjusting mechanism of interest rate. With cheap money, Enterprise could be relied upon to do the trick. Why, then, did Keynes urge other policies like public works in Britain at this time? Because, he could reply, cheap money was not on offer so long as Bank Rate had to be kept up in order to protect the high parity of sterling fixed under the Gold Standard. And Britain's return to Gold he now accepted as a *fait accompli*.

Keynes therefore joined forces with others who were prepared to consider appropriate action by government. He supported the proposals put forward by Mosley, then a minister in the Labour Government, for state development programmes. He pushed the EAC's committee of economists towards a programme of both public works and tariffs. He incurred the anger of many old Liberal colleagues by publicly questioning free trade. He drafted an addendum to the Macmillan Report, signed by five other members including the trade-union leader Ernest Bevin, arguing that some decisive break with existing policy, whether in the direction of wage cuts or tariffs or public works, was now necessary.

By the time the Macmillan Report was published in the summer of 1931, however, the mounting economic crisis at home and abroad marginalized such proposals, and events rapidly overwhelmed the Labour Cabinet. The government was caught in a spiralling financial and political crisis which threatened the pound sterling on the foreign exchanges. Only when the existing parity seemed untenable did Keynes himself opt for devaluation, though he was relieved when the new National Government found itself forced off Gold in September 1931.

4

After 1931 Keynes severed many of his direct political connections and, with an unaccustomed single-mindedness, devoted his energies to economic theory. Within a surprisingly short time he had stepped outside the analytical framework of the *Treatise* and was arguing out his new theory of effective demand. He was crucially stimulated at this point by the 'Circus' of younger economists at Cambridge, especially by the ideas of R.F. Kahn and J.E. Meade, suggesting a fresh approach to the problem of saving and investment. Instead of investment depending upon prior saving – the orthodox assumption – savings were seen as being generated by an initial act of investment through a process which multiplied income, output and employment.

Thus saving and investment were brought into equality by the equilibrating mechanism of changes in income or output. It followed that equilibrium might be reached while output was still below full capacity or full employment. It followed, too, that changes in output were now assigned the equilibrating task which was fulfilled under orthodox theory (including the *Treatise*) by changes in interest rate. What role, then, did interest play? Keynes proceeded to explain interest in terms of 'liquidity preference' – the premium which wealth-holders exacted for tying up their resources in ways which sacrificed the liquid advantages of holding cash.

The *General Theory* thus gave a wholly new account of how the economy worked – or failed to work. No longer did Keynes point to particular rigidities in the real world as the crucial reason why prices were prevented from making efficacious adjustments which would clear the market. He argued now that reductions in wages or interest rates, even if forthcoming, might simply be incapable of restoring full employment, which was a function of effective demand (that is, of prospective consumption plus investment). Keynes claimed that his theory would 'revolutionise the way the world thinks about economic problems'; but he acknowledged that it would necessarily be infused with political considerations in the process. The *General Theory* itself was largely silent on policy. Keynes, moreover, was fairly tentative and cautious in his subsequent practical recommendations, well aware that bottlenecks in production constrained the full use of resources, and reluctant to advance a practicable target for 'full employment' above a level of 95 per cent.

It was only with the Second World War that Keynes's ideas gained widespread acceptance. In 1940 he was invited back into the Treasury, where he served as a top-level adviser for the rest of his life. The 1941 Budget was based not simply on the need to raise revenue but on a macroeconomic approach – designed to contain inflation by restraining demand for finite resources. Conversely, the feasibility of maintaining full employment after the war was proclaimed in the Coalition Government's White Paper of 1944.

But Keynes's own attention was increasingly consumed by planning for the post-war international economy, seeking new means of discharging the functions of the historic Gold Standard. Keynes played a large part at the Bretton Woods conference (1944) which helped to set up the International Monetary Fund and the World Bank. In contrast to his advocacy of tariffs in the conditions of the 1930s, he now reverted to fundamentally liberal trade policies. His abilities as a negotiator were put to a supreme test at the end of the war when American support for Britain under the lend-lease agreement was abruptly terminated. Keynes was largely responsible for securing a large dollar loan from the USA and Canada to tide Britain over the transition to peace. It was an arrangement which he recognized as at once imperfect and necessitous – a case which he made with telling effect in the House of Lords in December 1945. There can be little doubt that these wearisome transatlantic negotiations taxed Keynes's strength – he had suffered a major heart attack in 1937 – and he died suddenly at Easter 1946, just before the Order of Merit, the supreme honour, could be conferred.

5

The ten essays in this volume were written at various times over the last fifteen years, and some account of the origin and purpose of each essay may be helpful in explaining my intentions at the time I wrote them. It should be remembered that, during the period of their composition, there has been little short of a transformation in the literature bearing on Keynes, so long dominated by Sir Roy Harrod's classic biography, *The Life of John Maynard Keynes* (1951). One important landmark was the completion of the Royal Economic Society's edition of *The Collected Writings of John Maynard Keynes*, in thirty handsome volumes (1971–89). Whatever credit is due elsewhere, especially to Sir Austin Robinson in launching this project, the expanding role assumed by his co-editor, Donald Moggridge, beginning in 1969, proved indispensable in escaping the dispiriting doldrums in which comparable enterprises have become becalmed. In 1992, moreover, Moggridge published his monumental study, *Maynard Keynes: An Economist's Biography*; and in the same year the long-awaited and justly acclaimed second volume of Robert Skidelsky's biography of Keynes, *The Economist as Saviour, 1920–37*, joined his earlier and more controversial volume, *Hopes Betrayed, 1883–1920* (1983). All these volumes, as they successively appeared, helped to shape my own work.

Chapter 1, 'The historical Keynes and the history of Keynesianism', is one of the most recent of my essays in composition, offering an overview of a number of problems explored in more detail later in the book. I wrote it to honour my colleague Derek Beales, whose professional commitment to the practice of both biography and history was signalled in the title given to his festschrift. It seemed to me that the tension between the two approaches was well illustrated by looking first at Keynes himself, with the focus on the immediate context within which he formed his own views, and then surveying the history of the doctrine to which his name was subsequently attached. As with other 'great eponymous isms', a process of ideological distortion could be observed, making 'actually existing Keynesianism' less a function of authorial intentions (which could in principle be recovered by biographical inquiry) and more an ideological outcome that needed historical explanation. If this was true of Keynesianism in Britain, it is hardly surprising that its protean character in other countries that adopted a professedly Keynesian analysis should turn out to be even more foreign to the intentions of its ostensible author. Recognizing this as a perfectly natural process of ideological accommodation, moreover, opens up the prospect of a realistic historical interpretation, rather than a simplistic dispute over alleged deviations from a supposedly unique revelation of true Keynesianism, with a consequent demonization of identified heretics for wilfully polluting the doctrinal wells.

One issue broached in chapter 1 is explored more fully in chapter 2, 'The best of both worlds', which was also written for a festschrift. Alas, John Clive, the intended recipient, died prematurely and the festschrift became a memorial volume; but his concern with finely nuanced explorations in intellectual biography lives on as an inspiration behind my essay. One theme is the uncritical use made by a number of subsequent writers, including Robert Skidelsky in *Hopes Betrayed*, of Keynes's own autobiographical essay, 'My Early Beliefs', thus giving currency to a rebarbative view of the young Keynes as simultaneously a callow hedonist and a callow rationalist. Sir Roy Harrod's concept of 'the presuppositions of Harvey Road' has likewise been used as a frame for this caricature.

It is, of course, this naive and two-dimensional Keynes who has become the butt of the influential 'public-choice' critique of Keynesianism, alleging its deficiency in worldly understanding of the political process. This was one reason why I felt it worthwhile to subject the relevant texts to rather close examination, in arguing the case for seeing a young Keynes who was already seized of more sophisticated ideas than a superficial reading of 'My Early Beliefs' might suggest. It is a theme to which I return in chapter 9.

A second theme in chapter 2, intertwined with the first, is the significance of Keynes's ideas about probability. Since this likewise requires alertness to a number of subtle textual points, this essay may prove as hard for the reader as, I confess, it often did for the writer (in the process of going through more drafts than almost anything else I have written). The reason is that I felt an obligation to do justice to the fine technical research that had been conducted on Keynes's philosophical thought, since this seemed to me to be insufficiently integrated with general accounts of his economic thinking. My own synthesis here rests on original research on Keynes's philosophy by other scholars, whom I hope I have fully acknowledged. The substantive conclusion is an important one since it bears on the epistemological assumptions which underpin Keynes's most important ideas. His concern with the linked concepts of probability, uncertainty and confidence has not, I argue, generally been given sufficient attention in interpreting his mature economic theory, still less in appreciating the tentative and conditional status of his precepts about economic policy. Moreover, the implications for Keynes's view of politics and public opinion, of which he unfortunately never presented an explicit account himself, have been almost entirely ignored. This too is a point to which I return in chapter 9, in discussing public-choice analysis of 'the democratic deficit'.

6

Chapters 3 and 4 belong together, despite the fact that the one was published before any other essays in this volume, while the other is now published for the first time. 'The politics of Keynesian economics, 1924–31', was my first attempt to write about Keynes, and I did so with the natural diffidence of a historian trespassing into territory which was more familiar to economists.

The essay was written, however, in the strong belief that these conventional disciplinary boundaries needed to be traversed. The volume of essays in which it originally appeared was concerned with the genre of historical writing about 'high politics' associated particularly with the name of Maurice Cowling and his college, Peterhouse, Cambridge. I had already identified myself as a critic of the 'Peterhouse school', as the editors well knew in commissioning this essay. Accordingly, one of its aims was to demonstrate to historians the inadequacy of 'high-political' interpretations if, enraptured by the play of tactical considerations, they simply ignored the substantive *content* of sophisticated arguments over economic policy. I did not challenge the notion that ideas are often self-serving, not least in politics; indeed the concept of ideology outlined in chapter 1 (to which I had explicitly been committed since at least 1978) took this for granted as a necessary but not a sufficient part of the explanation. 'How is it that self-serving ideas become current *in one form rather than another*?' I asked, pointing to the double process involved in the generation of ideologies. Adapting Marshall's metaphor of the two blades of a pair of scissors, I wrote of the importance of supply as well as demand in making a market for ideas. And in this context I was a supply-sider.

The other aim of the essay was, correspondingly, to suggest to economists that an 'internalist' history of Keynesianism might be enriched by some alertness to specifically historical 'externalist' factors. What I hoped to show, therefore, was not only how the analysis of the *Treatise on Money* (1930) informed all Keynes's policy advice around the time of its publication, but also how the generation of these theoretical ideas had been influenced by Keynes's own political agenda during the 1920s. His agenda, moreover, seemed to me an obvious extension of pre-war New Liberalism, which, I argued, had framed the political commitment of the young Keynes. What is not made explicit in chapter 3 is that this reading challenges the interpretation advanced by Robert Skidelsky in *Hopes Betrayed*, and does so, of course, for the same reasons more fully developed in chapters 1 and 2.

After publishing this essay, I envisaged that I might write a companion piece, of a similar length, exploring the making of the *General Theory* along similar lines, on the presumption that the immediate political context in which it was formed would prove to have been no less relevant than in the case of the *Treatise*. And I further supposed that, having accomplished this task, a political historian like myself would have exhausted his professional interest in the great economist. It did not work out like that. In the course of an intellectually stimulating period of research leave at the Australian National University in 1983, I became much more deeply enmeshed in problems of comprehending the ideas of the *General Theory*. The origin of these ideas seemed less easily explained by their political context than by their intellectual content. Joan Robinson's remark, that they were 'discovered' rather than 'invented', increasingly seemed a more promising line of investigation than any hypothesis on the process of causation I could suggest as a political historian.

Yet the *General Theory* remained a problem *for historians*, who could not properly ignore it by leaving issues of economic doctrine, in a scholarly division of labour, to the doctrine-historical specialists. This is why I drafted an article – at somewhat greater length than I had originally planned – offering a historical account of the making of the *General Theory*, but one informed by a sense of what was regarded as problematic in the specialist economic literature. This draft was, from the outset, deliberately intended for publication in a leading historical journal, not in one of the journals specializing in the history of economic thought. But the advice of one of the distinguished scholars who kindly read it for me, that I might find difficulty in reaching such an audience, turned out to be well-founded. Undeniably, the eventual negative decision of the journal to which I had submitted the article came as an immediate blow; the editor's kind profession of confidence that the article would nonetheless readily find a place in a doctrine-historical journal perversely reinforced my resolve not to seek alternative channels of publication. This setback induced me to conclude that the ideas which I had tried to encapsulate in a single article, albeit a long one, could best be made accessible to historians (as I still intended them to be) if recast into the more expansive mould of a book. *The Keynesian Revolution in the Making, 1924–36*, published by Oxford University Press in 1988, was the result.

Within that book I took the opportunity of revising and expanding the material in chapter 3, on the making of the *Treatise*; and chapter 4 now publishes for the first time my draft article of 1985, on the making of the *General Theory*. Compared with what later appeared in my book, this version is more dense in exposition but also more taut in argument; perhaps it assumes more prior knowledge on the part of the reader; perhaps it would, after all, have made most sense to a doctrine-historical constituency. Apart from questions of presentation, there are two significant differences from the text of my subsequent book in the evidence that could be cited.

In 1985 the unique surviving copy of Kahn's original paper of 1930, sketching a 'multiplier' effect for the EAC's committee of economists, could not be traced in the Keynes Papers. I therefore had to infer its contents from other accounts. In its absence, it seemed to me a document of tantalizing importance; once it turned up again, as it did in 1986, when Don Moggridge kindly sent me a copy, it seemed less momentous. But its temporary, accidental withholding left a permanent mark on my interpretation, I think, in alerting me to the important difference between Kahn's calculations about unemployment in 1930 and 'Mr Meade's Relation', as presented in the famous *Economic Journal* article of 1931, introducing the concept which subsequently became celebrated as 'the multiplier'. For it was the way that Meade generalized the relationship here that gave the multiplier its dynamic influence at the heart of the theory of effective demand. I am not sure if I would have seen this so clearly had the

Keynes Papers not been in the throes of removal and recataloguing at the time I was writing.

A second difference in the archival resources available to me turns on the Treasury file (T172/2095), the discovery of which, also in 1986, I describe fully in chapter 6 below. For this turned out to be the crucial source in establishing the nature of the 'Treasury View' of 1928–9, thus providing what I called the 'documentary spine' of chapter 3 in *The Keynesian Revolution in the Making*. It was one of the book's three innovative claims which I advanced in writing 'Keynes in history', reprinted below as chapter 6. 'Seeing the story in this way', I conclude there, 'partly depends on intellectual inferences from writings that have long since been published; but it also depends partly on finding a file that no one had looked at for half a century'. But the interpretation in my draft of 1985 – drafted, of course, without the benefit of consulting this file – now that I reread it today, looks relatively little different in outline from what I was able to substantiate more fully later. Finding the file, in short, seems to have played a rather less decisive role in forming my own interpretation than I came to think; though it admittedly armed my account with the authority of specific citation rather than having to rely on my own inferences to persuade others.

7

Towards the end of chapter 4 there is a rather brief discussion of the influence of J.A. Hobson on the formulation of the *General Theory*. This is a question which has long interested me; indeed, since I was a scholar of Hobson in the first instance, it constituted the path that first led me to study Keynes. The welcome growth in scholarly attention to Hobson's thinking in recent years is exemplified by the volume, edited by Michael Freeden, *Reappraising J.A. Hobson*, for which 'Hobson and Keynes as economic heretics' (chapter 5) was originally written. What had long struck me about the thought of the two economists was their common emphasis on what Hobson called 'the individualist fallacy', or what Keynesians generally term 'the fallacy of composition'. It was this rather than any technical economic concept which suggested an affinity in their thought, though looking for a more specific direct influence from Hobson to Keynes proved a fruitless quest. Nonetheless, this sort of logical distinction between what is true for the individual and what is true in aggregate seems to me to be worth very serious attention. This is why I have been tempted to call it 'the general theory behind the *General Theory*'. It is the fundamental conception which links Keynes to the development of macroeconomics and to game theory.

'Keynes in history' (chapter 6) was originally commissioned by the journal *History of Political Economy* as part of a symposium on Keynes as seen by other disciplines. I took the opportunity of offering not only a historiographical survey on Keynesian economics in Britain but also a methodological manifesto:

both of these served to introduce an appraisal of three aspects of the interpretation laid out in my book, *The Keynesian Revolution in the Making*. One of these, as has been noted above, concerned the new evidence on the Treasury View. Another was a restatement of the need to place Keynes in a fully rounded historical context, with attention to the different levels on which he was working and the different audiences he was addressing, in order to make sense of what he was saying as publicist, expert and theorist.

Finally, chapter 6 offers a recapitulation of my case for dating Keynes's intellectual revolution to 1932, subject to two qualifications. First, I accentuate a distinction between the theory of effective demand and the *General Theory*, given that I have come to attach more significance to uncertainty, notably as a result of Bradley Bateman's work, which is now happily published and susceptible of proper citation in chapter 6. My second qualification takes account of the publication of the Moggridge and Skidelsky biographies. In the light of their accounts, I suggest that what Keynes intuitively felt he *knew* in 1932 could only be *proved* by him in 1933. This whole dispute over dating the evolution of Keynes's ideas – which it is tempting to dismiss as scholastic quibble – has masked a deeper issue about the nature of those ideas and about the grounds on which they can be said to have been properly established. This, rather than technical in-fighting over a few months here or there, is the sort of argument that chapter 6 seeks to advance.

8

The remaining four chapters focus on economic policy rather than theory. 'The Treasury's analytical model of the British economy between the wars' was prepared for a conference in Washington, DC, in 1988 on the general subject of the role of economic knowledge in government; and cognate points from other participants in this conference are accordingly acknowledged in chapter 7. I wrote this essay having recently completed *The Keynesian Revolution in the Making*, and surveying some of the same arguments, but this time from the point of view of the Treasury rather than Keynes. As a result, I paid close attention to the extent to which Treasury policy changed over time, not only in its practical effect but in its intellectual orientation. The thinking of other economists – not just Keynes – played a part in explaining this; and the influence of Ralph Hawtrey within the Treasury struck me as particularly interesting as the source of notions of counter-cyclical macroeconomic management that owed little to the *General Theory*.

Chapter 8 pursues the question of the influence of theoretical ideas upon government. It was called 'The twentieth-century revolution in government' because it was written in 1989 in honour of Oliver MacDonagh, whose classic article, 'The nineteenth-century revolution in government' had, since its publication thirty years previously, proved seminal for the study of British administrative history. MacDonagh's point, that Benthamism had been unduly credited with influence on nineteenth-century government, on the basis of little more than sweeping inferences about the supposed influence of classic texts, prompted me to subject Keynesianism to similar scrutiny.

But if the influence of ideas, in forms faithful to their begetters, was not axiomatic, nor could the strong axioms of public-choice theory about bureaucratic self-aggrandizement adequately describe the dynamics of British government. So I argue in chapter 8, with special reference to the British bureaucratic tradition; and in chapter 9 I extend this critique to the British democratic experience. 'Keynes, Buchanan and the balanced budget doctrine' had its origin as a paper to the History of Economic Thought conference on Debt and Deficits at Gresham College in February 1996. It subjects James M. Buchanan's propositions about a Keynesian 'democratic deficit' to empirical scrutiny, measured against the historical record of British public finance. In chapter 1, the point is adumbrated that budgets were actually in surplus, by the established conventions of the day, during most of the Keynesian era; chapter 9 presents fuller statistics to substantiate the case, with some minor improvements in the method of calculation. Although it seems surprising, this is, so far as I am aware, the first time that such an exercise has been performed.

The other mission of chapter 9 is to report Keynes's own views on balanced budgets. Again, apart from a neglected paper by J.A. Kriegel, this appears not to have been attempted previously. Since Keynesianism continues to be associated so persistently with the advocacy of budget deficits, it is salutary to be reminded of just how little textual sanction for this view can actually be found in Keynes's own writings. Conversely, the regime of fiscal prudence which prevailed in Britain for a quarter of a century after his death represents a rare example of apparent fidelity in Treasury policy to the spirit, if not the letter, of his own precepts. Indeed the identification – or misidentification – of Keynes with proposals to overload the post-war British economy with the crippling burden of a welfare state provided the theme for a further essay, not reprinted here but speaking to the same point.[1]

Finally, in chapter 10 there is a study of the rhetoric rather than the content of post-war Keynesianism. This was originally conceived in 1995 as a paper to a conference in Sheffield, organized around the ideas of Albert O. Hirschman, whose suggestive study, *The Rhetoric of Reaction* (1992), informs my own text at several junctures. The stylized strategies of argument which Hirschman identifies – a hopeful appeal to 'synergy' in progressive rhetoric or a sceptical invocation of 'futility' in the rhetoric of reaction – can certainly be illustrated from British examples. Not only is it evident that so-called Keynesianism departed from the substance of the policy advice of the historical Keynes: it is also clear that the heirs of the post-war consensus took little heed – and even less as time went on – of the prudential caveats that initially hedged the Keynesian prospectus.

9

I trust that it will now be clear why I have called this book *The Keynesian Revolution and its Economic Consequences*. That there was a Keynesian revolution is a proposition of which I remain convinced. This revolution was not only in economic theory but also in economic policy. The relation between the two is not simple, as I hope to have shown; and the line of causal influence in the generation of new ideas did not necessarily run from theory to policy. Moreover, even when the influence of this particular academic scribbler did have economic consequences, these were often opaque rather than transparent, with highly imperfect fidelity to the utterances of the historical Keynes.

Yet as an inveterate political animal – as I persistently suggest him to have been – Keynes might have been less surprised, less disconcerted, about such consequences, than might be supposed. To say that he grew up in Harvey Road has a nice ambiguity about it: implying to some that a form of arrested development is the key to his later as well as his early beliefs; while, conversely, I would prefer to seize on the opposite implication that Keynes's thinking *matured* while he was a young man, reconciling to his own satisfaction the claims of public duty and private morality. And the changing form of his specifically economic ideas, which indeed underwent a revolution when he was approaching the age of fifty, should be understood as framed by interlocking assumptions, not only about the nature of knowledge itself, but about the inescapability of acting under conditions of imperfect information.

Hitherto the impact of Keynesianism upon policy has mainly been studied by economic historians, who have usually been concerned with the manipulation of policy from above by an administrative elite. This is a hydraulic conception of Keynesianism, imputing to government a claim to efficacy that has increasingly been mocked in the last thirty years – not only by economists and politicians but also, more tellingly, by events. By contrast, what might be called the Keynesian reception-literature has been less fully studied. Such a study would focus on the question of what was understood and propagated as Keynesianism in scholarly articles and books, in university courses, and in academic debates of a more popular character, especially in the twenty years after the Second World War.

If this doctrine-historical theme has yet to be fully explored, a third kind of historical inquiry has hardly begun at all – a study of the public rhetoric of Keynesianism. For this too helped shape what I call 'actually existing Keynesianism'; and just as it was the failure of 'actually existing socialism' in Eastern Europe that sealed the virtual demise of Marxist theory, so (albeit on a less cataclysmic scale) the practical deficiencies of ostensibly Keynesian economic management in the West inevitably proved damaging to the status of the *General Theory* itself. Now that the public rhetoric of Gladstonianism, as an earlier paradigm in British political economy, has been illuminated by historians of the calibre of H.C.G. Matthew and Eugenio Biagini, perhaps it is time for political historians of late twentieth-century Britain to emulate such research.

The problem of how professedly Keynesian precepts became imbricated with more immediate political arguments and priorities is one that the historical Keynes would have recognized. There is thus an agenda, of a kind that the penultimate page of the *General Theory* identified as needing to be addressed in 'a volume of a different character from this one', that now needs scholarly attention. The ideas of the historical Keynes about uncertainty and confidence, his hints about the complementary roles of expertise and public opinion, his sense of the potent encroachment of ideas rather than the inevitable entrenchment of vested interests, and his own commitment to the politics of persuasion, provide clues about the lines on which such a history might be written.

Note
1. This takes the form of a critique of the concept of 'New Jerusalem' as developed in two influential books by Correlli Barnett: *The Audit of War: The Illusion and Reality of Britain as a Great Nation* (1986) and *The Lost Victory: British Dreams, British Realities, 1945–50* (1995). See Peter Clarke, 'Keynes, New Jerusalem, and British Decline', in Peter Clarke and Clive Trebilcock (eds), *Understanding Decline: Perceptions and Realities of British Economic Performance* (Cambridge, 1997) pp. 145–65.

1 The historical Keynes and the history of Keynesianism

1

John Maynard Keynes lent his name to the most influential paradigm in the political economy of the mid twentieth century. During the last thirty years a distinction – though not always the same distinction – has increasingly been drawn between Keynes and Keynesianism. To study Keynes himself points towards problems which are essentially biographical, just as the impact of Keynesianism indicates problems which are more broadly historical; one approach enters into disputes about intentions, while the other is more concerned with assessing outcomes; and the two projects need to be linked.[1] Major biographies by Donald Moggridge and Robert Skidelsky have now modified important features of Sir Roy Harrod's great monument to his friend, and thereby helped to retrieve the historical Keynes: a child born in the year that Marx died, a Victorian in his eighteenth year at the end of the old queen's reign, a man of only sixty-two at his death in 1946. Recently, Keynes's early beliefs, of which he gave a famous account, and his work on probability have become the focus of lively debate among historians, philosophers and economists. All of this is relevant to understanding Keynes's own conception of political economy.

The historical fate of Keynesianism is likewise now seen in a new perspective. In the period up to the 1960s, naive Keynesian triumphalism postulated a conversion to Keynes's ideas which was at once inevitable, beneficent, and permanent; since then, vulgar anti-Keynesianism has been premised on Keynes's alleged deficiencies in analysis, foresight and practical wisdom. A more subtle line of criticism has discriminated between the posthumous doctrine and its original begetter, who was necessarily silent throughout subsequent decades of debate around his appropriated name. Axel Leijonhufvud was influential in challenging the academic consensus about the nature of Keynes's own theoretical contribution to economics, back in 1968, while Terence Hutchison was notable in posing similarly awkward questions for latter-day Keynesians about the nature of Keynes's own policy advice.[2]

As Skidelsky rightly says, 'People who give mechanical replies to the question of what Keynes would have done in the 1980s or 1990s ignore the supreme importance he attached to getting the character of the age right as a first step to theorising and policymaking.'[3] Among historians it is now well recognized that a text – or at least a dead author – cannot properly be made to speak on issues, however portentous, which lay outside the author's cognizance at the time of writing. It follows that the form in which influential ideas were conceived may well be different from that with which we have subsequently become familiar. Such 'ideological' distortions may have been a condition of their influence, as the price of the social purchase which they were thereby enabled to exert.[4] The present essay explores the tension between Keynes's own ideas and intentions, as formed in the course of his own lifetime (the biographical theme) and the ideological significance of Keynesianism, involving its selective reception and instrumental uses (the historical theme).

2

When Robert Skidelsky produced the first volume of his long-awaited study of Keynes, *Hopes Betrayed* was an apt subtitle for a book which disappointed and disillusioned many of Keynes's admirers, for a mixture of reasons, private as well as public. *Hopes Betrayed* was a big Bloomsbury biography, of Holroydian proportions, in which Skidelsky rounded up the usual suspects and washed their dirty linen in public. To those who found this sort of thing unnecessary, there were really two answers. First, it could be said, here was a wholly necessary correction to the hypocrisy of the received version. For a long time after his death, Keynes's homosexuality had not been widely known. It was passed over by Sir Roy Harrod, in his official biography of the great man in 1951. Harrod seems to have been fearful that, if Keynes himself did not appear respectable, the probity of Keynesianism might be impugned at a critical stage in its reception as the conventional wisdom of Anglo-American political economy. When, in a more permissive era, the gaff was duly blown and the Keynesian boom simultaneously faltered, it looked like Harrod's worst-case scenario.

Skidelsky's other rationale was intellectual, more abstruse and arcane in its implications. Quite deliberately, *Hopes Betrayed* shaped an account of a young man cocooned in a world where the cult of personal relations precluded just the sort of public concerns and commitments which later made him famous. The book exploited the availability of the ton or so of Keynes's own papers to throw many sidelights not only on the official career of the rising civil servant and don but on the charmed path he had trodden from 6 Harvey Road, Cambridge, to Eton and back to Cambridge as a Kingsman; it showed how he had become both an Apostle and a disciple (of the philosophy of G.E. Moore); and surely satiated the most avid reader's curiosity about Maynard and Lytton and Duncan and Leonard and Virginia and Vanessa. . . Thus Skidelsky's first volume only took his hero to his thirty-seventh year – at which age Keynes had published nothing that would cause his name to be remembered as an academic economist. The point of Skidelsky's interpretation was to show a Keynes who had so little that was 'Keynesian' about him.

Here is a biographical problem with both intellectual and political implications. Much of the trouble stems from Keynes's brilliant memoir, 'My Early Beliefs', posthumously published in 1949, which has sometimes been perused in cold print without recognizing its conventions of literary artifice. Keynes claimed that he, like other undergraduate Apostles who sat at the feet of G.E. Moore in Edwardian Cambridge, had 'a religion and no morals' and that 'we completely misunderstood human nature, including our own', through a misplaced attribution of 'rationality' to it.[5] This is the view endorsed in the first volume of Skidelsky's biography.[6]

Harrod's interpretation was governed by what he called 'the presuppositions of Harvey Road' – an overarching assumption, which Keynes inherited from his parents, 'that the government of Britain was and would continue to be in the hands of an intellectual aristocracy using the method of persuasion'.[7] Thus in Harrod's treatment of 'My Early Beliefs', the supposed influence of Moore in temporarily distracting his impressionable disciple is not directly contested; but though Keynes may have walked the tightrope of high philosophical speculation, the presuppositions were invoked by Harrod as a kind of moral safety net which prevented Keynes from falling very far or with any real damage.[8]

'My Early Beliefs' is not accepted uncritically by Skidelsky, for he admits that 'certain liberties with strict truth for the sake of effect and amusement would have been natural'. Yet despite saving phrases, the authority of 'My Early Beliefs' as a source remains integral to Skidelsky's interpretation. The point on which he fastens is that 'Moore provided no logical connection between ethical goodness and political, social or economic welfare'.[9] The logical connection between them is in fact through the theory which Keynes ultimately published as the *Treatise on Probability* (1921). It has been left to Keynes's other recent biographer, Donald Moggridge, to integrate these concerns.[10]

The fact is that Keynes's conception of probability offered a basis for actions to be judged on the basis of their *likely* consequences, rather than Moore's impossible requirement that consequences must be *certain* before any individual discretion could be justified. In general Keynes acknowledged that rules and conventions had a social utility, even though he made a persuasive case against Moore's insistence that they should *always* be obeyed. He was an immoralist in this narrow, tendentious, provocative, teasing definition rather than the broad, vernacular sense which Leonard Woolf correctly disputed. There was thus a firm common basis in Keynes's thinking about private and public claims; and, in licensing personal judgement, he implicitly assumed that it would have been formed and constrained by the same conventional morality which he refused to accept as a rigid and infallible commandment

It is one of the strengths of Skidelsky's second volume, *The Economist as Saviour*, that it restores Keynes to his proper historical context without diminishing the significance of his intellectual achievement. Keynes branches out of Bloomsbury and transcends the Treasury; neither involuted aesthete nor disembodied expert, he emerges as a multi-faceted figure, subject to a complex play of personal, intellectual and political influences. Moreover, it is clear that the related issues of expectations, confidence and uncertainty assume a large part in the story – bulking larger than they did a decade earlier in *Hopes Betrayed*. Part of the reason is technical: Skidelsky has now integrated the research which philosophers have been doing on Keynes's conception of probability into his account of Keynesianism as a whole, in practice as well as theory. This has important implications for the status of the contributions to economic theory which Keynes made in his two major academic works, the *Treatise on Money* (1930) and the *General Theory* (1936).

Keynes's challenge to conventional political economy can be seen in both theory and policy – but not in that order. His quest for remedial policies did not wait for the fruition of his theoretical insights. While he was still essentially a neo-classical economist himself, accepting the theoretical assumption that disequilibrium created its own self-correcting forces – albeit forces which might be thwarted in the real world – Keynes had already committed himself to a radical policy stance which invoked state intervention. His rationale was that government, representing the common interest, had a unique role to play. It could be described variously as that of supplying an initial impulse or a further acceleration, of priming the pump, or of offering a makeweight through public expenditure to a deficiency in effective demand. This is the vision of political economy which we immediately recognize as Keynesian.

'From 1924', Skidelsky suggests, 'Keynes knew what he wanted to do and, in very broad terms, why.'[11] This dating would not be accepted by some Keynesian scholars, most notably Moggridge; but it follows Harrod and it stands up well against the objections which have so far been raised against it. It sees the new departure in an article which Keynes wrote, under Lloyd George's prompting, in the Liberal weekly paper, the *Nation*, calling for a programme of public works. The reasoning was that the economy was 'stuck in a rut' and so needed 'an impulse, a jolt, an acceleration', to break the cycle of low confidence and instead generate 'cumulative prosperity'.[12]

One irreducibly biographical and personal factor may well be relevant to the maturing of Keynes's vision. He got married. The significance of this step has been attested over the years not only by his mother but by so austere a scholar as Lord Kahn. Moggridge provides a telling epigraph to his chapter, 'Lydia and Maynard', from another Cambridge economist, Walter Layton: 'I have long felt that marriage was the one thing left that could give a fresh stimulus to your brilliant career & develop your full powers by harmonising the big reserves of your emotional nature with your intellectual life.'[13] Such contemporary testimony is now given further biographical reinforcement by Skidelsky, who provides the most convincing account of a relationship which successively swept Keynes off his feet and put him on his feet.

Perhaps it is not surprising that Lydia Lopokova made such a big impression on Keynes when she returned to London with Diaghilev's ballet at the end of 1921. His sexually ambivalent nature was no protection against infatuation with her, whatever astonishment this caused in Bloomsbury. Their relationship was sensual and loving, revealing a mutually supportive sympathy that was an education to both of them. That they remained childless was not through choice. If Bloomsbury frowned on the match, so much the worse for Bloomsbury. Vanessa Bell, with whose family Keynes had shared 46 Gordon Square, began a vendetta which was maintained until the death of the two old ladies, ending separate lives in their Sussex farmhouses within a mile of each other. Lydia had a lot to put up with, but Maynard made his choice without equivocation or regret. The fractured friendships of Bloomsbury yielded, albeit with some nostalgic sadness, to the allure of the fractured syntax of 'Lydiaspeak' which provided so many fresh insights on the world. As Lydia said of one critic, 'he does not know that it is poor of him not to allow you to be more than economist, all your "walks of life" make a piquant personality'.[14]

It was, paradoxically, when Keynes became 'more than economist' that his distinctive vision as an economist became apparent. This happened when he was dragged out of the Bloomsbury orbit, not only by Lydia but also by the gravitational pull of public affairs, and in particular the peculiar magnetism of Lloyd George. Keynes's overt political commitment in the 1920s was marked by his emergence as a leading publicist for the Liberal Party, now reinvigorated under the leadership of Lloyd George – the one political leader who sensed that the politics of the future lay in central issues of economic management, thus signalling the need for a more robust political economy than the axioms of 'laissez-faire'. 'I approve Keynes, because, whether he is right or wrong, he is always dealing with realities' was Lloyd George's compliment on Keynes's unemployment initiative in the *Nation* (a remark which Keynes recorded in a characteristic letter to Lydia).[15]

Keynes saw his opportunity for redefining the agenda of government in a way that spoke to new issues, which we immediately recognize as macroeconomic. He began as a critic of the policy of deflation which was the necessary prelude for a return to the orthodox principles of sound finance, hallowed by Britain's pre-war prosperity. The rationale of deflation was to reduce costs to a competitive level, as a transitional adjustment to a new equilibrium, which would in turn permit Britain to return to the Gold Standard at the pre-war parity. Gradually it dawned on Keynes that, in the real world, the adverse consequences of deflation might be rather more than transitional. In that case it was frivolous to claim that 'in the long run' equilibrium would be restored. Keynes's point was that 'this *long run* is a misleading guide to current affairs. *In the long run* we are all dead.'[16] Hence the campaign which Keynes waged against the return to Gold, if it entailed throttling trade through dear money. 'In a longer perspective',

Skidelsky comments, 'it was the start of the Keynesian Revolution.'[17] In short, Keynes challenged laissez-faire as a *policy* well before he had developed a critique of the orthodox economic *theory* of the self-adjusting tendencies of the free market.

3

The theoretical message of the *Treatise* was that savings and investment, being different activities carried on by different people, could not simply be presumed to be identical. It required interest rate to bring saving and investment into equilibrium. As Moggridge has reminded us, it was the *natural* rate of interest which would do this, rather than the *market* rate which actually prevailed at any particular time; and 'the primary task of monetary policy was to prevent their divergence and to provide price stability at full employment.'[18] A reading of the *Treatise* which emphasizes its 'orthodoxy' would point to the tendency towards equilibrium which Keynes's model assumes, so long as the natural rate prevails and is not thwarted in its assigned role. What Skidelsky chooses to emphasize, by contrast, is the *Treatise*'s preoccupation with the economics of disequilibrium, when the economy is in a position of sub-optimal output and hence unemployment. If the rate of interest – or 'bank rate' as Keynes normally said – is what restores equilibrium, it follows that banking policy plays a crucial role in stabilizing the system. 'Order has to be created', Skidelsky asserts: 'it is not natural.'[19] Put in this way – and it is persuasively put – the *Treatise* carries us a long way into the world disclosed by the *General Theory*, in which the absence of self-righting forces in the economy is affirmed.

The inescapable point in the *Treatise* was that disequilibrium was a product of thwarted expectations. When entrepreneurs made their investments, they did so with an expectation of normal profit which failed to materialize. Only when expectations were fulfilled was equilibrium achieved; conversely, disequilibrium was only the problem so long as expectations were not fulfilled. Describing the *Treatise* in this way brings out the centrality of expectations to its model of the economy; but the epistemological frailty or subjectivity of those expectations, in generating the confidence necessary for investment, had still not become central to Keynes's theoretical analysis, still less to his policy advice. Indeed he often spoke at this time as though all that was needed was a magic tool-kit to sort out a mechanical problem. Confidence would be generated by recovery, not vice versa.[20]

Keynes's experience of actual historical developments – from the Wall Street crash of 1929 to the flight from sterling in 1931 – nudged him towards a partial recognition of the importance of business psychology in sustaining or undermining self-reinforcing cycles which took on a life of their own. Keynes had already given some hints, implying perhaps more than he fully intended, in the *Treatise*, where his analysis of 'bullishness' and 'bearishness' built directly upon the experience of boom and bust on Wall Street. His analysis concentrated on 'the fact that *differences* of opinion exist between different sections of the public'. The subjective nature of the estimates of the probabilities involved is the point to note; for it surely represents a shift from the strictly objective epistemology which had formerly underpinned Keynes's academic research on probability. Hitherto he had allowed for probabilistic judgements of the likely consequences of actions – but only for correct or incorrect judgements of those probabilities, given the same access to information, as in a market. Some passages of the *Treatise*, however, paint a picture with a different look to it. On the one side there was was an untrammelled 'bullishness of sentiment'; on the other, stretching the established sense of a 'bear' as one who sold short on the stock exchange, he identified as bears those 'persons who prefer to keep their resources in the form of claims on money of a liquid character realisable at short notice'.[21] Who was in the right frame of mind, the bulls or the bears? It all depended, surely, on whether it was a bull market or a bear market. And what helped to determine that? Why, the relative numbers who were in a bullish or bearish frame of mind, of course! Keynes's arguments imply this, even if his intuitions may have run ahead of his strict formal intentions.

Keynes's concept of liquidity preference built on such foundations. What the *General Theory* did was to develop it as his theory of interest, once he had abandoned the conventional explanation of interest rate as the equilibrator of the economy. The *Treatise* too had attributed this role to interest rate, simply adding the twist that it was an inefficient equilibrator. But the *General Theory* attributed unemployment not to a disequilibrium but instead to an equilibrium – one which was not disturbed by any self-righting pressure from under-employed resources. Moreover, those bargaining over the price of their capital or their labour were impotent in the face of market failure of this kind. The strategies available to individuals (going liquid, cutting wages, reducing spending) were collectively self-defeating. Keynes thus broke the chain of rationality between individual decisions and an optimal outcome for the community which was implicit in the concept of 'the invisible hand' and which had long been regarded as a piece of common sense. 'It is natural to suppose that the act of an individual, by which he enriches himself without apparently taking anything from anyone else, must also enrich the community as a whole', the *General Theory* acknowledged. But its revolutionary message was that the theory applicable to the individual firm did not provide a theory of output *as a whole*.[22]

Though Keynes never used the term himself, plainly there is here a concept of macroeconomics, conceived as the study of the system as a whole, not simply of one sector, however great in magnitude, nor of any sub-set of economic agents, however numerous. Book Two of the *General Theory*, concerned with 'Definitions and Ideas', leads up to a clinching assertion in its concluding sentence of 'the vital difference between the theory of the economic behaviour of the aggregate and the theory of the behaviour of the individual unit'.[23] Indeed in the preface to the French edition Keynes tried to pretend that this was why he had termed it

> a *general* theory. I mean by this that I am chiefly concerned with the behaviour of the economic system as a whole, – with aggregate incomes, aggregate profits, aggregate output, aggregate employment, aggregate investment, aggregate saving rather than with the incomes, profits, output, employment, investment and saving of particular industries, firms or individuals.[24]

His criticism of neo-classical microeconomics – or what he celled 'classical economics' – was precisely that it failed to grasp this macroeconomic dimension.

Keynes himself made two repeated claims about his own thinking during the early 1930s: first, that it underwent a revolution, and secondly, that this rested upon ideas which were 'extremely simple and should be obvious'.[25] There is surely strong reason to regard the fallacy of composition as the overarching concept which informed the creation of the theory of effective demand in the early 1930s. Though the concept was hardly new to the author of the *Treatise on Probability*, it took another decade before the author of the *General Theory* seized upon it as a key which could turn in the lock of a door which he needed to open. When Keynes explained his new theory of effective demand for the first time, in his university lectures in the Michaelmas Term of 1932, he did so by outlining 'two fundamental propositions', both distinguishing between the choices open to individuals and the outcome necessarily true in the aggregate.[26] This distinction provided an analytical tool that could be applied to a variety of decisions: about holding money, about saving and spending, about cutting wages. In this sense, it is the general theory behind the *General Theory*.

'The precise use of language comes at a late stage in the development of one's thought', Keynes said in one of his lectures in 1933. 'You can think accurately and effectively long before you can so to speak photograph your thought.'[27] In the light of this remark, it is interesting to ponder an article which he had written a year previously, while he was struggling to express his new insights, about the essentially circular nature of economic behaviour. 'When we transmit the tension, which is beyond our own endurance, to our neighbour, it is only a question of a little time before it reaches ourselves again travelling round the circle.'[28] Here is an image which could equally well illustrate the centrality of the fallacy of composition in Keynes's current thinking – or the centrality of confidence, through the self-fulfilling nature of the expectations which it generated. The ambiguity may arise because Keynes was not yet in a position to photograph his thought, rather than because the sort of thinking which had now seized him was inaccurate or ineffective. In short, there may be more than one helpful way of describing the revolutionary shift in Keynes's ideas.

A further question arises about how Keynes's own agenda was to be implemented. This is really a political issue, about power and how to mobilise it. The conventional, constitutional mechanism under the parliamentary system is via public opinion, via the ballot box, via the election of sympathetic representatives, and via the formation of a ministry committed to the required policy. Keynes tried this road. He was instrumental in persuading the Liberal Party to stake its fate in the 1929 General Election on a pledge to reduce unemployment by means of a public investment programme. Keynes assumed a high public profile during the campaign with the pamphlet *Can Lloyd George Do It?*, written with Hubert Henderson. But the electoral verdict gave Lloyd George no chance to do it. Instead a minority Labour Government was returned, to which Keynes thereupon turned his attention. He sought to influence its policy through the various channels open to him in 1930, notably the new Economic Advisory Council and the Macmillan Committee on Finance and Industry, to both of which he had been appointed.

Keynes was certainly lucky to have another hat to wear, as an expert, now that his politician's hat had been knocked off. But does that justify Skidelsky in interpreting Keynes's politics as simply statist and elitist, or in identifying Keynes as a Liberal who ended up as a Whig? 'Keynes's anti-market, anti-democratic bias was driven by a belief in scientific expertise and personal disinterestedness which now seems alarmingly naive', Skidelsky states. 'This runs like a leitmotiv through his work and is *the* important assumption of his political philosophy.'[29] There is something in this; but some qualification is also necessary. When Keynes explicitly called himself a 'leftish Liberal' in the 1920s, it seems perverse to insist that he did not know what he was talking about. Likewise, in the face of his reiterated appeals for a dialogue with Labour, and his uniformly dismissive comments on the lack of appeal of Conservatism, not to mention his apparent Labour vote in 1935, to conclude that 'it is easy to imagine Keynes at home, or as at home as he would ever be, in the Conservative Party of Macmillan and Butler' seems rather over-imaginative.[30] In this at least, it should be said, Lord Skidelsky is at one with Sir Roy Harrod, forty years earlier.

Exaggerating Keynes's technocratic bent, at the expense of his experiments in the method of democratic persuasion, creates not only a distorted impression but also a factitious problem. For it then becomes difficult to make sense of his explanation (in 1934) of why his policies had not yet been adopted: 'Because I have not yet succeeded in convincing either the expert or the ordinary man that I am right'. Only when *both* were convinced, he maintained, would economic policy, 'with the usual time-lag, follow suit'.[31]

The *General Theory* supplied a logical reason why there was no effective chain from understandable (and in that sense rational) microeconomic decisions to optimal (and in that sense rational) macroeconomic outcomes. This was a world necessarily bounded by uncertainty, and one therefore in which potent economic decisions had to be based on uncertain expectations. It follows that Keynes's politics of persuasion were part of a process whereby appropriate economic expectations were formed. Indeed Skidelsky shows clearly that such a climate of enlightened confidence constituted the context and premise for the successful implementation of Keynesian policies. Conversely, in the absence of either confidence or enlightenment, the best that could be hoped was to do good by stealth. As Keynes – willing, as usual, to settle for second-best – confided in June 1932, once Neville Chamberlain was firmly installed at the Treasury, 'There are enormous psychological advantages in the *appearance* of economy.'[32] A real iron Chancellor might be a disaster in a slump, but there was some compensation in having one who was lath painted to look like iron. Even so, Keynes's real thrust is better expressed in another comment on Chamberlain: 'Unfortunately, the more pessimistic the Chancellor's policy, the more likely it is that pessimistic anticipations will be realised and *vice versa*. Whatever the Chancellor dreams, will come true!'[33]

4

What might be called the reception-literature on Keynesianism has hitherto focused mainly on its administrative impact. The actual behaviour of the policy-makers has been the focus – some would say the butt – of the public-choice school: essentially a model of decision-making which stresses the policy-makers' own microeconomic motives. Like other men, it is held, bureaucrats are to be seen as motivated by rational self-interest, in ways that subvert the purity of those naive presuppositions of Harvey Road.[34] The simplicities of the public-choice model may themselves be simplistic; but it is well worth asking what Treasury mandarins got out of their job, even if the answer turns on exploring a syndrome of psychic satisfactions rather than identifying crude material benefits accruing to them in pay or perks or even power. The social anthropology of Heclo and Wildavsky within the 'Whitehall village' suggests a more subtle and fruitful line of approach.[35]

The appeal of Keynesianism to the mandarin temperament should certainly not be overlooked. In the inter-war years the Treasury had been intellectually captive to the elegance of the self-acting model of the economy which legitimated 'sound finance'. The model of Keynesianism which they came to adopt in the post-war period also bore a mandarin stamp. Busy policy-makers, of course, did not spend their time poring over the *General Theory* to tease out its doctrine. It is interesting that Sir Richard Hopkins did not read the *General Theory* until he had formally retired as Permanent Secretary at the Treasury in 1945 (though he then read it twice in preparing for the National Debt Enquiry) while Hugh Dalton reread it both on becoming Chancellor of the Exchequer and after resigning from that post.[36] What politicians and civil servants wanted was a handbook readily applicable to specific policy issues – which was not, alas, what Keynes had purported to offer in the *General Theory*. 'It would need a volume of a different character from this one', he stated, 'to indicate even in outline the practical measures in which they might gradually be clothed'.[37]

In the fullest study of wartime and immediately post-war macroeconomic policy-making, Alan Booth suggests that 'the "embedding" of Keynesian analysis in Whitehall' was the result of 'a complex interaction between economic theory, political power, administrative organisation and Britain's economic history in the period 1939–49'.[38] Even so, Keynes's own role is difficult to discount; his influence was felt in virtually every corridor of Whitehall. But he was not the only economist who found and exploited new elbow room as a wartime policy adviser. Lionel Robbins, as Director of the Economic Section, emerged as 'a willing and effective public relations officer for the Keynesian cause' – and one whose credentials were the more impressive in view of his pre-war opposition to Keynes. Conversely, James Meade, already one of the architects of the *theory* of effective demand, now systematized a policy for its practical management. His work with Richard Stone in producing aggregate figures for national income can justly be described as 'a revolutionary departure in British official statistics'.[39] This led to the operationalization of the concepts of the *General Theory* in a way which spoke to the macroeconomic issue raised by the war: how to control inflation.

Keynesian economic theory may have been devised at the bottom of the slump, but it was symmetrical in its policy implications, as its author explicitly affirmed. 'The best we can hope to achieve is to use those kinds of investment which it is relatively easy to plan as a make-weight, bringing them in so as to preserve as much stability of aggregate investment as we can manage at the right and appropriate level', he wrote in 1937, at the peak of pre-war British economic recovery. 'Just as it was advisable for the Government to incur debt during the slump', he argued, 'so for the same reasons it is now advisable that they should incline to the opposite policy'.[40]

Still, there is an obvious irony in the circumstances under which Keynesian ideas achieved their administrative breakthrough. Devised as a strategy to 'conquer unemployment' (as the claim had been made in 1929), a Keynesian macroeconomic analysis was in fact adopted by a hitherto sceptical Treasury in order 'to pay for the war' (in the language of 1939–40). Insofar as the Treasury became Keynesian it was not – in some belated act of intellectual atonement – to adopt a policy of expansion under conditions of deflation, but to impose a policy of restraint under conditions of incipient inflation. This explains the framework adopted in the 1941 Budget, defining the problem of war finance in Keynesian terms, as one of mobilizing maximum resources. The Treasury could now seize upon the same intellectual arguments, which they had previously contested as the premise for expansionist policies, to support the sort of restrictionist measures which they characteristically favoured. Who had converted whom is a moot point.

Another great landmark was when the Coalition Government's White Paper on Employment in 1944 opened with its ringing commitment to 'the maintenance of a high and stable level of employment after the war'. True, many caveats followed, especially the remarkable comment in one paragraph that 'None of the main proposals contained in this Paper involves deliberate planning for a deficit in the National Budget in years of sub-normal trade activity'.[41] Keynes's comment on the penultimate draft was that this section, with its feast of 'budget humbug', had 'the air of having been written some years before the rest of the report'.[42] It derived and survived, as he well knew, from drafts written by Sir Wilfrid Eady, Joint Second Secretary at the Treasury from 1942 to 1952. Keynes had played some part in the debates within Whitehall and evidently found Eady's coy characterization of his Treasury colleagues as 'obtuse, bat-eyed and obstinate' altogether too near the truth. Keynes brushed aside Eady's professions of incomprehension of the theoretical issues at stake, claiming that 'after all, it is very easily understood! There is scarcely an undergraduate of the modern generation from whom these truths are hidden.'[43] One difference that the *General Theory* made to policy-making was that its widespread acceptance by the rising generation of academic economists put the Treasury on the defensive, no longer confident of the sanction of orthodoxy.

With the danger of going down with the sinking ship staring it in the face, the Treasury took its cue from Sir Richard Hopkins, whose tussles with Keynes, stretching back to the sittings of the Macmillan Committee on Finance and Industry in 1930, had been an education for both of them. The bland drafting of paragraph 77 (which we now know to have been by Hopkins) shows the Treasury style at its best, effortlessly fudging a form of words which gave few hostages to fortune, claiming consistency with the past while simultaneously acknowledging a new departure:

> There is nothing to prevent the Chancellor of the Exchequer in future, as in the past, from taking into account the requirements of trade and employment in framing his annual Budget. At the same time, to the extent that the policies proposed in this Paper affect the balancing of the Budget in a particular year, they certainly do not contemplate any departure from the principle that the Budget must be balanced over a longer period.[44]

The provenance of the White Paper is thus evident, as a Keynesian message, strained and filtered through the fine mesh of careful Treasury prose. The fact remains that everything else in it is by way of qualification to its initial and central claim.

> The Government accept as one of their primary aims and responsibilities the maintenance of a high and stable level of employment after the war. This Paper outlines the policy which they propose to follow in pursuit of that aim. A country will not suffer from mass unemployment so long as the total demand for its goods and services is maintained at a high level.

That this claim was founded on a Keynesian multiplier analysis was subsequently made explicit.[45] 'My own feeling is that the first sentence is more valuable than the whole of the rest', Keynes said privately.[46]

The policy to be followed included not only strictly Keynesian measures for the counter-cyclical regulation of public investment but also parallel measures, chiefly due to Meade, for controlling swings in consumption expenditure by varying the rates of social insurance contributions. But if New Jerusalem was the ultimate goal, it was only to be reached by a hard and stony road. While the government professed 'no intention of maintaining wartime restrictions for restriction's sake', they were nonetheless 'resolved that, so long as supplies are abnormally short, the most urgent needs shall be met first', and trusted that 'the public will continue to give, for as long as is necessary, the same wholehearted support to the policy of "fair shares" that it has given in war-time'.[47]

The White Paper, in short, was not only a Keynesian document but one approved by Keynes himself, and attempts to suggest otherwise seem misguided. Keynes called the draft 'an outstanding State Paper which, if one casts one's mind back ten years or so, represents a revolution in official opinion'.[48] He had had to wait until nearly the end of his life to capture the ear of the opinion-forming elite; but that he had now done so was unmistakable. The White Paper went as far as was decent in making this plain:

> Not long ago, the ideas embodied in the present proposals were unfamiliar to the general public and the subject of controversy among economists. To-day, the conception of an expansionist economy and the broad principles governing its growth are widely accepted by men of affairs as well as by technical experts in all the great industrial countries.[49]

Though the canonical status of the *General Theory* was increasingly assured, however, it was more by vague invocation than by specific citation. What came to be justified under the rubric of Keynesianism might, in some respects at least, have surprised the historical Keynes.

The case for macroeconomic regulation of the economy was commonly meshed into a debate about planning, the buzz-word of the 1940s. It was in this guise that Keynesianism was assimilated to conventional arguments for socialism.

True, Keynes had a longstanding record of wishing to regulate investment so as to make full use of resources, and in the *General Theory* he accordingly suggested 'a somewhat comprehensive socialisation of investment'. The Labour Party's nationalization measures, however, hardly fulfilled his criteria of controlling the overall volume of investment, whether public or private – 'it is not the ownership of the instruments of production which it is important for the State to assume.'[50] Nonetheless, Labour appealed to a synergy between its nationalization programme and a full-employment policy, under the elastic rubric of planning. In 1944 Dalton identified counter-cyclical control of investment as 'one of the strongest reasons for nationalisation' in the Labour Party's confidential discussions of post-war policy.[51]

In regulating the level of effective demand, Keynes's instincts were always to concentrate on investment. Practically all that the *General Theory* said about consumption was: 'The State will have to exercise a guiding influence on the propensity to consume partly through its scheme of taxation, partly by fixing the rate of interest, and partly, perhaps, in other ways.'[52] In practice, consumption proved easier to regulate than investment. Under the Labour Government, there was a commitment to macroeconomic management of the level of demand through fiscal policy, supplemented by the use of direct controls to keep inflationary pressure in check. 'Really, therefore', Dalton confided in his diary, 'though this is not the way anyone puts it – "always have a bit of inflationary pressure, but use physical controls to prevent it breaking through"'.[53] Publicly, this is how Sir Stafford Cripps explained the matter in his Budget speech of 1950: 'Excessive demand produces inflation and inadequate demand results in deflation. The fiscal policy of the Government is the most important single instrument for maintaining that balance.'[54]

By contrast, the use of monetary policy as an economic regulator smacked of the bad old deflationary days of the Gold Standard, and was abjured by Labour. In taking this line Dalton could initially claim both theoretical and practical endorsement from Keynes. Keynes repeatedly stressed the desirability of bringing down the rate to a low *and stable* level (in this sense 'fixing' the rate). True, there was a reference in the Employment White Paper to 'the possibility of influencing capital expenditure by the variation of interest rates', following a period of cheap money.[55] Keynes had simply commented: 'I have never myself been able to make much sense of that paragraph.'[56] In the last months of his life, furthermore, Keynes had joined Joan Robinson in supporting Dalton's attempt at securing 'cheaper money' in the structure of long-term rates for government borrowing.[57]

Whatever the technical merits of this policy of fixed, minimal interest rates, both its provenance and its ideological dimension were clearly indicated in the *General Theory*. 'The outstanding faults of the economic society in which we live are its failure to provide for full employment and its arbitrary and inequitable distribution of wealth and incomes', Keynes claimed. Not only did he suggest that both flaws could be mitigated through a redistribution of income, which would raise the propensity to consume: he claimed that his theory held 'a second, much more fundamental inference' about inequalities of wealth, via the role now assigned to interest rates. If high interest rates became unnecessary to assure adequate saving, a regime of cheap money 'would mean the euthanasia of the rentier, and, consequently, the euthanasia of the cumulative oppressive power of the capitalist to exploit the scarcity value of capital'.[58] It is little wonder that this apophthegm made a natural appeal to Labour supporters, not least Dalton himself. Indeed it led him to push cheaper money to a point where it became unsustainable, thereby disclosing a perverse effect of his monetary policy upon capital values. Though he was still bullish in November 1946 – '"The euthanasia of the rentier" is proceeding apace' – the moment of truth came that winter, with the issue of government stock ('Daltons') at the unprecedentedly low level of 2.5 per cent. Its failure left the issue largely in the hands of the authorities. The perverse consequence came through an appreciation of the value of assets with a prospective annual return higher than these rock-bottom official interest rates. Here was the basis for the strategy, later urged by Crosland, Labour's pre-eminent revisionist, for raising interest rates as a means of depreciating capital values. When this point was put to Dalton in 1951, he noted ruefully: 'This is a new argument, not to be found in Keynes.'[59]

Though the Bank of England's discount rate remained fixed at the level of only 2 per cent until the Labour Government lost office at the end of 1951, there is evidence that Gaitskell, the new Chancellor, was ready to contemplate a rise in long-term rates to fight inflation.[60] It was left to the incoming Churchill Government to restore a flexible Bank Rate. There was no talk of 'monetarism' in those days; but the scheme (ROBOT) that was broached for allowing sterling to float, under rather complex arrangements, went a long way down that road. The thrust of ROBOT was to charge the Bank of England with implementing a monetary policy that would make the defence of sterling its prime objective, necessarily at the expense of the full-employment objective. This would obviously have made life simpler for the Bank. In 1944 the Deputy Governor was reported to be 'uneasy at the prospect of our entering the post-war period without having any clear idea of what dials to watch in determining bank policy. Under the Gold Standard there were well understood indicators.'[61] The wistfulness of the authorities for the good old days of the 'knave-proof' fiscal constitution should not be underestimated. Though ROBOT was overruled on political grounds by the Churchill Government – since the Conservatives wanted to live down their reputation as the party of unemployment and the Prime Minister himself had had quite enough of the Gold Standard for one lifetime – the new government naturally imparted its own bias to the Keynesian consensus, just as the Labour Government had.

The Conservative version of demand management was to reinforce fiscal fine tuning with a monetary policy that now used interest-rate changes to the same ends. After twenty years at 2 per cent Bank rate was symbolically raised to 2.5 per cent in November 1951 and to 4 per cent a few months later. By 1957 the market was used to rates at around 5 per cent, and Peter Thorneycroft's 'September measures' that year went to a 7 per cent rate, unprecedented since the disinflationary squeeze introduced in April 1920 by the Lloyd George Coalition. During 1957–8, however, it took only fourteen months for the rate to decline to 4 per cent – and a further thirty-two months before Bank rate again reached its crisis level of 7 per cent in July 1961. 'Stop-go', of course, was one name for this kind of economic policy. In terms of intellectual consistency this was hardly Keynesian: instead, credit regulation to control the cycle of disinflation and reflation derived faithfully from the views which Ralph Hawtrey had long urged upon his colleagues (as some old Treasury hands recognized). It needs to be appreciated that the old dogs of the Treasury were not just learning new tricks but performing some of their old tricks too.[62]

Indeed, as the nature of the post-war economic problem revealed itself, the Treasury found itself in an all too familiar position. At the end of the war there had been a general expectation that the post-1945 experience would parallel that of post-1918: a couple of years of inflationary boom, with a slump around the corner. This fear was implicit in the 1944 White Paper. It was constantly in Dalton's mind, not only through his own memories but through reminders from Evan Durbin and the XYZ group of Labour economists. True, Dalton's Budget speech in April 1947 said that inflation rather than deflation was now the immediate danger. Yet Meade, writing in 1948, when inflation was already at the front of his own mind, prefaced his arguments with the comment:

> We are all agreed that measures must be taken to stimulate total monetary demand and to prevent it from falling below the level necessary to sustain a high output and high employment when the time next comes – as sooner or later it assuredly will come – when a deficient total demand threatens to engulf us in a major depression.[63]

Right through to 1949 fears of deflation continued, though by now intermittently, to grip the minds of the policy-makers, not least Sir Stafford Cripps; and in 1950 his successor, Gaitskell, was still keen to introduce a Full Employment Bill, despite the obvious lukewarmness of the old guard at the Treasury, led by Sir Bernard Gilbert and Sir Wilfrid Eady.[64]

It was only in 1951 that it really became clear that the scenario had changed. Here was the crucial turning-point, in perceptions of unemployment as much as in its incidence. It is hardly too much to say that in the next twenty years full employment came to be taken for granted. The attribution of this happy state of affairs to Keynesian influence may well rest on the unargued assumption, *post hoc ergo propter hoc.* Certainly the Keynesian triumphalist literature of the 1960s implies an economic-historical role for the *General Theory* which now looks implausible as a sufficient explanation for the long post-war boom. Yet it is not clear that the narrower question of why people stopped worrying about a slump in 1951 ought to be answered without reference to the historical Keynes, still less to Keynesianism.

After all, in the last slump Keynes had made his name by proposing a programme of public works, to be spread over two years, which would have raised government expenditure by about 2 per cent of gross domestic product (GDP). What he had actually wanted was roads or houses; but, in a famous passage in the *General Theory* he ironically allowed for the conventional 'preference for wholly "wasteful" forms of loan expenditure rather than for partly wasteful forms', which still served to stimulate the economy so long as they provided the requisite 'pretext for digging holes in the ground'.[65] Suppose, then, that a rise in wasteful public expenditure – not by a mere 2 per cent of GDP but nearer double that – were to have been planned by government over two years beginning in 1951, would that not in itself have been enough to release loyal Keynesians from any fear of deflation? This is, of course, exactly what the Labour Government's rearmament programme amounted to in its macroeconomic impact. Though its implementation was trimmed back by the incoming Conservative Government, the impact of defence spending is clear. The flaw in this analogy is obviously that this was not deficit finance; but nor was the *increase* in spending covered by revenue; so in effect rearmament boosted demand through cutting the budget surplus by 5 per cent of GDP between 1951 and 1953 (see table 1.1).

Table 1.1   Government income and expenditure as a percentage of GDP

	Revenue	Expenditure	Balance	Defence
1951	36.6	30.1	+6.5	6.8
1952	36.6	33.4	+3.2	8.8
1953	33.7	32.8	+0.9	10.2

Source: Appendix to chapter 9; and see n. 68.

This stimulus to the economy may not have been beneficial, and it imperfectly furfilled Keynes's dictum that 'wars have been the only form of large-scale loan expenditure which statesmen have thought justifiable'.[66] Nonetheless its part in changing perceptions about the British economy needs to be remembered.

It is, however, a further step – and a long one – to suggest an axiomatic identification of Keynesianism with a 'democratic deficit'. Notably through the

influence of the Nobel laureate James Buchanan, such an axiom has become a
staple of public-choice analysis. Here the 'specific hypothesis is that the
Keynesian theory of economic policy produces inherent biases when applied
within the framework of political democracy'.[67] Though this analysis was
prudently limited by its authors to the political history of the United States, it
may be thought curious that a hypothesis of such explanatory power, relying
on a bias alleged to be inherent, should not yield equally demonstrable insights
about the political legacy of Keynesianism in Britain.

Yet the fact is that during the period which is now regarded, for better or for
worse, as the heyday of Keynesian influence, the Treasury maintained a
generally tight fiscal stance. The two draconian budgets which Dalton introduced
in 1947 finally removed the wartime deficit in government expenditure.
Throughout the next quarter-century, a surplus was realized in every year
except one. The exception was 1964–5, following Maudling's 'dash for growth',
when an apparent deficit, itself amounting to less than 1 per cent of GDP, may
well be a product of a change in accounting conventions. Only from 1973 did
a series of deficits mount steadily, reaching a peak in 1976 at nearly 7 per cent
of GDP.[68]

After the Second World War, the total level of the public debt reached 275
per cent of GDP in 1947. Yet within five years it had fallen to 200 per cent, and
in 1965 the national debt was less than current GDP for the first time since 1916.
By 1980, after thirty years of alleged Keynesian profligacy, the debt amounted
to less than six months' current production, whereas the national debt had
been more than two years' production in 1931, supposedly the end of the era
of sound money.[69] These figures may well conceal as much as they reveal; but
they suggest the need for more sophisticated historical research on the empirical
relationship between Keynesianism and government deficits.

The simplest interpretation is that the budget was balanced because low
levels of unemployment provided no reason to unbalance it. It was a backhanded
tribute to the success of full employment that other, and more traditional,
priorities in budget-making found influential champions within the government
apparatus. In this sense lip-service to Keynesianism served to license the
Treasury's timeless mission – to act as a check upon human nature. Sir Bernard
Gilbert, with his longstanding view of the Treasury's function as that of
'scraping the butter back out of the dog's mouth', perfectly exemplifies a cast
of mind hardly ruffled by the advent of 'full-employment' rhetoric.[70] 'For
some years it is likely that that the policy will involve keeping the brake on with
varying degrees of pressure, on both capital and consumer expenditure', Gilbert
noted presciently in 1945. 'I see no difficulty about that, it is in harmony with
all our past training and experience, and the constitution of the machinery of
Government is well fitted for the exercise of negative controls.'[71] The result was
a highly circumspect approach towards any possibility of an unbalanced budget.

The prospect of a deficit, which suddenly (and misleadingly) appeared during the making of Butler's 1954 budget, thus 'produced a sudden reversion to pre-war principles', according to Sir Robert Hall, currently Economic Adviser to H.M. Government. Not only Butler and Gilbert but Sir Edward Bridges, as Permanent Secretary to the Treasury, apparently regarded the predicted deficit as worse than the predicted fall in employment with which it was associated, and Hall thus had 'quite a struggle to get them to realize that the principle of the Budgets since 1948 made the surplus or deficit accidental.'[72] Accidental? It sounds like *Animal Farm* Keynesianism, with some budget outcomes (deficits) plainly more accidental than others (surpluses).

6

Keynes had, of course, addressed his magnum opus chiefly to his 'fellow economists', with a qualifying hope that it would be 'intelligible to others.'[73] How the *General Theory* was received, understood, and propagated by academic economists is an important topic which has not yet found its historian. There is a story to be told here in which names like Robertson, Hicks, Harrod, Hawtrey, Meade and Robbins will bulk large. But so will that of A.W. Phillips, and not only because of the eponymous 'Phillips curve' which came to express the supposed trade-off between unemployment and inflation. If the conception of Keynesianism which flourished by the 1950s can be called hydraulic, it was surely the ingenious Professor Phillips who set his stamp on this metaphor by causing an actual 'Phillips machine' to be constructed. It was developed at the London School of Economics in 1949–50, simulating the economy by pumping coloured liquids through transparent tubes, thus demonstrating to the sceptical how the flows could be manipulated by pulling the right levers.[74] Clearly Phillips himself was an engaging man and his machine achieved pedagogical triumphs which anticipated the advent of computer modelling. It is surely plain, however, that the inspiration for such mechanical exercises, so redolent of Heath Robinson, is hardly that of the historical Keynes.

The *General Theory*'s insight about the fundamental role of expectations under conditions of uncertainty in influencing the behaviour of the economy was overlooked by the policy-makers of the 1960s and 1970s at their peril. 'This is because they had inherited Keynes's machinery, but not the philosophy which sets limits to the scope and effectiveness of that machinery', is how Skidelsky puts it. 'Their hubris was inevitably succeeded by nemesis.'[75] In examining the ideological impact of Keynesianism in post-war Britain, it should not surprise historians to discover infidelity to Keynes's original intentions. Indeed such distortions may have been a price that had to be paid for the influence of the doctrine. It is not determinist or reductionist to recognize a natural selectivity in the reception of ideas by those to whom they appeal. Just as the Labour dialect of Keynesianism embraced planning and nationalization as the means of economic management, so the Conservative patois spoke of regulation through monetary policy, while the mandarin idiom dwelt on the beauties of restraint and fine-tuning by an omnicompetent Treasury.

The opaque historical consequences of Keynesianism were certainly not foreseen by the historical Keynes – only the fallibility of foresight itself. As Keynes told Shaw in 1935: 'When my new theory has been duly assimilated and mixed with politics and feelings and passions, I can't predict what the final upshot will be in its effects on action and affairs.'[76] He lived long enough, moreover, to glimpse his transformation from the begetter of ideas which he could recognize as his own to the status of father of an 'ism'. After he had dined with a group of Keynesian economists in Washington, D.C., in 1944, he said at breakfast the next morning: 'I was the only non-Keynesian there.'[77]

Notes

1. This is essentially what I aim to do in this essay, integrating themes which I explore more fully in several essays reprinted below, which are cited hereafter by short title and chapter number in this volume. I am grateful to Bradley Bateman, Stefan Collini, Susan Howson, John Thompson and Maria Tippett for constructive criticism of earlier drafts.
2. Axel Leijonhufvud, *On Keynesian Economics and the Economics of Keynes* (1968); T.W. Hutchison, *Keynes versus the 'Keynesians'. . .?* (Institute of Economic Affairs, 1977).
3. Robert Skidelsky, *John Maynard Keynes, Vol. 2: The Economist as Saviour, 1920–1937* (1992), p. 270.
4. Here I am recapitulating a point made in my historiographical survey, 'Keynes in history', ch. 6 below.
5. *JMK*, vol. 10, pp. 436, 448. This and the next three paragraphs summarize a case which I have more fully substantiated in 'J.M. Keynes, 1883–1946: "the best of both worlds"', ch. 2 below.
6. Robert Skidelsky, *John Maynard Keynes, Vol. 1: Hopes Betrayed* (1983), pp. 119, 124, 229, 233, 262.
7. Roy Harrod, *The Life of John Maynard Keynes* (1951), pp. 192–3.
8. Harrod, *Keynes*, p. 80.
9. Skidelsky, *Keynes*, vol. 1, pp. 143, 146.
10. See Donald Moggridge, *Maynard Keynes: An Economist's Biography* (1992), chs 5 and 6, at p. 165.
11. Skidelsky, *Keynes*, vol. 2, p. 173; cf. pp. 178, 184.
12. *JMK*, vol. 19, pp. 219–23. Moggridge, *Keynes*, pp. 420ff, disputes the interpretation in Harrod, *Keynes*, pp. 345ff, as supported in Clarke, *Keynesian Revolution in the Making*, pp. 24, 76–8.
13. Layton to Keynes, 19 August 1925, in Moggridge, *Keynes*, p. 395; cf. Richard Kahn, *The Making of Keynes's General Theory* (Cambridge, 1984), p. 169.
14. Skidelsky, *Keynes*, vol. 2, p. 303.
15. 'To you I can make boastings and not fear to be misunderstood – it is an internal boasting', he had to explain on finding that Lydia had treated his confidences as the sort of gossip too good to keep to herself. See Polly Hill and Richard Keynes (eds), *Lydia and Maynard: The Letters of Lydia Lopokova and John Maynard Keynes* (1989), pp. 205, 207: an edition to which all scholars are now indebted.
16. *JMK*, vol. 4, p. 65.
17. Skidelsky, *Keynes*, vol. 2, p. 147.
18. Moggridge, *Keynes*, p. 486, referring to the Wicksellian origin of this distinction.
19. Skidelsky, *Keynes*, vol. 2, p. 410.

20. I have been led to appreciate the significance of this point by the insights in the work of Bradley Bateman [now published as *Keynes's Uncertain Revolution* (Ann Arbor, Michigan, 1996)], which has caused some modification of the interpretation set out in 'J.M. Keynes, 1883–1946: "the best of both worlds"', ch. 2 below.
21. *JMK*, vol. 5, pp. 223–5; cf. pp. 128–31. The notion of liquidity preference is clearly glimpsed here – though not yet its significance as the explanation of interest rates.
22. *JMK*, vol. 7, pp. 20, 293.
23. *JMK*, vol. 7, p. 85.
24. *JMK*, vol. 7, p. xxxii.
25. *JMK*, vol. 7, p. xxiii (preface to the *General Theory*). I have substantiated the argument in this paragraph more fully in *The Keynesian Revolution in the Making, 1924–36* (Oxford, 1988), pp. 269–72 and in 'Hobson and Keynes as economic heretics', ch. 5 below.
26. Lecture notes of R.B. Bryce, 24 Oct. 1932, transcript by Thomas K. Rymes (Marshall Library, Cambridge).
27. Lecture notes by Marvin Fallgatter, 6 Nov. 1933 (Rymes transcript).
28. *JMK*, vol. 21, p. 213 (*New Statesman and Nation*, 24 Dec. 1932).
29. Skidelsky, *Keynes*, vol. 2, p. 228.
30. Skidelsky, *Keynes*, vol. 2, p. 232; cf. p. 536 for Skidelsky's statement that Keynes, in the 1935 General Election, 'for the first and only time in his life, voted Labour'.
31. *JMK*, vol. 28, p. 35 (*New Statesman*, 24 Nov. 1934).
32. *JMK*, vol. 21, p. 110 (Keynes to Macmillan, 6 June 1932).
33. JMK, vol. 21, p. 184 (*The Times*, 5 April 1933).
34. See Gordon Tullock, 'Public choice', in John Eatwell, Murray Milgate and Peter Newman (eds), *The New Palgrave*, 4 vols (1987), vol. 3, pp. 1040–4, at p. 1043. This sort of analysis is directly applied to Keynesianism in Britain in J.M. Buchanan, R.E. Wagner and J. Burton, *The Consequences of Mr Keynes* (Institute of Economic Affairs, 1978).
35. Hugh Heclo and Aaron Wildavsky, *The Private Government of Public Money*, 2nd edn (1981), esp. pp. lxxii, 2. I have developed these points in 'The twentieth-century revolution in government: the case of the British Treasury', ch. 8 below.
36. Susan Howson, *British Monetary Policy, 1945–51* (Oxford, 1993), pp. 18–19, 305–6. My treatment of many issues below is fundamentally indebted to this study.
37. *JMK*, vol. 7, p. 383.
38. Alan Booth, *British Economic Policy, 1931–49: Was There a Keynesian Revolution?* (1989), p. 51.
39. Ibid., p. 67.
40. *JMK*, vol. 21, pp. 387, 390 ('How to avoid a slump', Jan. 1937).
41. *Employment Policy*, Cmd 6527 (May 1944), foreword and par. 74.
42. *JMK*, vol. 27, p. 367 (note by Keynes, 14 Feb. 1944).
43. *JMK*, vol. 27, p. 325 (Eady to Keynes, 26 May 1943; Keynes to Eady, 27 May 1943).
44. Cmd 6527, par. 77.
45. Cmd 6527, p. 3 (foreword); cf. par. 40.
46. Moggridge, *Keynes*, p. 709 (Keynes to A. Robinson, 5 June 1944); and see pp. 709–14 for a full and cogent account of Keynes's part in the drafting of the White Paper.
47. Cmd 6527, par. 17. Correlli Barnett has tendentiously presented this debate as a triumph for the 'glib confidence' of 'New Jerusalemism'; see *The Audit of War* (1986), pp. 257–63.
48. *JMK*, vol. 27, p. 364 (note by Keynes, 14 Feb. 1944).
49. Cmd 6527, par. 80.
50. *JMK*, vol. 7, p. 378.
51. Howson, *British Monetary Policy*, pp. 92–3. See Elizabeth Durbin, *New Jerusalems* (1985), esp. pp. 216–18, for the earlier link between socialization and full employment policies argued by the New Fabian economists; and Donald Winch, *Economics and Policy* (1969), pp. 215–18, for a pioneering dissection of the muddled arguments for Keynesianism and 'planning'.
52. *JMK*, vol. 7, p. 378.
53. Ben Pimlott (ed.), *The Political Diary of Hugh Dalton* (1986), p. 465 (24 Jan. 1950).
54. Sir Stafford Cripps, quoted in Edward Bridges, *The Treasury* (1966), p. 93.

55. Cmd 6527, par. 59. On this ambiguity see Howson, *British Monetarv Policy*, pp. 44ff.
56. *JMK*, vol. 27, pp. 377–9 (Keynes to Sir Alan Barlow, 15 June 1944).
57. Howson, *British Monetary Policy*, pp. l49, 152.
58. *JMK*, vol. 7, pp. 372–6.
59. See the authoritative treatment in Howson, *British Monetary Policy*, pp. 134–5, 191–5, 305–7; quotations from Dalton's diary at pp. 191, 305. Meade and Robbins had long advocated short-run variations in interest rates; see pp. 46, 49.
60. Howson, pp. 291–2.
61. Note of a conversation with B.G. Catterns by Lucius Thompson-McCausland, 14 Feb. 1944, quoted in Howson, *British Monetary Policy*, p. 59. On ROBOT see Alec Cairncross, *Years of Recovery: British Economic Policy. 1945-51* (1985), ch. 9. The persistence of the 'knave-proof appeal of the Gold Standard for the Treasury mind, as illustrated in this and the next paragraph, is one theme of my study, 'The Treasury's analytical model of the British economy between the wars', ch. 7 below.
62. See G.C. Peden, 'Old dogs and new tricks: the British Treasury and Keynesian economics in the 1940s and 1950s', in Barry Supple and Mary Furner (eds), *The State and Economic Knowledge* (Cambridge, 1990).
63. J.E. Meade, *Planning and the Price Mechanism* (1948), p. 12; cf. Howson, *British Monetary Policy*, pp. 146–7, 163.
64. Cairncross, *Years of Recovery*, p. 426; Howson, *British Monetary Policy*, pp. 303–4.
65. *JMK*, vol. 7, pp. 129–30.
66. *JMK*, vol. 7, p. 130.
67. J.M. Buchanan and Richard E. Wagner, *Democracy in Deficit: The Political Legacy of Lord Keynes* (1977), p. x. It is congruent with their argument that they should see Keynes as an anti-democratic elitist (p. 7), imprisoned in the presuppostions of Harvey Road (p. 78).
68. [See Appendix to ch. 9, which presents revised figures, based on a slightly improved method of calculation from that used when the original version of this chapter was published in 1996.]
69. Calculated from B.R. Mitchell, *British Historical Statistics* (Cambridge 1988), table 7, pp. 602–3; Table 4, pp. 829–30 (GDP).
70. B.W. Gilbert in 1931, quoted in Eunan O'Halpin, *Head of the Civil Service: A Study of Sir Warren Fisher* (London, 1989), p. 54.
71. Gilbert to Bridges, 20 March 1945, in Jim Tomlinson, *Employment Policy: The Crucial Years*, *1939–1955* (Oxford, 1987), pp. 81–2.
72. Alec Cairncross (ed.), *The Robert Hall Diaries, 1954–61* (1991), p. 8 (8 April 1954).
73. *JMK*, vol. 7, p. xxi (preface to the *General Theory*).
74. A.W. Phillips, 'The relation between unemployment and the rate of change of money wages in the United Kingdom, 1861–1957', *Economica*, vol. xxv (1958), pp. 283–99; and see Nicholas Barr, 'The Phillips machine', *LSE Quarterly*, vol. 2 (1988), pp. 305–37.
75. Skidelsky, *Keynes*, vol. 2, p. 410.
76. *JMK*, vol. 28, p. 42.
77. Austin Robinson in Hutchison, *Keynes versus the 'Keynesians'. . .?*, p. 58.

2   J.M. Keynes, 1883–1946: 'The best of both worlds'

1

It has increasingly been recognized in recent years that Keynes's work cannot properly be appreciated if he is regarded narrowly as 'an economist'. Indeed an expertise in current economics may be misleading rather than enlightening. Keynes himself talked of his mature theoretical insights, for which he made such notoriously high claims, as simple, basic ideas. He went so far on one occasion as to claim that, while what he had to say was 'intrinsically easy', it was 'only to an audience of economists that it is difficult'.[1] This reflected a longstanding belief that economics was 'an easy subject – at which, however, very few excel!' The paradox was that the avocation of the economist required a combination of gifts: not only as mathematician and historian, but also as statesman and philosopher.[2] This essay explores the relation between these two latter roles – the one pre-eminently concerned with politics and public duty, the other intractably preoccupied with the foundations of personal morality.

A substantial body of research has recently been devoted to uncovering the philosophical underpinnings of Keynes's work.[3] Its general trend is to suggest that Keynes's *Treatise on Probability* (hereafter *Probability*), effectively begun in 1907, must be seen as one of the foundation stones of his *General Theory*, published nearly thirty years later – a thesis which, in its rigorous form, argues for a textual continuity in the treatment of the linked themes of uncertainty and probability. But it is not so easy to find agreement on how, or how securely, the economic edifice reposes upon its supposed philosophical footings. Marxian scholars will be familiar with the basic variants of this game of 'What Keynes Really Meant'. Thus the traditional position, as represented by Richard Braithwaite, is that there is a discontinuity between the philosophical thought of the Young Keynes and the Old Keynes.[4] This view has now met two revisionist arguments for a continuity thesis: one maintaining that the Old Keynes was clearly immanent in the Young Keynes and the other that the Young Keynes was faithfully reproduced in the Old Keynes.

Keynes's own account of his early beliefs put into circulation two influential notions, which are intertwined at the heart of the puzzle. The first was that he, like other undergraduate Apostles who sat at the feet of G.E. Moore in Edwardian Cambridge, had 'a religion and no morals'.[5] The other was his declaration that 'we completely misunderstood human nature, including our own', through a misplaced attribution of 'rationality' to it.[6] The young Keynes was, on this reading, obsessed with questions of personal relations and private ethics but indifferent to public and civic responsibilities – a view persistently conveyed in Skidelsky's biography.[7]

This reading of 'My Early Beliefs' is also consistent with much of the Keynesian debunking of the last two decades. For it is a short step from the impression of an apolitical young Keynes to the view of the mature economist as either an unreconstructed rationalist or an over-confident technocrat – and, in either case, betraying an impatience with, or an incomprehension of, the political processes of the real world. Now it must be acknowledged that Keynes presented such critics with plenty of ammunition, not least in the conclusion to the *General Theory*, with its assertion that 'soon or late, it is ideas, not vested interests, which are dangerous for good or evil' – famous last words indeed![8] At the time A.L. Rowse denounced this as a 'rationalist fallacy, the fatal defect of the liberal mind, the assumption that human beings are rational, will respond to a rational appeal, that ideas in themselves are effective and need only to be thrown out upon the waters' of discussion for the right ones to prevail'.[9] Fifty years on, this had become the crux of the public-choice theorists' critique of Keynesianism: 'Keynes did not envisage the application of his policy views in a vulgar contemporary political setting, in which parties of all persuasions are continuously tempted to yield to such pressures as numerous private vested-interest groups, including the bureaucracy, and the necessity of vote-gathering in order to win elections.'[10]

These two lines of interpretation are neatly conflated by a reference to Roy Harrod's influential concept of 'the presuppositions of Harvey Road' – an assumption, which Keynes inherited from his parents, 'that the government of Britain was and would continue to be in the hands of an intellectual aristocracy using the method of persuasion'.[11] It would, however, be rash to suppose that Harrod and Skidelsky – let alone Keynes – were in fact subscribing to exactly the same account. This takes us back to a biographical and historical problem which has too often been treated in cursory or downright misleading ways.

Let us begin with what Keynes himself said. Part of the trouble is that his brilliant memoir, 'My Early Beliefs', has been read as a document in ways alien to the circumstances of its composition. Written for his friends as the Munich crisis brewed in 1938, it made a profound impression upon them as they listened to its evocative account of a lost age of innocence, while the light slowly drained out of the bleak autumnal sky. 'The beauty and unworldliness of it' struck Virginia Woolf, even though it made her feel 'a little flittery and stupid'. Maynard had contrived his effects with an artist's sureness of touch: it made for 'a very human satisfactory meeting'.[12] Posthumously published, the essay has sometimes been perused in cold print without recognizing that literary artifice has its own conventions and that strict veracity is not necessarily among them.

In Harrod's interpretation, essentially from the perspective of 1938, the supposed influence of Moore in temporarily diverting his impressionable disciple from the path of public duty is not directly contested. Thus Keynes may have had a passing prepossession with the problem of the 'good'; but this was countered and contained by the presuppositions of Harvey Road.[13] If Harrod was inclined to discount the iconoclasm of Keynes's account and to disclose instead an implicit recognition of public duty, to Skidelsky this stood out as another example of how the authorized biography had reflected a pious and unhistorical commitment to defend Keynes's reputation even from the self-inflicted barbs of autobiography.

Not that 'My Early Beliefs' is accepted uncritically by Skidelsky, for he acknowledges that 'certain liberties with strict truth for the sake of effect and amusement would have been natural'.[14] Moreover, he also acknowledges that Leonard Woolf was one Apostle who directly repudiated its reading of Moore and his influence, maintaining that 'we were not "immoralists"'.[15] Yet this testimony is brushed aside by Skidelsky, on the grounds that Woolf's undisputed commitment to political objectives must have derived from 'something else'. Despite saving phrases, therefore, the authority of 'My Early Beliefs' as a source remains integral to Skidelsky's interpretation. The point on which he fastens is that 'Moore provided no logical connection between ethical goodness and political, social or economic welfare'; hence a Moorite – and 'Keynes always remained a Moorite' – was consistent in evincing no interest in such matters.[16] Yet the curious feature in what Skidelsky contends about the lack of connection between Moore's doctrine and Keynes's politics is that elsewhere in his volume the author goes so far in supplying an account of the logical connection between them – through Keynes's theory of probability. Donald Moggridge explicitly integrates these concerns by making out a case for 'the important role of the period of the creation of *Probability* in bringing Keynes out from the inwardness and ultra-rationality of his "early beliefs" towards a view of the world that could link "science and art", his duty to his friends and an active role in the wider phenomenal world'.[17]

Nor can probability be safely ignored in studying Keynes's mature writings, which persistently suggest the salience of conceptions of uncertainty and risk in the formation of economic expectations. In his last major theoretical contribution, 'The General Theory of Employment', published in the *Quarterly Journal of Economics* in 1937, uncertainty is a leitmotif running through the article. What was wrong with the orthodox theory was its assumption 'that we have a knowledge of the future of a kind quite different from that which we actually possess'. It was this 'hypothesis of a calculable future', with its 'underestimation of the concealed factors of utter doubt, precariousness, hope and fear' which was at the root of the trouble.[18]

Now if this were the whole burden of Keynes's message it would substitute a fundamentally irrationalist for a purely rationalist theory of the economy. This is the direction in which Shackle's suggestive insights about the role of uncertainty as Keynes's 'ultimate meaning' tend to lead.[19] But Keynes gives a clear hint that a more subtle epistemology is in fact proposed. He thought it worthwhile to digress on the distinction between what is 'probable' and what is 'uncertain'. 'The game of roulette is not subject, in this sense to uncertainty; nor is the prospect of a Victory bond being drawn.' What is uncertain is the outbreak of war or other matters where 'there is no scientific basis on which to form any calculable probability whatever'. It is this intractable lack of relevant knowledge which 'compels us as practical men to do our best to overlook this awkward fact and to behave exactly as we should if we had behind us a good Benthamite calculation of a series of prospective advantages and disadvantages, each multiplied by its appropriate probability, waiting to be summed'.[20]

Over the years, several economists took up this hint that readers of the *General Theory* might also turn with profit to *Probability*. But none of them, it is fair to say, turned with the requisite rigour and persistence; and only in the 1980s was professional expertise in this field allied with archival access to Keynes's writings on probability stretching back to the Edwardian period. Once we apprehend that a sophisticated concern with probability was part and parcel of the same bundle of early beliefs – of which Keynes wrote his classic account within a couple of years of dropping these ripe hints about the ubiquitousness of uncertainty – it becomes apparent that some technical understanding of his ideas in this field is likely to illuminate his more accessible beliefs about economics and policy and politics.

2

The current state of the literature has not produced a consensus. The common ground between the different accounts is, however, sufficiently extensive to permit some clear conclusions to be drawn. In the first place the significance of Moore's work can now be better appreciated. Moore asked two questions in his *Principia Ethica*: 'What kind of things ought to exist for their own sakes?' and 'What kind of actions ought we to perform?' His answer to the first was the basis of Keynes's 'religion': that we know what is good on the basis of intuition. But with actions, as Bateman has nicely put it, we enter a field of 'objective consequentialism' which is close to classical utilitarianism in insisting on the causal effects of our actions as the relevant test of whether they are good or bad. Moore's point about 'moral rules or laws, in the ordinary sense' was that it was 'generally useful, under more or less common circumstances, for everybody to perform or omit some definite kind of action'. So it is not surprising that his system faced a critical choice between what modern philosophers dub rule utilitarianism and act utilitarianism. Should *the individual* always follow the rules? Or are individuals ever justified in judging particular cases for themselves? In his 1903 opus Moore insisted on following the rules because the probability of an individual turning out to have been correct in deciding otherwise in any particular case was unknowable.[21] These were the rule-bound 'morals' which Keynes, as a principled immoralist, rejected.

The difference between them, however, was much more narrowly defined than Keynes's subsequent broad-brush picture suggests. The provocative language of 'immoralism', with its suggestion that rules were only there to be flouted, masked the real point at issue, which was the caveat that rules need not *invariably* take precedence over a soundly argued objection. What the young Keynes rejected was not a consequentialist social ethic as such but the conception of probability on which Moore had implicitly relied in deciding that personal discretion could never be justified.

'My Early Beliefs' claimed that the Apostles 'took not the slightest notice' of Moore's chapter on 'Ethics in relation to conduct'. But, as O'Donnell has pointed out, to gloss this as 'ignored' is wildly inaccurate, since Keynes in fact devoted close attention to a discriminating critique of this chapter, notably in a paper which he gave to the Apostles on this theme.[22] The gist of Keynes's criticism was to indict Moore for employing a frequency theory of probability, which sought to measure probability by the observed frequency of subsequent events. To Keynes this seemed absurd – as though the actual frequency with which a coin happened to come down heads or tails in a series of tosses could disturb the proposition that each outcome had, on each toss, been equally likely. Probability for Keynes was already seen as a rational judgement *ex ante*, a way of summing expectations, not a statement *ex post*.

If this were so, Keynes argued, then probability, properly understood, offered the basis for actions to be judged on the basis of their likely consequences. Moore's impossible requirement for complete certainty of knowledge in order to justify personal judgement was thus made redundant. Moreover, Bateman has shown that Moore took the point. Keynes argued out his position in his King's College Fellowship dissertation of 1908, which formed the backbone of his *Probability* as finally published in 1921. The impact of Keynes's work is demonstrated by Moore's abandonment of his earlier argument when he published a new book on ethics in 1912, and his adoption instead of a terminology about probability which avoided Keynes's criticisms. Moore now allowed for the exceptional case in which it could reasonably be foreseen that following a rule would probably lead to bad results, which ought to be avoided – even though there could be no absolute certainty that things would have turned out that way.[23] In short, by means of probability Keynes seems to have made an 'immoralist' of his mentor. If Keynes was a Moorite, there are senses in which Moore became a Keynesian.

The technical dimension to this discussion is inescapable, however rebarbative it seems to connoisseurs of the deceptively easy style in which Keynes couched 'My Early Beliefs'. What Keynes rejected was an *aleatory* conception of probability, based on observed frequency of occurrence; what he proposed instead was an *epistemic* conception, dependent on the degree of prior knowledge of the likelihood of an event. Now aleatory theories are necessarily objective, and epistemic theories may be subjective. But the distinctive feature of *Probability* was that it presented an *objective epistemic* theory. It argued for a unique, given, determinate, calculable set of probabilities in the world, susceptible of correct perception through logical inference from the available evidence.[24]

Maybe the essential point about Keynes's early beliefs can be made without adopting such a tight taxonomy. Thus Carabelli prefers to argue that *Probability* extended the logic of probability to arguments of a non-demonstrative and non-conclusive character. Such arguments, dependent on limited rather than perfect knowledge, were part of a logic which had its own rationality while resting also on intuition.[25] Indeed, this leads Carabelli to identify a clear subjectivist element in Keynes's theory from the time he first began drafting it in 1907; and to argue that he had already broken with the sort of rationalism which he caricatured in 'My Early Beliefs', which might accordingly be retitled 'My Very Early (around 1903–6) Beliefs'.[26]

There is no need here to assimilate these varying emphases. More striking is their common reading of the work on probability which Keynes had substantially completed before the outbreak of the First World War, though not published as *Probability* until afterwards. What he upheld was a probabilistic theory of ethics with a strong consequentialist emphasis. In general he acknowledged that rules and conventions had a social utility, even though he made a persuasive case against Moore's earlier insistence that they should always be obeyed. He was an immoralist in this sense rather than that which stuck in Leonard Woolf's autobiographical gorge.

There was thus no chasm in his thinking between private and public claims, even though he saw many practical dilemmas in living out his ideas in the world. Moreover, in licensing personal judgement, he implicitly assumed that it would have been formed and constrained by the same conventional morality which he refused to accept as an infallible commandment – a post-Victorian attitude in more ways than one. In this respect there is a revealing passage in Virginia Woolf's diary, recording a discussion about Christianity with Keynes in 1934.

> Morality. And JM [Keynes] said that he would be inclined not to demolish Xty if it were proved that without it morality is impossible. 'I begin to see that our generation – yours and mine V., owed a great deal to our fathers' religion. And the young, like

Julian [Bell], who are brought up without it, will never get so much out of life. Theyre trivial: like dogs in their lusts. We had the best of both worlds. We destroyed Xty & yet had its benefits.' Well the argument was something like that.[27]

3

Recent attempts to demonstrate the continuity in Keynes's thought from the composition of *Probability* to the *General Theory* have encountered – maybe created – one major problem. This concerns his apparent shift of view in 1931, when he responded to criticism of his theory of probability from Frank Ramsey, who argued that the confidence with which expectations were formed and held depended on subjective factors and not just on logical inference from objective reality. Ramsey was a brilliant young mathematician whose premature death Keynes mourned, and personal sympathy may explain the tone which he adopted in a review of Ramsey's subsequently published papers. But can it explain away Keynes's capitulation? 'So far I yield to Ramsey – I think he is right', Keynes wrote, accepting that 'the basis of our degrees of belief – or the *a priori* probabilities, as they used to be called – is part of our human outfit, perhaps given us merely by natural selection, analogous to our perceptions and to our memories rather than to formal logic'.[28] If this were so, then probabilities were not unique, assessed correctly or incorrectly by those who grasped or failed to grasp the appropriate logical relationships. Instead, probabilities might reasonably be assessed differently by different people – albeit on the basis of the same evidence.

This retraction has usually been taken at face value; only with the work of Carabelli and O'Donnell has it been argued – on different grounds – that Keynes's position remained substantially unchanged. For Carabelli this is obviously because she has already detected in the Young Keynes a full perception of subjectivism which the Old Keynes did not need to learn at Ramsey's posthumous knee.[29] For O'Donnell, conversely, the evidence that the Old Keynes did not abandon the logical basis of the Young Keynes's theory is sufficient evidence that no conversion to a radically subjectivist model took place.[30] It has been left to Bateman to reassert that there was a real shift, albeit within the same basic model, from an objective epistemic theory to a subjective epistemic theory. He uses this discontinuity to argue against a fundamentalist influence of probability theory in Keynes's economic thinking.[31]

The relevance of a probability model to the *General Theory* does not, however, depend on maintaining that there was continuity in Keynes's thought. It may be fruitful to ask instead whether the early 1930s saw a shift towards subjectivism in Keynes's thinking about *both* probability and economic behaviour. If the first shift in Keynes's views in the early 1930s was towards recognizing a clearly subjective element in his model of rational behaviour, his other shift – in economic theory itself – was complementary. It turned on the relation between expectations and equilibrium, as seen in their contrasting treatment in the *Treatise on Money* and the *General Theory*.

Keynesianism already existed as a set of practical policy axioms before Keynes sought to challenge the theoretical postulates on which, as he liked to say, he had been brought up. In 1930 the *Treatise on Money*, for all its striking novelty in expression, did not doubt that market forces tended towards an equilibrium at which all resources in the economy, including labour, would be fully employed. What the *Treatise on Money* did was to dwell on the unhappy consequences of disequilibrium. It made the point by stressing the difference between saving and investment. For if decisions to save and to invest were taken by different people, there was an obvious need to reconcile them. Interest rate classically did this job, finding a level that was not too high (for that would choke off Enterprise) and not too low (for that would fail to reward Thrift) but just right. Disequilibrium between saving and investment was a symptom of a rate of interest that was wrong. If it was too low ('cheap money'), an investment boom occurred, accompanied, of course, by inflation. But that was hardly the problem in 1930. The real issue at the time was what happened when dear money caused entrepreneurs to make losses. This was the practical problem in Britain after the return to the Gold Standard in 1925, because Bank Rate had to be kept high to maintain the pound at an overvalued parity.

Keynes had, of course, made his name as an economic publicist in the 1920s, disputing the Gold Standard policy on pragmatic grounds; what he did in the *Treatise on Money* was to theorize his critique. He explained the inability of interest rates to fall to their proper domestic level by pointing to the *modus operandi* of Bank Rate in responding to international pressure on the exchange rate. The level of interest rates required for internal equilibrium between saving and investment was precluded by external commitments. That, at least, is how Keynes preferred to put the matter. He could not, however, deny the fact that if British labour costs had exhibited the flexibility assumed in orthodox thinking, and fallen in tandem with the price level, the trick could have been turned.

The salient point in the *Treatise on Money* was that disequilibrium was a product of thwarted expectations. When entrepreneurs made their investments, they did so with an expectation of normal profit which failed to materialize. Bank rate was stuck too high to allow them to prosper. Not only did dear money raise the cost of investment and set a correspondingly high target for the returns needed to make it profitable, but it also provided savers with an excessive incentive. The excess of saving over investment measured the windfall losses which entrepreneurs suffered as a consequence. How so? Because, had this slice of income not been devoted to excessive saving but to consumption, it would have provided the slice of extra spending on consumption goods which would have allowed their producers to make their anticipated level of profit. Instead, the goods would have to be sold for knock-down prices, visiting disappointed entrepreneurs with windfall losses on a scale which exactly equalled the excess of saving over investment. Only when expectations were fulfilled was equilibrium achieved; conversely, disequilibrium was only the problem so long as expectations were not fulfilled.

This way of describing the *Treatise on Money* brings out the centrality of expectations to its model of the economy. Not only does it raise the question: why are expectations not fulfilled? It also prompts a further question: should expectations that are not fulfilled be regarded as irrational? 'Rational expectations' these days are axiomatically those which are fulfilled. But for Keynes, as has been seen, an appeal to the subsequent fact of non-fulfilment would have been quite improper. It would have imported exactly the aleatory test of probability which he always rejected as appropriate to human behaviour.[32] The right question was: had the expectations been reasonable at the time the relevant decisions had been taken? Not altogether, Keynes suggested.

Keynes's experience of developments in the real world from the Wall Street crash of 1929 to the flight from sterling in 1931 brought home to him the full importance of business psychology in sustaining or undermining confidence in self-reinforcing cycles which took on a life of their own. Did such insights help prompt his sympathetic response to Ramsey's argument for the irreducibility of subjective beliefs? After all, Keynes published his review, not in an abstruse philosophical journal, but in the *New Statesman and Nation*, and he did so the week after Britain was forced off the Gold Standard. It was then that he conceded that 'the basis of our degrees of belief' was 'part of our human outfit' rather than derived from formal logic.[33]

Keynes had already gone a long way down this road in the *Treatise on Money*, where his analysis of 'bullishness' and 'bearishness' built directly upon the experience of boom and bust on Wall Street. His analysis concentrated on 'the fact that *differences* of opinion exist between different sections of the public'. No unique objective probabilities here! On the one side there was an untrammelled 'bullishness of sentiment'; on the other, stretching the established sense of a 'bear' as one who sold short on the stock exchange, he identified as bears those 'persons who prefer to keep their resources in the form of claims on money of a liquid character realisable at short notice'.[34] The notion of liquidity preference is clearly glimpsed here – though not yet its significance as the explanation of interest rates.

Further issues arise: not only whether bulls or bears were acting rationally (or entertaining reasonable expectations) but whether such behaviour had a self-fulfilling effect. A suggestive passage in the *Treatise on Money* is that in which, with Keynes's practised ability to find uncanny adumbrations of his current ideas in earlier writers, he turned to 1 Kings 17:12–16. The parable of the Widow's Cruse was always an unlikely story. Keynes used it to illustrate 'one peculiarity of profits (or losses) which we may note in passing'. It was that however much of their profits entrepreneurs spent, profits as a whole would not be depleted because the effect would be to increase the profits on consumption goods by the same amount.[35] Alas, it was a fallacy, as he subsequently came to realize in the course of criticism from the so-called Circus in Cambridge, because he had illicitly assumed that only prices and not output would rise. This objection, however, does not have the same force against his parallel example, when entrepreneurs making losses seek to recoup them by curtailing consumption, thus converting the cruse to a Danaid Jar which can never be filled up. These paradoxes intrigued Keynes at the time, as his references to them before the Macmillan Committee indicate. The Widow's Cruse was an example of non-rational behaviour which was apparently self-fulfilling in generating economic rewards for those who indulged in it. The Danaid Jar was an example of how individual rationality merely reinforced an adverse outcome for all concerned – through a wholly natural desire to run away from bears.

These paradoxes were resolved by two insights which lay at the heart of Keynes's rapidly evolving theory of effective demand. The first he presented in his university lectures of October 1932. He had now formulated a concept which he termed liquidity preference and which he acknowledged as 'somewhat analogous to the state of bearishness'. The novelty, however, was not in the language but in the way he put it to work as his explanation of interest rates. It was a notion, as he later claimed, 'which became quite clear in my mind the moment I thought of it'.[36]

Keynes's other insight was more fundamental, for it broke the chain of rationality between individual decisions and an optimal outcome for the community. 'It is natural to suppose that the act of an individual, by which he enriches himself without apparently taking anything from anyone else, must also enrich the community as a whole', the *General Theory* acknowledged; but its message was that the theory applicable to the individual firm did not provide a theory of output *as a whole*.[37] The analysis of the *General Theory* thus shifted the focus away from whether individuals formed reasonable expectations. Instead the problem turned on the psychological forces which governed the state of the market. It was compounded, moreover, by the inability of individuals to buck the trend in a falling market. Even rational individual strategies (going liquid, cutting wages, reducing spending) were collectively self-defeating.

Once seized of this point, Keynes expressed it pithily, variously and frequently, in ways that it would be otiose to document here. The fallacy of composition thus provided a logical reason why individuals, even if they acted rationally to save themselves, might not be able to do so, since competitive strategies could not simultaneously succeed for all. It is tempting to go further. One might say that the *General Theory* disclosed a class of actions about which individuals had no means of determining epistemic probabilities which could warrant the description objective. But this is to forge a more rigorous link between Keynes's evolving ideas about epistemology and economics than is (probably) justifiable. In the absence of specific textual support, it is hazardous to infer what 'must have been in his mind' and to look for a tight, formal consistency in the thinking of a man who allowed his intuition free rein to pierce the different problems he tackled. It is safer to rest with the observation that both in his economic analysis, which occupied most of his attention in the early 1930s, and in his fugitive reappraisal of his theory of probability, Keynes now showed a readiness to allow more weight to subjective feelings.[38]

4

In the *Treatise on Money* expectations can be seen as a *deus ex machina*. Their importance was given a new twist in the *General Theory*, where they became an integral part of the analysis. Expectations about demand were problematic in both books. Hence the *Treatise on Money* included as 'income' not only the realized receipts of entrepreneurs but also their expected profits (which they actually suffered as windfall losses). The *General Theory* gave a simpler account with its concept of effective demand, comprising actual investment and immediately prospective consumption. The common point is that expectations are always, necessarily, the basis of investment decisions. In the *Treatise on Money*, however, the problem is how expectations are thwarted, producing a position of disequilibrium. In the *General Theory*, conversely, the problem is equilibrium itself – because it may be sub-optimal, with persistent unemployment.

Here Keynes's story no longer depended on expectations not being realized. As he told Harrod in 1937, 'the theory of effective demand is substantially the same if we assume that short-period expectations are always fulfilled.'[39] Indeed one could argue that expectations are always self-fulfilling via the multiplier, which necessarily increases aggregate income in a determinate way. The catch, of course, is that such an increase in income may not be reflected in an increase in output, but only in prices. To this extent inflation is the escape valve in the model. The elasticity of the supply curve is crucial; Keynes envisaged it responding to increases in effective demand with increasing output until full employment is reached, at which point further pressure on demand would simply produce inflation.

In the *Treatise on Money*, although Keynes had recognized that savings and investment might be in disequilibrium, he had still clung to the theoretical axiom that different forces, acting in opposite directions, had a tendency to bring them back towards equilibrium. In the *General Theory* the self-righting forces had disappeared, and when Keynes generalized further in the 1937 *QJE* article he offered his most comprehensive explanation. Here confidence became the psychological premise of decisions to invest, just as it was of decisions to save. Saving took place in a world permeated by subjective apprehensions. Keynes argued that 'partly on reasonable and partly on instinctive grounds, our desire to hold money as a store of wealth is a barometer of our distrust of our own calculations and conventions concerning the future'.[40] Hence the inadmissibility of direct extrapolation from barter transactions in devising simple models of how a monetary economy actually worked. The behaviour of a monetary economy was unique since it dealt with uncertainty by putting a price upon it, and allowed people to opt for money itself rather than the goods or assets which it could purchase. Keynes's theory of interest, as expressing the liquidity preference of lenders, was founded on this conception. Saving was thus no longer a confident, rational calculation, acting out the virtue of thrift; it was rooted in the precarious psychology of fear and distrust.

Investment, likewise, was not derived from an objective computation of actual yields; instead the *General Theory*'s identification of 'animal spirits' stressed the volatility of business confidence. Thus investment, the motor of the economy, 'depends on two sets of judgments about the future, neither of which rests on an adequate or secure foundation – on the propensity to hoard and on opinions on the future yield of capital assets'. To speak of a *propensity* imports nothing more purposeful than inclination or bias; to speak of *opinions* suggests the disputable and infirm nature of decisions. A dim view of the future would not only stimulate hoarding, and thus depress investment, it would also depress investment by reducing expectations of profit. Since both were expressions of optimism or pessimism, they tended to fluctuate in the *same* direction, as business psychology peaked and drooped. So 'the only element of self-righting in the system arises at a much later stage and in an uncertain degree.'[41] Keynes concluded: 'This that I offer is, therefore, a theory of why output and employment are so liable to fluctuation.'[42]

5

Despite other discrepancies in the secondary literature, there is an impressive measure of agreement over the probabilistic model of behaviour which underpins the *General Theory* and was made more explicit in the *QJE*. Unlike Shackle's reading of Keynes in an irrationalist sense, this stresses Keynes's attempt to salvage and identify a modified role for rationalism. O'Donnell makes a persuasive case for seeing this as a 'theory of rational behaviour under irreducible uncertainty'.[43] Fitzgibbons writes of 'the twilight of probability' in which we live, carrying the inference that 'it is best to recognize our limitations and act upon them instead of representing to ourselves that our methods of knowledge are more powerful than they actually are'.[44] Carabelli makes the point that 'when stressing the practical cognitive side of uncertainty, Keynes, unlike Shackle, considered it as a condition of knowledge rather than of ignorance (even when the actual knowledge was minimal)'.[45] It follows that it is reasonable to rely upon conventions where knowledge is insufficient to supply better reasons for acting.[46]

In short, it is not uncertainty as such but *our knowledge of uncertainty* which commands the situation. It is under these conditions that we are persuaded to act, in ways that seem reasonable to us at the time when decisions need to be made. Our current beliefs, opinions and expectations are crucial in moulding the plastic shape of the future. Moreover, if individuals were impotent to realize their goals in the market, as Keynes saw it, this was no excuse for fatalism but a demonstration of the need for those decisions which cannot safely be left to the market to be taken within the polity. Although the role of persuasion in achieving this had a directly political element, it was also a question of forming expectations.[47]

The self-sustaining effect of confidence turned economic problems into psychological problems. If effective demand drives the economy, and investment plus expectations of consumption drive effective demand, and confidence drives investment, and expectations drive confidence, then the involuted role of expectations in driving the economy is inescapable. Part of Keynes's project was to conquer public opinion and thereby produce the climate of expectations in which the economy could flourish.

The conquest of public opinion admittedly had a directly political dimension. Keynes obviously wanted to persuade decision-makers to adopt his policies. But his model of opinion-forming surely amounted to more than an elitist or intellectualist fallacy. Though it was rooted in liberal assumptions, it pointed to a coherent conception of social-democratic change – an ongoing process of persuasion at more than one level. It may be that he underestimated not only the difficulties involved in the transmission of ideas but also the perils of mis-understanding along the way. Hume's dictum that reason is the slave of the passions is relevant here, but it was undoubtedly Keynes's hope that the relationship implied between the horse and the rider would permit purposive choice.[48] Keynes was not oblivious of what I would call the ideological problem – the way in which his ideas, in the process of finding the sort of social purchase necessary to make them effective, would necessarily undergo a selective process of simplification and distortion.

In 1934 Keynes advanced a short explanation of why government had not adopted his policies: 'Because I have not yet succeeded in convincing either the expert or the ordinary man that I am right'. The impediment did not lie, he contended, in the self-interest of the ruling classes but in 'the difficulty of knowing for certain where wisdom lies' and in the related difficulty of persuading others. In arguing that it was 'not self-interest which makes the democracy difficult to persuade' he provided a snapshot of how he expected public opinion to move.

> In this country henceforward power will normally reside with the Left. The Labour
> Party will always have a majority, except when something happens to raise a doubt

in the minds of reasonable and disinterested persons whether the Labour Party are in the right. If, and when, and in so far as, they are able to persuade reasonable and disinterested persons that they are right, the power of self-interested capitalists to stand in their way is negligible.[49]

A little over a month later Keynes made his better-known claim to Shaw about his hopes to revolutionize economic thinking; and this letter helpfully amplifies the parallel statement at the end of the *General Theory* about ideas ruling the world. For Keynes was concerned with political problems in a far more persistent and fundamental way than has generally been credited, even if he did not succeed in formulating fully adequate solutions, nor purport to do so. He told Shaw: 'When my new theory has been duly assimilated and mixed with politics and feelings and passions, I can't predict what the final upshot will be in its effects on action and affairs.'[50] His own expectations thus remained bounded by uncertainty; but this did not inhibit him from backing his own judgement about politics and public opinion, as about other, more private concerns. Of course not. This was the same Keynes who said in 1938 'I remain, and always will remain, an immoralist.'[51] He still wanted the best of both worlds.

Notes

1. *JMK*, vol. 14, p. 124. In exposition this essay has benefited from discussion of my paper at the Harvard symposium in memory of John Clive in April 1992 and from the criticism of successive drafts by Bradley Bateman, Stefan Collini, John Thompson and Maria Tippett.
2. *JMK*, vol. 10, p. 173.
3. R.M. O'Donnell, *Keynes: Philosophy, Economics and Politics* (1989); Anna M. Carabelli, *On Keynes's Method* (1988); Bradley W. Bateman, 'Keynes's changing conception of probability', *Economics and Philosophy*, vol. 3, 1987, pp. 97–120; idem,'G.E. Moore and J.M. Keynes: a missing chapter in the history of the expected utility model', *American Economic Review*, vol. 78, pp. 1098–1106; Athol Fitzgibbons, *Keynes's Vision* (Oxford, 1988).
4. R.B. Braithwaite, 'Keynes as philosopher', in Milo Keynes (ed.), *Essays on John Maynard Keynes* (Cambridge, 1975), pp. 237–46.
5. *JMK*, vol. 10, p. 436.
6. *JMK*, vol. 10, p. 448.
7. Robert Skidelsky, *John Maynard Keynes*, vol. 1 (1983), pp. 119, 124, 229, 233, 262; cf. pp. 106, 117, 157, 209–10, 245–6, 400–1, cited by O'Donnell, p. 116, making the related point that Skidelsky's Keynes allegedly kept personal ethics in one compartment and relegated public duty to another.
8. *JMK*, vol. 7, p. 384.
9. A.L. Rowse, *Mr Keynes and the Labour Movement* (1936), p. 61.
10. John Burton, *Keynes's General Theory: Fifty Years On* (Institute of Economic Affairs, 1986), p. 15.
11. Roy Harrod, *The Life of John Maynard Keynes* (1951), pp. 192–3.
12. Anne Olivier Bell (ed.), *The Diary of Virginia Woolf*, vol. 5 (Penguin edn, 1985), pp. 168–9.
13. Harrod, p. 80.
14. Skidelsky, p. 143.
15. Leonard Woolf, *Sowing* (1970), pp. 144–56, at p. 148.
16. Skidelsky, p. 146.
17. See Donald Moggridge, *Maynard Keynes* (1992), chs 5 and 6, at p. 165.
18. *JMK*, vol. 14, p. 122.
19. See G.L.S. Shackle, *The Years of High Theory* (Cambridge, 1967), esp. ch. 11.

52   *The Keynesian revolution and its economic consequences*

20. *JMK*, vol. 14, pp. 113–14.
21. G.E. Moore, *Principia Ethica* (Cambridge, 1903), pp. 162–3, explicated in Bateman, 'A missing chapter', pp. 1098–1100.
22. O'Donnell, pp. 149–50. The dating of this paper to 1904, as supplied by O'Donnell and Skidelsky, without further comment in either case, proved troubling to both Carabelli and Bateman, who pointed out that no evidence of date could be found and that references within the paper anticipated the drafts of 1907 (Carabelli, p. 5 n. 5 at p. 252; Bateman, 'A missing chapter', p. 1101 n. 5). Moggridge now proposes to resolve this discrepancy by making a plausible argument for 1907 (Moggridge, *Maynard Keynes*, ch. 5, App. 1). Bateman meanwhile has shifted towards 1904 [my reference was to an unpublished draft of Bradley Bateman, *Keynes's Uncertain Revolution* (Ann Arbor, Michigan, 1996)]. Happily, whichever dating is preferred, there is little dispute over the substance of the case which Keynes outlined and subsequently developed.
23. Bateman, 'A missing chapter', pp. 1103–4.
24. Bateman, 'Keynes's changing conception', pp. 99–100. A subjectivist position, it should be noted, need not be irrationalist if – as in Ramsey's version, considered below – it still demands that, whatever basis individuals have for adopting their beliefs, these must nonetheless be constrained by consistency and coherence. Betting is thus the favourite analogy here, where the fact that each punter is free to back his favourite is consistent with the fact that a book can be made which sums all the bets. See O'Donnell, pp. 23–4. O'Donnell's taxonomy cuts the cake in a different way from Bateman's, grouping not only the frequency concept but also the logical concept which Keynes upheld, as two variants of objectivist theories. These stand distinct from subjectivist theories, which are dependent on the confidence with which individuals entertain their beliefs, howsoever generated.
25. Carabelli, pp. 16–17, 27.
26. Carabelli, pp. 99–100. Indeed, only in Fitzgibbons does a literalist reading of 'My Early Beliefs' meet no explicit challenge, and even here its account is implicitly undercut by the author's exposition of Keynes's all-embracing probabilistic vision. Fitzgibbons begins with the principle of indifference, which Keynes regarded as facile because 'the world is too complex to be explained by a theory that applies to the tossing of a coin'. He relied instead on intuition to grasp a logic of probability that was 'the logic of ordinary discourse' and hence applicable to real-world decisions. Fitzgibbons, pp. 12, 17.
27. Anne Olivier Bell (ed.), *The Diary of Virginia Woolf*, vol. 4 (Penguin edn, 1983), p. 208.
28. *JMK*, vol. 10, p. 339.
29. Carabelli, pp. 96–7
30. O'Donnell, pp. 139–48.
31. Bateman, 'Keynes's changing conception', p. 107. These interpretations, it should be noted, disagree more sharply about the position from which Keynes began than about that at which he ended, the more so since O'Donnell acknowledges that Ramsey had an indirect influence on Keynes in moving him towards a preference for 'weak rationality' rather than the 'strong rationality' which had previously underpinned his theories (O'Donnell, p. 147).
32. Thus it is surely misguided to suggest that some of Keynes's ideas anticipate a rational expectationist position, as in Allan H. Meltzer, *Keynes's Monetary Theory: A Different Interpretation* (Cambridge, 1988), pp. 7, 13–14, 68 n. 10, 141, 175; though Meltzer also recognizes the discrepancy at p. 144. For a clarification see Bateman, 'Keynes's changing conception', pp. 116–17.
33. *JMK*, vol. 10, p. 339.
34. *JMK*, vol. 5, pp. 223–5; cf. pp. 128–31.
35. *JMK*, vol. 5, p. 125. and Peter Clarke, *The Keynesian Revolution in the Making* (Oxford, 1988), pp. 250–1.
36. Clarke, p. 263.
37. *JMK*, vol. 7, pp. 20, 293.
38. I have had the benefit of reading Bateman's unpublished paper, 'Finding confidence', which offers support for a discontinuity thesis while differing in its treatment of the role of expectations as outlined in my next two paragraphs.
39. *JMK*, vol. 14, p. 181.

40. *JMK*, vol. 14, p. 116.
41. *JMK*, vol. 14, p. 118.
42. *JMK*, vol. 14, p. 121.
43. O'Donnell, p. 261. Not, as Bateman shows, 'rational expectations' in the modern sense, since Keynes's point about how expectations are formed under uncertainty was 'that people use epistemic probabilities in decision making and this was still his position at the time he wrote *The General Theory*' (Bateman, 'Keynes's changing conception', pp. 116–17).
44. Fitzgibbons, p. 142.
45. Carabelli, p. 103.
46. Carabelli, pp. 161, 163.
47. As Carabelli puts it, 'the analysis of the passivity of *individual* economic behaviour put forward by Keynes did not imply a denial of the possibility of intervention of and on economic agents *as a whole* and of social institutions in an active way in the future' (p. 228).
48. See Eduardo da Fonseca, *Beliefs in Action* (Cambridge, 1991), pp. 90–2, 184–5, 186, 188–9.
49. *JMK*, vol. 28, pp. 35–6.
50. *JMK*, vol. 28, p. 42.
51. *JMK*, vol. 10, p. 447.

3   The politics of Keynesian economics, 1924–31

1

In speaking of the politics of Keynesian economics, one might legitimately have in mind a topic to which considerable attention has been paid over the years. There is a fecund literature about how, and why, and when, and to what extent, and from whom, the Keynesian revolution in economics encountered political resistance or acceptance.[1] The present essay does not purport to contribute to that literature. Thus it is not concerned with the impact of Keynes but with a prior question about the political considerations which may have influenced Keynes during a crucial stage in his economic thinking. It is implicitly directed against two reductionist approaches, each with its own temptations. Although the two are methodologically distinct, they are able to enjoy a sort of peaceful co-existence which it is one object of this essay to provoke and disturb.

The first approach has its stronghold in the technical history of economic theory, whereby Keynes can be placed within a self-contained tradition of economic thought and his conceptual contribution to it appraised accordingly. It is the internal logic of the development of a discipline which is to the fore here, and the frame of reference is fundamentally teleological. The aim is to identify the Keynes patent on certain functional parts of the working model which economists have assembled and tested in use. Keynes's thought can thus be reduced to his apprehension of a number of original propositions, the essence of which can be captured in their fully-developed exposition. This essay, however, is less concerned with Keynes's thought than with his thinking. Why and how did he arrive at certain conclusions? Was he led to them or driven to them? The path of reasoning by which he got there should certainly be examined, but so should his reasons for choosing it.

But if economics is not a walled garden, it follows that one does not jump over the wall into a peculiar territory, called politics, where the rules are different. It is surely no less reductionist to suppose that the significance of Keynesian policies can be comprehended simply by putting the sharp inquiry, *cui bono*? The methodology of high politics has taught historians to identify some of the tactical functions which issues can serve, but this does not exhaust the question of their substantive content. How is it that self-serving ideas become current in one form rather than another? Accepting, for the sake of argument, the high political dictum that politicians' interest in ideas is governed by

solipsism, one might suppose that there would be nothing like a slump for
fostering economic panaceas. It would follow that Keynes was saying what
politicians wanted to hear. But why Keynes rather than Hobson or Major
Douglas? And why the striking vicissitudes over time in the reception accorded
to Keynesian ideas? Adapting a famous metaphor, one might say that a
concentration on the imperatives of high politics neglects supply in favour of
demand – an explanation relying on one blade of a pair of scissors to cut
through the problem. This essay cannot provide a methodological paradigm to
banish such difficulties. It can try to illuminate a necessarily complex dialectical
relationship between the formulation of sophisticated ideas, with their own rules
of congruence and logic, and the political predispositions helping to determine
their thrust.

2

On 14 September 1930, John Maynard Keynes finished writing the *Treatise on
Money*, which had occupied him for much of the previous seven years. He told
his mother: 'Artistically it is a failure – I have changed my mind too much during
the course of it for it to be a proper unity.'[2] In the preface, written the same day,
he said virtually the same, that 'there is a good deal in this book which represents
the process of getting rid of the ideas which I used to have and of finding my
way to those which I now have. There are many skins which I have sloughed
still littering these pages.'[3] It was, however, a work to which he attached
considerable importance – the 'strict logical treatment of the theory' which he
had promised his fellow members of the Macmillan Committee on Finance and
Industry the previous March.[4] The theoretical nature of the Treatise did not,
therefore, divorce it from the practical policy questions which the Macmillan
Committee was considering in 1929–31. The rather technical brief of the
committee was likewise related to broader issues of economic policy, on which
Keynes was giving advice to the authorities at this time, chiefly under the
auspices of the Economic Advisory Council. This advice in turn had direct
political bearings, especially insofar as it touched on proposals which were matters
of party controversy.

Now Keynes was no political innocent. His authorship of the pamphlet *Can
Lloyd George Do It?* during the 1929 election campaign had given him a
prominent polemical role as an advocate of public works. The *Treatise*, however,
suggested the primacy of cheap money in promoting recovery. Nor was this the
only source of bewilderment about Keynes's views at this time. A notorious
opponent of Britain's return to the Gold Standard, he spoke up against
devaluation. An advocate of a national treaty to reduce all incomes, he poured
scorn on wage cuts. A free trader all his life, he began arguing for tariffs. The
relationship between these matters is what first needs to be established.

When the *Treatise* was published, it was generally agreed that its most original contribution to economic analysis was the emphasis laid upon the distinction between saving and investment.[5] This was enhanced in late revisions of the book in 1929–30. The notion itself had been 'gradually creeping into economic literature in quite recent years', and Keynes paid tribute to the work of his Cambridge colleague, D.H. Robertson, here.[6] Nonetheless, the way Keynes put the concept to work opened up a whole new field. In a homely exposition, added at a late stage to Volume Two, he pointed out that it was usual to think of the world's wealth as having been accumulated by thrift, whereas the truth was that another economic factor – enterprise – was really responsible. 'If enterprise is afoot, wealth accumulates whatever may be happening to thrift; and if enterprise is asleep, wealth decays whatever thrift may be doing.'[7] Saving in itself achieved nothing until investment employed the resources thus made available. Investment depended on entrepreneurs, and their confidence was best generated by cheap credit and inflationary expectations. Keynes's chapter, 'Historical illustrations', is virtually a hymn to inflation. What use could be made of monetary policy to encourage enterprise by facilitating investment? This was the practical question to which Keynes's theory gave rise.

In the *Treatise* Keynes declared that 'the real task' of monetary theory was 'to treat the problem dynamically' in order 'to exhibit the causal process by which the price level is determined, and the method of transition from one position of equilibrium to another'.[8] He considered that this was the chief failure of the quantity theory (the contention that a rise in the price level was the result of an increase in the money supply). Keynes held that equilibrium supplied the unique condition under which it was true. He stated his argument initially for a closed system, where the problem was to balance saving and investment. Since they responded inversely to changes in interest rates, the way was open for the banking system, as 'a free agent acting with design', to control the final outcome.

It could *achieve* a balance by throwing the weight of official interest rates to one side or the other. 'Booms and slumps', Keynes maintained 'are simply the expression of the results of an oscillation of the terms of credit about their equilibrium position'.[9] If this was a relatively simple task inside a closed system, it became appallingly difficult when considered within the real world of the international economy. For not only had saving and investment to be kept in equilibrium, so also had the country's international earnings and its foreign lending. Since the banking system had to work with the same instrument on these two different problems, it followed that 'the conditions of international equilibrium may be incompatible for a time with the conditions of internal equilibrium'.[10] How, then, could it be supposed that a balancing act of such complexity could ever be brought off?

Keynes worked out his answer in chapter 13 of the *Treatise*, 'The *modus operandi* of Bank Rate'. This was a rigorous theoretical account, designed to cover all possibilities. In order to assess where the weight of analysis fell, however, it is necessary to bear in mind the special conditions which were at the forefront of Keynes's own mind. Britain's return to the Gold Standard at an overvalued parity in 1925 set the conditions of the problem. The existing monetary mechanism coped best when it followed the market, up or down, not when it tried to fight the market: in particular, it was 'singularly ill adapted' to impose lower real earnings via high interest rates.[11] Yet the 1925 measures had required credit restriction, 'with the object of producing out of the blue a cold-blooded income deflation';[12] Bank Rate had been given the job of reducing British costs to a level which would restore international competitiveness. Keynes claimed that neither economists nor bankers had been clear enough about the causal process involved, and hence both were 'apt to contemplate a deflation too light-heartedly'.[13] For the chain of causation here was: first, the deliberate choking of investment by high interest rates: second, its effect in inflicting abnormal losses upon entrepreneurs; third, the consequent withdrawal of offers of work; fourth, the reduction of money earnings as a result of unemployment.

Backed by this analysis, in February and March 1930, Keynes conducted his evidence to the Macmillan Committee like a seminar. He expounded the *modus operandi* to the committee, inviting admiration for its jewelled mechanism. It was, he stressed, 'not a doctrine peculiar to myself', but the classical theory underpinning all notions of 'traditional sound finance in this country'.[14] His orthodox exposition prepared the ground for the more disturbing contention that the return to Gold, requiring wage reductions of 10 per cent, had the effect of 'setting Bank rate policy a task it had never been asked to do before in the economic history of this country'.[15] The external constraints had to be met, and could be met; but the price was an interest rate structure inappropriate for the achievement of an internal equilibrium. When Keynes thereupon broached his own distinction between saving and investment, he was able to produce Bank Rate as the key to the position. But it was a key which would not turn in the lock. As Keynes acknowledged, 'if we did not belong to an international system I should have said there was no difficulty whatever; one could simply reduce the Bank rate to that level where savings and investments were equal.'[16] Under those conditions, 'the rate of interest would always tend to fall to the yield of the next thing which was worth doing.'[17] When international conditions dictated higher rates, the mechanics of the system should in theory have produced lower costs and lower prices. 'But if you jam the machine halfway through so that you have a chronic condition in which business men make losses, you also have a chronic condition of unemployment, a chronic condition of waste; and the excess savings are spilled on the ground.'[18] It was when Bank Rate was used to regulate income downward that this 'jam' or 'hitch' occurred, preventing the process from working through to its final conclusion, and creating 'the worst possible condition, to be left in this jammed state'.[19]

Keynes had thus begun by investing some of the classical propositions with his own lucidity. Pigou acknowledged that the *Treatise* gave 'an account of the *modus operandi* of bank rate much superior, as it seems to me, to previous discussions'.[20] It was when Keynes used this as a basis on which to build his own distinctive analysis that his efforts found less ready acceptance. As long as saving and investment remained undifferentiated, increased saving seemed a plausible solution to the problem of under-investment; likewise, investors would presumably be attracted once wage costs were cut back to realistic levels. But at this stage in the argument Keynes pointed to the mental leap he required from his hearers, claiming that 'it makes a revolution in the mind when you think clearly of the distinction between saving and investment'.[21] In practice, wage cuts had never been an easy way out, but in theory they had constituted a simple answer. Keynes now challenged this. He had constructed his own squirrel cage, and he was to spend most of 1930 and 1931 darting around inside it, exploring possible exits.

3

What were the main features of this cage? The fundamental constraint on Britain's international position was inadequate foreign earnings. They were insufficient to finance British investment abroad. The Bank of England therefore stepped in to safeguard the gold reserves, which backed the exchange rate of sterling. Its sole weapon was a high interest rate, which indeed discouraged foreign lending but only at the cost of domestic enterprise. With home investment held back, and foreign lending blocked off, the result was that 'a certain amount of our savings is spilled on the ground' in a wasteful dissipation of potentially useful resources. Savings were eaten up in financing business losses rather than profitable investment. 'Our investment abroad is fixed by the cost of production, our investment at home is fixed by rate of interest, and the two together fall short of our savings, and the difference is accounted for by the loss to the business world.'[22] To what solution did this way of posing the problem point? The logic of the analysis was such that in itself it did not imperatively demand any single remedy, but rather established criteria by which a range of remedies might be judged. This was the technical virtue of formal economic analysis, but it did not foreclose the political choices that then arose.

Before the Macmillan Committee, Keynes spoke blandly of 'classifying the suggested remedies in such a manner as to fit in neatly with this general analysis and diagnosis'. This served to declare his professional credentials, which were accepted by his colleagues with little demur. The chairman, indeed, cut in to supply the right word when Keynes was, for once, momentarily at a loss.[23]

'I propose, as a scientist to be – '
'Remorseless.'

The remorseless method involved a systematic appraisal of the relevance of a variety of proposals. At this stage Keynes identified seven classes of remedy, as follows:

1. *Devaluation*. Revaluation of gold (the usual way of putting it) was an obvious possibility in view of Keynes's view that the return of Gold in 1925 lay at the root of Britain's immediate problems. But an opportunity missed was an opportunity lost, so far as Keynes was concerned, and he did not see devaluation as desirable in 1930, because of the consequences for credit and confidence. It was a last resort, if all else failed.
2. *A national treaty*. This would provide for an agreed reduction of all domestic money incomes. It was really a way of living with the Gold Standard by short-circuiting deflation as the path to a lower level of domestic costs. Keynes had advocated it on these grounds in 1925, but by 1930 he pretty clearly recognized that it was not practicable. 'Its feasibility is almost entirely a matter of psychological and political, and not economic factors', he commented.[24]
3. *Bounties to industry*. These, too, constituted a theoretically attractive possibility in that they would use taxation to place the burden of maintaining competitive prices upon the whole community rather than upon certain sections of industry. 'It may be', Keynes argued, 'that our social feelings have caused us to fix wages at a higher level than the economic machine grinds out. If we were to balance that by a bounty that would be the public subscribing to meet the difference out of the common purse.'[25] This was a variant on a plea he had made earlier in the year for seeing the social wage, rather than high earnings, as the economically viable road to social amelioration.[26]
4. *Rationalization* This was the vogue word in 1930 for schemes to cut unit costs, especially through economies of scale. Clearly any improvement in efficiency was desirable; the real question was whether this alone could be relied upon to turn the situation around.
5. *Tariffs*. Protection was an old political battle-axe with a new economic cutting edge – new because several of the traditional, free trade arguments now struck Keynes as inverted arguments for tariffs. Would tariffs not increase the profits of entrepreneurs at the expense of the rest of the community? 'That is precisely what we want. . . .' Would they not act as 'a surreptitious way of decreasing real wages'? Or induce a rise in prices? Indeed, 'also something we want', said Keynes.[27] Moreover, the classical theory of free trade bore a striking likeness to the *modus operandi* of Bank Rate – in fact, it was mere prolegomenon insofar as trade transactions

worked through international gold movements to *activate* changes in Bank Rate. Thereafter, the precision of the compensating effects depended likewise upon the fluidity of wages and the flexibility of employment. But again, the immediate problem was what to do 'supposing we get jammed at the point of unemployment'? The choice was not between making more or less suitable articles according to a perfect international division of labour, but between making something (albeit unsuitable ideally) and making nothing. Keynes's conclusion was, therefore, that 'the virtue of protection is that it does the trick, whereas in present conditions free trade does not'.[28] Protection was thus helpful even if it was 'not anything like adequate to the situation'.[29]

6. *Home investment.* Keynes called this 'my favourite remedy' without further ado.[30] He proceeded to justify it by a process of elimination. New employment, he reasoned, might arise from exports (though the snag there was high wages); or from import substitution (the protectionist solution). Alternatively, consumption might rise at home. Although the spending power of the newly employed would create a favourable repercussion, 'you cannot start the ball rolling in this way'.[31] Less saving would also be of some advantage, though it was 'very low in my category of remedies'.[32] There remained a fourth possibility: that of creating new capital assets. 'It is the only remedy left, if one holds that the other three remedies are either impracticable in the position today or are inadequate, or are in themselves undesirable.'[33] There were various devices by which private enterprise might be encouraged to invest more at home, but the crux of the case was 'that it must be Government investment which will break the vicious circle'.[34]

7. *International measures.* High interest rates were choking investment, so reducing them would pave the path to recovery. Cheap money in one country, however, was not much of a slogan. Concerted action by the central banks was, therefore, in the long term, the most important thing of all.

Keynes endorsed all these proposals as having some point. 'While I have my preferences, practically all the remedies seem to have something in them', he claimed.[35] Rather than argue for one panacea, in season and out, therefore, he suggested that almost any of them might be worth a trial, given particular circumstances. Thus, as far as his Macmillan Committee evidence goes, devaluation was a last resort; a national treaty was a spent hope; bounties were probably impracticable; rationalization was insufficient in itself; tariffs were helpful at the margin; public works remained the favourite emergency measure; and in the long term the international economy needed cheap money. In the *Treatise*, Keynes commended four solutions: rationalization, tariffs, public works and cheap money. But this was *given* that the Gold Standard obtained (no devaluation), and *given* also that wage reductions were ruled out; so only bounties failed to make both lists.

The close correspondence here is hardly surprising, since Keynes was putting the finishing touches to the *Treatise* while giving his evidence to the Macmillan Committee. But it serves to show that there is little reason to charge Keynes with inconsistency on the ground that his polemical advocacy of public works in 1929–30 did not match up with his theoretical prescription of cheap money in the *Treatise*. The economic reasoning was the same in both cases, in that both met his criteria for stimulating investment. Thus the *Treatise* insisted that 'the great evil of the moment' lay in 'the unwillingness of the central banks of the world to allow the market rate of interest to fall fast enough', and asserted that 'we cannot hope for a complete or lasting recovery' until such a fall had taken place.[36] But whether to leave a long-term solution in the hands of central bankers – hands tied by national constraints and paralysed by mutual suspicions – was a question of practical judgement. Even in the *Treatise*, therefore, Keynes added that 'there remains in reserve a weapon by which a country can partially rescue itself when its international disequilibrium is involving it in severe unemployment'[37] and this was, if course, domestic involvement promoted by the government.

4

Keynes can be called inconsistent, therefore, only in the sense that he was led to investigate various methods of escaping from the squirrel cage; but it formed a structure within which all his moves were circumscribed; and his set aim was to get out. This consistency of approach, if not of methods, can be seen in four further attempts at analysis of the problem which he made, in slightly differing contexts, six months either side of the *Treatise*'s publication in October 1930. Indeed, the main difference between them is one of emphasis, depending largely on the starting point in each case. The way in which the remedies presented in his evidence to the Macmillan Committee (numbered as Evidence 1 to 7 below) fared under those conditions can be followed in remorseless detail.

The first of these statements was his letter to the Governor of the Bank of England, Montagu Norman, of 22 May 1930.[38] This started, naturally enough, with the international difficulties on account of which the Bank felt inhibited from taking further action. 'But that is why I twist and turn about trying to find some aid to the situation', Keynes countered. Again his analysis turned on the *Treatise* proposition that unemployment *must* stem from an excess of savings over investment, in which case only an increase of investment, at home or abroad, was a real solution. Increased foreign investment implied higher exports (which implied lower costs); or lower imports (which implied lower costs or tariffs); or more loans. Any of these were compatible also with increased home investments; but these would not materialize unaided. A further alternative –

'a counsel of despair' – was to decrease savings. Thus *given* the Gold Standard, and *given* existing interest rates (which eliminated Evidence 1 and 7), the options were to cut domestic costs (Evidence 2 and 4), to resort to protection (Evidence 5), and to stimulate home investment (Evidence 6).

Two months later, Keynes tried again, this time in response to the Prime Minister's questions to the Economic Advisory Council.[39] His scheme remained the same. 'Our dilemma in recent years, as I see it, is that if we raise the rate of interest aufficiently to keep our foreign lending down to the amount of our favourable balance, we raise it too high for domestic enterprise.' The touchstone in appraising remedies was therefore whether they increased either the foreign balance or the outlet for savings at home. The former could be accomplished in five ways: first, by decreasing the costs of production (rationalization, tax deductions, or wage cuts – really reiterating Evidence 2 and 4); second, by protection (Evidence 5), which was the quickest, easiest method; third, by import boards (a new idea); fourth, by arrangements with the Dominions, of which Keynes was sceptical; fifth, by increasing world trade, which was primarily an international rather than a local matter (Evidence 7). This cluster of measures would work on the foreign balance; the alternative was to concentrate on the problem of home savings, for which four proposals were enumerated as appropriate (all of them varieties of Evidence 6). A home development programme, to which 'the greatest possible importance' was attached, came first. Next, subsidies to private enterprise. Thirdly, there were ways of helping domestic enterprise to afford high interest rates. On inspection, two of these merely restated options already considered – a decrease in costs (Evidence 2 and 4) and protection (Evidence 5) – so the only new consideration was the desirability of promoting confidence. Keynes's fourth proposal on home investment was to make lenders accept less. How? A tax on foreign loans was one possibility; so was an outright embargo upon them; and lower world interest rates would clearly help, though to say this only reiterated the desirability of international measures (Evidence 7). The residual means of influencing lenders turned on confidence, already adumbrated as a factor influencing borrowers; and by this route Keynes came to a specific Budget proposal. Confidence, he told MacDonald, should be sought by postponing improvements in the social services, by looking for economies in 'abuses of the dole', and finally – the square at the bottom of every snake and the top of every ladder of Keynes's board – tariffs (Evidence 5).

His third survey of the problem took shape in the Report of the Committee of Economists for the Economic Advisory Council in October 1930.[40] Keynes's influence upon the report was considerable, but in its drafting he was in the hands of formidable professional colleagues, only one of whom (Stamp) was in full accord with him. That he managed to carry Pigou and Henderson with him in the final report, and Robbins for a good part of the way, is evidence of Keynes's adroitness in committee work rather than of like-minded unanimity between the experts. The marks show. Keynes seems to have bought assent for his proposals by accepting his colleagues' way of specifying the problem. Thus Keynes's draft of the report defined the remedies at the outset as confronting the problem of a disparity between wages and prices.[41] Forced to start from here, Keynes proceeded to classify the options in terms of their relevance to this relationship.

The initial class of remedies were those which permitted present wages to be paid: by tackling restrictive practices, conditions for the dole, and productivity (Evidence 4). Next came those which involved raising prices. This might be achieved through a rise in world gold prices or by a sterling devaluation (Evidence 1). An intermediate category followed, which gave Keynes plenty of elbow room. It became, in the first place, a means of justifying measures to promote home investment – the 'confidence' package for the Budget, including tariffs (Evidence 5), fiscal incentives to favour domestic projects, and, of course, public works (Evidence 6). It also turned into an advocacy of ways of increasing investment abroad, one method again comprising tariffs (Evidence 5). Finally, it ushered in, naked and explicit, the tariff-bounty proposal (Evidence 3 and 5) which Keynes had been working out.[42] The final group of remedies were for wage cuts (Evidence 2 and 4).

In Keynes's original scheme, the classes covering Evidence 3, 5 and 6 were preferred, with 1 better than those parts of 2 and 4 which implied wage cuts.[43] In the agreed Report, after concessions to Henderson and Pigou, the emphasis on wage cuts received fuller endorsement in Section VII, but Sections IX, X and XI elaborated the variants under Keynes's umbrella category covering Evidence 3, 5 and 6.[44]

The fourth document stating Keynes's overall view on economic policy in this period is the Macmillan Report, published in June 1931, especially Addendum I as signed by Keynes and five other members. The Report accepts Keynes's account of the *modus operandi* of Bank Rate.[45] In other sections drafted by him, it rejects devaluation as expedient, and indicates the opening for government enterprise in breaking the vicious circle.[46] In the Addendum, Keynes was able to impose his own logic more cogently. He stated the alternatives as being: more exports, import substitution, or further home investment. The practical courses open to achieve this were three. First, real wages might be reduced. The available means were: devaluation, which was theoretically best fitted for this task (Evidence 1); tariffs and bounties (Evidence 3 and 5), which produced the same effects while not disturbing confidence; and a national treaty (Evidence 2), despite its practical difficulties. Second, there might be some control on imports or aid to exports – tariffs again (Evidence 5). Third, there might be an encouragement of home investment, requiring government initiative in such fields as housing, the re-equipment of staple industries, and railway electrification (Evidence 6). In the year or so since Keynes had outlined his seven options in evidence before the committee, therefore, the proposal for tariffs (Evidence 5) had been combined with bounties (Evidence 3) as a functional alternative both to devaluation (Evidence 1) and to a national treaty (Evidence 2); and was also advocated as a support for a public works programme (Evidence 6). Rationalization (Evidence 4) had faded considerably, meanwhile, and international measures (Evidence 7) looked even less promising as a short-term answer.

5

It can be seen, therefore, that, wherever Keynes began in analysing the problem, he always ended up with the same handful of remedies. He was constrained within these options by his commitment to the theoretical proposition of the *Treatise*, that '*if* our total investment (home *plus* foreign) is less than the amount of our current savings (i.e. that part of their incomes which individuals do not spend on consumption), then – in my opinion – it is absolutely certain that business losses and unemployment *must* ensue'.[47] True or false? 'I can only say', Keynes told Norman, 'that I am ready to have my head chopped off if it is false!'[48]

Which course Keynes advocated at any one time depended partly on what was taken as given. Saving exceeded investment because Bank Rate was too high. The only way to reduce it was by international action, which in this sense was at the top of the list as a theoretically sound long-term solution. But from a local point of view, it was at the bottom of the list as a likely source of relief. Devaluation was admitted to be the most direct means of escape from the shackles imposed by international commitments; but until the summer of 1931 Keynes accepted the existing exchange rate as given. This left four real options: rationalization, tariffs (and bounties), wage cuts, and public investment. *Something* had to be done. It was Keynes's opinion that 'we should probably abolish our existing economic system if present conditions looked like lasting indefinitely'.[49] As to which of the relevant policies should be tried, Keynes told MacDonald that 'the peculiarity of my position lies, perhaps, in the fact that I am in favour of practically all the remedies which have been suggested in any quarter'. It was the negative attitude that was unforgivable – 'the repelling of each of these remedies in turn'.[50]

How far could economics be expected to provide the correct answers? Keynes held a generally high opinion of his calling and expressly urged that the government should take professional advice. He encouraged the Prime Minister to appoint a committee consisting solely of professional economists, who had 'a language and a method of their own', so that issues could be properly isolated. 'There is no reason', he added, 'why the results should not be expressed in a manner intelligible to everyone'.[51] He stated more than once that economics was at an awkward transitional stage, making it difficult to expound to laymen.[52] Technical questions had to be settled among economists – not least whether the theoretical framework of the *Treatise* was generally acceptable.

Meanwhile, however, it was no good leaving everything to the experts. 'In a sense there are no experts', he told a radio audience in 1931.[53] So the fact that public works were 'agreeable to common sense' was a strong recommendation, although there were also some cases 'where uninstructed common sense tends to believe exactly the opposite of the truth'.[54] The worst combination was the sort of bastard economic reasoning he detected behind the Treasury View, 'half-way between common sense and sound theory; it is the result of having abandoned the one without having reached the other'.[55] Expert appraisal might properly be conceived as a filter, separating cogent propositions from plausible fallacies. The real choices could thus be made apparent through professional skill. But, as the Report of Economists put it, at this point 'wider considerations of policy must necessarily come in than those merely of economic cause and effect'; and on these, 'economists, like other people, differ among themselves'.[56] Likewise the Addendum to the Macmillan Report concluded that the ultimate differences were 'not so much matters of theory as of the practical judgement of probabilities and of what is most prudent'.[57]

Whereas Keynes's economic analysis endorsed a range of proposals as relevant to Britain's current predicament, his own political predispositions naturally affected the relative priorities which he assigned to them. Some remedies were innocuously uncontentious. Nearly everyone nodded approvingly when the desirability of rationalization or of international measures to promote recovery was preached. Conversely, nearly everyone shook their heads sagely when devaluation was mentioned. The other remedies, however, were more highly charged politically. This was most obvious in the case of protection. For a quarter of a century the Conservatives had been identified with tariffs, while the Liberals were immemorially free traders. Hence, the unmistakeable frisson in the Macmillan Committee when Keynes revealed his sympathy for tariffs in his evidence of 28 February 1930.[58] He argued that protection was 'radically unsound, if you take a long enough view, but we cannot afford always to take long views . . .' In treating protection as a technical question of this kind, rather than as a moral absolute, he immediately sensed himself to be on dangerous ground, confessing that it was 'extremely difficult for anyone of free trade origin, so to speak, at this juncture to speak in a way that he himself believes to be quite truthful and candid without laying himself open to misrepresentation and to being supposed to advocate very much more than he really does'.[59] The chairman delicately drew attention to the 'political considerations' and 'gibes about inconsistency' which this new topic was bound to arouse.[60] He was 'frankly rather concerned' about whether it fell within his committee's terms of reference, since 'a report dealing with tariff reform' would be 'an unexpected result of our appointment'.[61] Worthy recommendations about credit, banking and finance were no doubt what Macmillan had envisaged, but it suddenly came home to him that 'our Report might become a document of first-rate political importance'.[62]

A large part of Keynes's advocacy of tariffs was an attempt to dissipate the conventional political connotations of the issue. When he made a public declaration of his position in March 1931, he suggested that 'Free traders may, consistently with their faith, regard a revenue tariff as our iron ration, which can be used once only in emergency'.[63] The question then was whether the emergency had arrived, not whether the traditional free trade case had been misconceived. But the controversy he provoked was not, of course, conducted by such a reappraisal but by wheeling out the time-honoured maxims which had seen service against Joseph Chamberlain, not to mention Lord George Bentinck.[64]

Keynes concluded that 'new paths of thought have no appeal to the fundamentalists of free trade', who had forced him 'to chew over again a lot of stale mutton, dragging me along a route I have known all about as long as I have known anything', and which was nothing but 'a peregrination of the catacombs with a guttering candle'.[65] He was, however, fully ready to exploit the ideological purchase of the protectionist cry. Indeed he laid increasing emphasis upon it as a means of promoting confidence among businessmen because it matched up with their general prejudices. Keynes was hoping, moreover, to achieve a more ambitious finesse, by marrying his own proposals for public works with those for import duties. 'For the bad effect of the former on business confidence and on the foreign exchanges would be offset by the good effects of the latter; whilst both would increase employment.' In his own mind, this combination made good economic sense, with the principle being the same on both counts.[66]

In the case of protection, Keynes was seeking to discuss it as a technical economic device, by ignoring its emotive political and social overtones. When it came to wage cuts, however, he acted in a contrary fashion. In the *Treatise* his analysis showed that an equilibrium rate of interest, appropriate to the needs of home investment and the foreign balance, was only feasible if 'the money rate of efficiency earnings of the factors of production' were flexible.[67] Since every other means of achieving this mobility had been covered under other heads, the remedy of income reduction stood as one prominent option every time Keynes had to produce an exhaustive list. He did not deny that the economic position would be improved by wage cutting: indeed the fact that 'the resistance to it has been tenacious and on the whole successful' was cited to explain 'why the phase of unemployment had been so exceedingly prolonged'.[68]

Keynes, however, never showed much stomach for breaking down this resistance. After the General Strike, when such a policy might have been feasible, 'Mr Baldwin decided – quite rightly – that it would be socially and politically inexpedient to take advantage of the situation in this way'.[69] Keynes repeated in 1930 that it was 'impracticable and undesirable to seek the remedy of reducing wages'.[70] In the *Treatise* he described an attempt to cut wages as 'a dangerous enterprise in a society which is both capitalist and democratic'.[71] He gave the Macmillan Committee his opinion 'that for centuries there has existed an intense social resistance to any matters of reduction in the level of money incomes'.[72] Listening to the employers' evidence, he found their unwillingness to recommend this solution 'truly remarkable', even when they had been pressed to fall back upon it.[73] The Addendum to the Report foresaw 'immense practical difficulties, perhaps insuperable difficulties', in the way of such cuts, and warned that 'the social costs of an attempt which failed would be incalculable'.[74] Keynes had, at the drafting stage, categorized such an endeavour as requiring 'the utmost determination and ruthlessness, an iron will, and a readiness to face, almost for certain, a violent social struggle'.[75] When he prepared a memorandum for the committee of economists, advocating the tariff-bounty proposal, he contrasted it with a direct attempt to reduce money wages, which could only be enforced 'as a result of a sort of civil war or guerilla warfare carried on, industry by industry, all over the country, which would be a hideous and disastrous prospect'.[76] In response to Hubert Henderson's charge that this was to run away from the problem, these references were cut out of the agreed report.[77] But in saying, during his exchanges with Henderson, that 'an assault on wages' represented a 'view which I have hitherto been rejecting and still on the whole, I think, reject',[78] Keynes had conveyed a disingenuous impression of the strength of his opposition. Did he merely think – 'on the whole' – that 'a hideous and disastrous prospect' should be rejected?

Keynes's persistent approach was thus to admit the theoretical possibility of the wage-cut remedy but to discount it as impracticable. The requisite mobility of wage rates was simply 'not one of the alternatives between which we are in a position to choose. We are not offered it. It does not exist outside the field of pure hypothesis.'[79] Having closed this avenue, Keynes could blandly suggest that 'if we are to avoid putting wages lower we must look around for some other method'.[80] Thus, despite his readiness to admit that there was something in 'practically all the remedies that have been suggested in any quarter', he managed to 'twist and turn about' in a way that always led him away from the most widely canvassed common-sense remedy of all. As Henderson trenchantly noted on Keynes's draft for the economists' report, after half-recognizing the case for cuts, it 'runs right away from it, and proceeds to twist and wriggle and turn in a desperate attempt to evade the logic of the situation'.[81] Henderson, moreover, was surely right in identifying Keynes's politics as the fundamental explanation of the course taken in his economic reasoning.

6

No one was better placed to acquire an insight into Keynes's political values than Hubert Henderson. He had been appointed editor of the *Nation* by Keynes in 1923, after the paper had been taken over as an organ of the sort of Liberalism with which the Summer Schools were associated. As editor and chairman of the board, the two men worked closely together. Keynes wrote for the *Nation* himself, and used it to launch his most telling public initiatives – especially, it may be noted, in bringing the issue of unemployment to the fore. In his economics Keynes was finding that the tradition in which he had been brought up was no longer relevant to the new problems of the 1920s. But the same was not really true in his politics. Despite the vicissitudes of the Liberal Party in recent years, and despite the novelty of Labour's rise to office, Keynes's political outlook in the mid 1920s remained in essentials that of the new Liberalism which had flourished in the Edwardian period when he was a young man.

There are four salient respects in which Keynes can be identified with the new Liberalism. In the first place, he proclaimed the end of laissez faire – 'not enthusiastically, not from contempt of that good old doctrine', he claimed in 1924, 'but because, whether we like it or not, the conditions for its success have disappeared'.[82] Two years later he was pointing to the Conservative party as the place 'for those whose hearts are set on old-fashioned individualism and laissez faire in all their rigour'.[83] This decisive rejection of the economic navigation of the older Liberal tradition cleared the decks for a new agenda in politics.

Secondly, salvation could not be looked for in socialism and class warfare. Keynes therefore rejected, on the one hand, the theoretical prescription of doctrinaire state socialism, 'because it misses the significance of what is actually happening'. For example, he insisted that there was 'no so-called important political question so really unimportant, so irrelevant to the reorganisation of the economic life of Great Britain, as the nationalisation of the railways'.[84] On the other hand, he also rejected the class war as the appointed means of achieving socialism. He could 'conceive nothing worse for us all than a see-saw struggle on class lines between the Haves and the Have-nots'.[85] Moreover, the appearance in the latter guise of trade unionists – 'once the oppressed, now the tyrants' – merely masked their 'selfish and sectional pretensions'.[86] Hence the fundamental inadequacy of this whole approach. 'I do not believe', he wrote in 1927, 'that class war or nationalisation is attractive or stimulating in the least degree to modern minds'.[87]

Thirdly, therefore, Keynes envisaged 'a reformed and remodelled Liberalism, which above all, shall *not*, if my ideal is realised be a *class* party'.[88] The experimental use of the state to achieve the ends of social justice did not imply a strategy of catastrophe but rather the application of hard thinking to see how the system could be made to work more acceptably. Keynes concluded 'that capitalism, wisely managed, can probably be made more efficient for attaining economic ends than any alternative system yet in sight, but that in itself it is in many ways extremely objectionable'.[89] Even when it functioned well, it was unfair; when it functioned badly, it became intolerable. Keynes was seeking 'the development of new methods and new ideas for effecting the transition from the economic anarchy of the individualistic capitalism which rules in Western

Europe towards a regime which will deliberately aim at controlling and directing economic forces in the interests of social justice and social stability'.[90]

Finally, this meant in practice that there was a large amount of common ground between Liberalism and ordinary or moderate Labour. If Liberals were 'inclined to sympathise with Labour about what is just', then their task was 'to guide the aspirations of the masses for social justice along channels which will not be inconsistent with social efficiency'.[91] As things stood in the mid 1920s, there was little immediate likelihood of 'a progressive Government of the Left capable of efficient legislation' unless cooperation with Labour was established,[92] and Lloyd George's efforts in this direction were a major reason why Keynes swung into his orbit, despite the strong pull of old Asquithian loyalties.

These four cornerstones of the new Liberalism were built into the foundations of Keynes's political thinking. He specifically described his aspirations as 'the true destiny of a New Liberalism'[93] – an odd turn of phrase if it was merely a random choice of words. This outlook not only made him a committed Liberal in party terms but also placed him self-consciously on the left of the British political spectrum – 'I am sure that I am less conservative in my inclinations than the average Labour voter', he reflected.[94] It meant, moreover, that Keynes looked on the Liberal Party not as a route to power (in which case 'I agree that one is probably wasting one's time')[95] but rather as a means of putting policies on to the political agenda. There was some consolation in 'supplying ... Labour governments with ideas'.[96] Keynes's stance, furthermore, gave a specific direction to his proposals on tackling unemployment. It is not just that these were first published in a Liberal journal, subsequently discussed under Liberal auspices, and increasingly identified as the policy of the Liberal Party in the late 1920s: there are also indications that their origin was more political than economic.

Now it would be foolish to deny the centrality of the Gold Standard in conditioning Keynes's thinking on economic policy in these years; but all is not as it seems. When, in his advice on different occasions up to the summer of 1931, Keynes ruled out devaluation as a remedy, he was accepting Churchill's decision to return to Gold as a *fait accompli*. His advocacy of other courses, as has been seen, ran logically from this premise. It is accordingly no surprise to find Keynes, in April 1929, defending his consistency by claiming 'that I began advocating schemes of National Development as a cure for unemployment four years or more ago – indeed, as soon as I realised that, the effect of the return to gold having been to put our money rates of wages too high relatively to our foreign competitors we could not, for a considerable time, hope to employ as much labour as formerly in the export industries'.[97] He wrote in the same vein in May 1929 that, since the return to Gold, he had 'spent the four years trying to find the remedy for the transitional period and to persuade the country of its efficiency'.[98] His unemployment proposals could thus be viewed as an economic response to the imposition of the Gold Standard. There is only one snag in this account. Churchill announced the return to Gold in April 1925; Keynes's article, 'Does unemployment need a drastic remedy?', had been published in the *Nation* nearly a year previously, in May 1924.

Taking his cue from Lloyd George, Keynes in this article for the first time outlined proposals for national development as a cure for unemployment. The seeds of some of his most fruitful notions were planted here. He was already claiming that 'we must look for succour to the principle that *prosperity is cumulative*'. He contended that 'the mind must be averted' from wage cuts, in favour of seeking 'to submerge the rocks in a rising sea'.[99] In response to his critics, he defied them to 'maintain that England is a finished job, and that there is nothing in it worth doing on a 5 per cent basis'.[100] Such notions were developed in a series of statements over the next five years or so, bringing Keynes into close cooperation with Lloyd George's efforts to revitalize Liberalism. Whatever Keynes's motives for becoming involved in a crusade against unemployment, mere chronology suggests that they cannot simply be ascribed to the economic consequences of Mr Churchill.

The Liberal proposals to cure unemployment, authoritatively outlined in the 'Yellow Book' of 1928, were peculiarly Keynes's responsibility.[101] He obviously intended that they should help the party electorally. The pamphlet he wrote with Henderson during the 1929 election campaign, *Can Lloyd George Do It?*, took a robustly partisan line and drew him directly into party political controversy. But the results of the 1929 election dealt a mortal blow to the Liberals' chance of power, and they were condemned to a peripheral role once MacDonald's Labour Government took office. Keynes remained an advocate of the 1929 programme through thick and thin. 'I am keener than ever on schemes of home development', he wrote in May 1931, 'and indeed on much of the Yellow Book'.[102] For his collaborator, Henderson, however, the intervening period had been one of disillusionment and reappraisal, confronted with the responsibilities of his new posts as secretary to the Economic Advisory Council.

Henderson's doubts surfaced by May 1930, when he told Keynes of his 'shifting of opinion from my position a year or so ago', i.e. the publication of *Can Lloyd George Do It?* No longer believing a public works programme would be merely transitional, he denounced any impression that its cost would be trifling as 'a sheer fake and fraud'.[103] By October 1930 the world slump had convinced him that it was no use bilking 'the disagreeable reactionary necessity of cutting costs (including wages)'. Rather than face up to it earlier, he acknowledged that he had 'in recent years supported recourse to temporary expedients and makeshifts'; but he now found it 'impossible to maintain such an attitude any longer'.[104] He could not accept that public works were in any real sense an alternative. Keynes seemed to him in danger of 'going down to history as the man who persuaded the British people to ruin themselves by gambling on a greater illusion than any of those which he had shattered'.[105] Henderson, moreover, had no doubt about the explanation of this extraordinary perversity. It seemed to him that 'the really important issues' which had arisen to divide them were 'of a broad and almost temperamental nature'.[106] He told Keynes of his feeling that 'you're over-moved by a sense that it's inconsistent with your self-respect to accept anything savouring of a conservative conclusion'.[107] The plain moral of economizing was that 'drawn by the ordinary, conservative, unintellectual businessman', and it was no doubt 'disagreeable to admit that the ordinary businessman can possibly be right'.[108] If only Keynes had 'considered the question really objectively and without regard to Left prepossessions'![109]

7

As Henderson must well have realized, a Keynes lacking 'prepossessions' would have trodden a different path from 1924 onward. By 1931, however, the claims of 'objectivity' were hardly likely to deflect him: rather the reverse. After the return to Gold, Keynes had once written that 'I am trying with all my wits, now in this direction and now in that, to face up to the new problems, theoretically and practically, too'.[110] Theoretically, he had not at this juncture succeeded in establishing much of a hold, at least as far as any justification for public works was concerned. In his early drafts of the *Treatise* he maintained that capital expenditure financed by public borrowing could 'do nothing in itself to improve matters' and might 'do actual harm'.[111] No hint here of a gap between savings and investment which state action could be summoned to close. As late as the summer of 1927 Keynes was commending the use of tax revenue so long as the Government 'itself *saves* it in some shape by diverting it into productive channels',[112] when the option of *investing* it in this way was how the *Treatise* would have made the point. It was at this stage that Keynes's activities as a publicist threatened to outrun even his formidable technical capacities as an economist. Although the author of *Can Llovd George Do It?*, brimming with common sense and self-confidence, had been well into his stride by 1924, the author of the *Treatise* was still groping for the right words several years later. It was only when they were both summoned to appear before the Macmillan Committee that they turned out to be the same person.

Notes
1. See especially Donald Winch, *Economics and Policy* (1969); Robert Skidelsky, *Politicians and the Slump* (1967); idem, 'The reception of the Keynesian revolution', in Milo Keynes (ed.), *Essays on John Maynard Keynes* (Cambridge, 1975), pp. 89–107; Susan Howson and Donald Winch, *The Economic Advisory Council! 1930–1939* (Cambridge, 1977); and Roger Middleton, 'The Treasury in the 1930s: political and administrative constraints to acceptance of the "new" economics', *Oxford Economic Papers*, xxxiv (1982), pp. 48–77. For its sources, this essay is manifestly under a considerable debt to Donald Moggridge's exemplary edition

of recent volumes in *The Collected Writings of John Maynard Keynes*. I am grateful to Michael Bentley, Stefan Collini, Michael Hart, Murray Milgate, Mary Short, John Thompson and Donald Winch for their helpful comments on an earlier draft.

2. *JMK*, vol. 13, p. 176.
3. *JMK*, vol. 5, p. xvii.
4. *JMK*, vol. 20, p. 136 (evidence of 6 March 1930).
5. See reviews by Norman Angell, *Time and Tide*, 8 Nov. 1930; A.C. Pigou, *Nation*, 24 Jan. 1931; Barbara Wootton, *The Listener*, 26 Feb. 1931; Anon., *New Statesman*, 31 Jan. 1931.
6. *JMK*, vol. 5, p. 154n.
7. *JMK*, vol. 6, p. 132. The stages in the composition of the *Treatise* can be followed from material in *JMK*, vol. 13, ch. 2.
8. *JMK*, vol. 5, p. 120.
9. *JMK*, vol. 5, pp. 164–5.
10. *JMK*, vol. 5, p. 165.
11. *JMK*, vol. 5, p. 245.
12. *JMK*, vol. 6, p. 163.
13. *JMK*, vol. 5, p. 244.
14. *JMK*, vol. 20, p. 53 (evidence of 20 Feb. 1930).
15. *JMK*, vol. 20, p. 56 (ibid.).
16. *JMK*, vol. 20, p. 84 (evidence of 21 Feb. 1930).
17. *JMK*, vol. 20, p. 79 (ibid.).
18. *JMK*, vol. 20, p. 75 (ibid.).
19. *JMK*, vol. 20, p. 82 (ibid.).
20. Review of the *Treatise* by Pigou, *Nation*, 24 Jan. 1931.
21. *JMK*, vol. 20, p. 87 (evidence of 21 Feb.1930).
22. *JMK*, vol. 20, p. 95 (evidence of 28 Feb. 1930).
23. *JMK*, vol. 20, p. 99 (ibid.).
24. *JMK*, vol. 20, p. 102 (ibid.).
25. *JMK*, vol. 20, p. 108 (ibid.).
26. 'The question of high wages', *Political Quarterly*, Jan.–March 1930, in *JMK*, vol. 20, p. 3ff.
27. *JMK*, vol. 20, p. 113 (evidence of 28 Feb. 1930).
28. *JMK*, vol. 20, pp. 114–15 (ibid.).
29. *JMK*, vol. 20, p. 125 (evidence of 6 March 1930).
30. Ibid.
31. *JMK*, vol. 20, p. 126 (ibid.).
32. *JMK*, vol. 20, p. 127 (ibid.).
33. *JMK*, vol. 20, p. 128 (ibid.).
34. *JMK*, vol. 20, pp. 146–7 (ibid.).
35. *JMK*, vol. 20, p. 99 (evidence of 28 Feb. 1930; cf. p. 125 (evidence of 6 March 1930).
36. *JMK*, vol. 6, pp. 185, 344.
37. *JMK*, vol. 6, p. 337.
38. *JMK*, vol. 20, pp. 350–6. Since section 4 does not advance the argument, but merely substantiates it in detail, readers who find this rebarbative are advised to take it on trust and move on to section 5.
39. *JMK*, vol. 20, pp. 370–84 (Keynes answers, 21 July 1930).
40. See Keynes's memorandum for the committee, dated 21 Sept. 1930, in *JMK*, vol. 13, pp. 178–200; his 'Proposal for tariffs plus bounties', 25 Sept.1930, *JMK*, vol. 20, pp. 416–19; and the 'Draft Report', 4 and 6 Oct.1930, *JMK*, vol. 20, pp. 423–50. The final report, 24 Oct. 1930, is printed in Howson and Winch, *The Economic Advisory Council*, pp. 180–227, which gives (pp. 71–2) an authoritative account of its composition.
41. *JMK*, vol. 20, p. 429 (draft report).
42. 'Proposal for tariffs plus bounties', 25 Sept. 1930, *JMK*, vol. 20, pp. 416–19, introduced into section XII (b) of the Report, Howson and Winch, pp. 212–13.
43. *JMK*, vol. 20, p. 429 (draft report).
44. Moreover, even in section VII, Keynes largely succeeded in drawing the teeth of the wage-cut recommendation by adding his own summary (par. 51), in which clause (5) stated that

'every other remedy with any serious balance of argument in its favour should be tried first' (Howson and Winch, p. 195). This paragraph alone was put in the summary of conclusions (p. 219).

45. Report of the Committee on Finance and Industry, Cmd. 3897 (1931), pars 215ff.
46. Ibid., pars 256, 316 (authorship from *JMK*, vol. 20, p. 309).
47. *JMK*, vol. 20, p. 350 (Keynes to Norman, 22 May 1930); cf. *JMK*, vol. 5, pp. 161–2.
48. *JMK*, vol. 20, p. 351 (Keynes to Norman, 22 May 1930).
49. *JMK*, vol. 20, pp. 273–4 (comments on Brand's memorandum, 7 April 1931).
50. *JMK*, vol. 20, p. 375 (answers to the Prime Minister's questions, 21 July 1930).
51. *JMK*, vol. 20, p. 368 (Keynes to MacDonald, 10 July 1930).
52. *JMK*, vol. 20, p. 269 (Macmillan evidence, 5 Dec. 1930); p. 477 (lecture on 'The internal mechanics of the trade slump', 6 Feb. 1931).
53. *JMK*, vol. 20, p. 515 (CBS broadcast, 12 April 1931).
54. *JMK*, vol. 20, p. 129 (Macmillan evidence, 6 March 1930); p. 305 (Macmillan Report, Addendum I).
55. *JMK*, vol. 20, p. 130 (Macmillan evidence, 6 March 1930).
56. *JMK*, vol. 20, pp. 449–50 (draft report of committee of economists, Oct. 1930).
57. Cmd. 3897, Addendum I, par. 53; printed in *JMK*, vol. 20, p. 307.
58. *JMK*, vol. 20, pp. 113ff.
59. *JMK*, vol. 20, p. 120 (evidence of 6 March 1930).
60. *JMK*, vol. 20, p. 121 (ibid.).
61. *JMK*, vol. 20, p. 123 (ibid.).
62. *JMK*, vol. 20, p. 123 (ibid.).
63. *JMK*, vol. 9, p. 238 ('Proposals for a revenue tariff', *New Statesman and Nation*, 7 March 1931).
64. Cf. A.J. Balfour's complaint a generation earlier: 'Those who are protectionists are assumed to be protectionists after the manner of Lord George Bentinck. Those who are free traders are assumed to be free traders after the manner of Mr Cobden.' *Economic Notes on Insular Free Trade* (1903), p. 3.
65. *JMK*, vol. 20, p. 505 (*New Statesman and Nation*, 11 April 1931).
66. *JMK*, vol. 20, p. 488 (foreword to Rupert Trouton, *Unemployment: its causes and their remedies*, published in 1931; cf. pp. 300–1 (Addendum to the Macmillan Report); 386 (*Manchester Guardian*, 14 Aug. 1930); 416 (proposal for tariffs plus bounties, 25 Sep. 1930).
67. *JMK*, vol. 5, p. 165.
68. *JMK*, vol. 19, p. 772 (Book review in *Britannia*, 2 Nov. 1928).
69. *JMK*, vol. 19, p. 763 ('How to organise a wave of prosperity', *Evening Standard*, 31 July 1928).
70. *JMK*, vol. 20, p. 11 (The question of high wages', *Political Quarterly*, Jan.–March 1930).
71. *JMK*, vol. 6, p. 346.
72. *JMK*, vol. 20, p. 64 (evidence, 20 Feb. 1930).
73. *JMK*, vol. 20, p. 377 (answers to the Prime Minister's questions, 21 July 1930).
74. *JMK*, vol. 20, p. 308 (para. 53, iv).
75. *JMK*, vol. 20, p. 280 (notes on the majority draft, 20 May 1931).
76. *JMK*, vol. 20, p. 419 (25 Sept. 1930).
77. Compare *JMK*, vol. 20, pp. 416–19, with Howson and Winch, pp. 212–15; Henderson's memorandum is in *JMK*, vol. 20, pp. 452–6.
78. *JMK* vol. 20, p. 365 (Keynes to Henderson, 6 June 1930).
79. *JMK*, vol. 20, p. 497 (letter to the *New Statesman and Nation*, 16 March 1931).
80. *JMK*, vol. 20, p. 322 (radio talk, *The Listener*, 26 Feb. 1930); he had argued in the same steps in a letter to *The Times*, 15 Aug. 1929, *JMK*, vol. 19, p. 833.
81. *JMK*, vol. 20, p. 453 (Henderson's memorandum, 13 Oct. 1930).
82. *JMK*, vol. 19, p. 228 ('A drastic remedy; reply to critics', *Nation*, 7 June 1924).
83. *JMK*, vol. 9, p. 300 ('Am I a Liberal?', *Nation*, 8 Aug. 1925).
84. *JMK*, vol. 9, p. 290 ('The end of laissez-faire', 1926).
85. *JMK*, vol. 19, p. 324 (letter of support to the Liberal candidate in Cambridge, 18 Oct. 1924).
86. *JMK*, vol. 9, p. 309 ('Liberalism and Labour', *Nation*, 20 Feb. 1926).

87. *JMK*, vol. 19, p. 640 (speech on 'Liberalism and industry', 5 Jan. 1927).
88. *JMK*, vol. 19, p. 441 (lecture on 'The economic transition in England', 15 Sept. 1925).
89. *JMK*, vol. 9, p. 294 ('The end of laissez-faire').
90. *JMK*, vol. 19, p. 439 ('The economic transition in England', 15 Sept. 1925).
91. *JMK*, vol. 19, pp. 639–40 ('Liberalism and industry', 5 Jan. 1927).
92. *JMK*, vol. 19, p. 327 ('The balance of political power at the elections', *Nation*, 8 Nov. 1924).
93. *JMK*, vol. 19, p. 439 ('The economic transition in England'); cf. p. 647 ('Liberalism and industry') and *JMK*, vol. 9, p. 305 ('Am I a Liberal?'). The balance of historical evidence thus seems to me to invalidate the philosophically plausible view stated by Maurice Cranstom, 'Keynes: his political ideas and their influence', in A.P. Thirlwall (ed.), *Keynes and Laissez-Faire* (1978), pp. 111–14.
94. *JMK*, vol. 9, pp. 308–9 ('Liberalism and Labour').
95. *JMK*, vol. 19, p. 733 (Keynes to J.L. Garvin, 9 Feb. 1928).
96. *JMK*, vol. 9, p. 310 ('Liberalism and Labour').
97. *JMK*, vol. 19, p. 812–13 (letter to the *Evening Standard*, 30 April 1929).
98. *JMK*, vol. 19, p. 824 (review of the Treasury White Paper, *Nation*, 18 May 1929).
99. *JMK*, vol. 19, p. 221 ('Does unemployment need a drastic remedy?', *Nation*, 24 May 1924).
100. *JMK*, vol. 19, p. 228 (reply to critics, *Nation*, 7 June 1924).
101. *Britain's Industrial Future* (1928); for Keynes's contributions see *JMK*, vol. 19, p. 731. There is a good account of this episode in John Campbell, *Llovd George: The Goat in the Wilderness* (1977), ch. 7.
102. *JMK*, vol. 20, p. 527–8 (Keynes to Aubrey Herbert, 29 May 1931).
103. *JMK*, vol. 20, p. 358 (Henderson to Keynes, 30 May 1930).
104. *JMK*, vol. 20, p. 452–3 (Henderson memorandum, 13 Oct. 1930).
105. *JMK*, vol. 20, p. 364 (Henderson to Keynes, 5 June 1930).
106. *JMK*, vol. 20, p. 454 (Henderson memorandum).
107. *JMK*, vol. 20, p. 360 (Henderson to Keynes, 30 May 1930).
108. *JMK*, vol. 20, p. 452 (Henderson memorandum).
109. *JMK*, vol. 20, p. 363 (Henderson to Keynes, 5 June 1930).
110. *JMK*, vol. 20, p. 450 (*Manchester Guardian Commercial*, 2 Nov. 1925).
111. *JMK*, vol. 13, p. 23 (draft from 1924–5).
112. Italics added. *JMK*, vol. 19, p. 676 ('The Colwyn Report', *Economic Journal*, June 1927).

4 Keynes's *General Theory*: a problem for historians

As a fellow genius, Bernard Shaw was well placed to appreciate that his young friend had no need for false modesty, nor for any other kind. 'To understand my state of mind, however', Keynes confided to him on New Year's Day, 1935, 'you have to know that I believe myself to be writing a book on economic theory, which will largely revolutionise – not, I suppose, at once but in the course of the next ten years – the way the world thinks about economic problems.'[1] The Keynesian revolution was not to be achieved by a stealthy Fabian outflanking strategy but by outright assault on the citadel. 'I want, so to speak, to raise a dust', Keynes told Harrod.[2] From the outset, therefore, the reception of the General Theory has been a matter for controversy and confrontation, polemics and heroics.

The economic literature is formidable. Broadly speaking, until the end of the 1960s its tone was triumphalist, celebrating the more or less complete victory of the forces of light over the forces of darkness.[3] The post-war consensus in economic policy, maintaining full employment by fiscal techniques of demand management, ostensibly derived from the *General Theory*. At the academic chalkface, Hicks's ISLM diagram[4] simplified the theoretical relationships in an income-expenditure model of the economy. This 'neo-classical synthesis' legitimized Keynesian policies in the real world (where rigid wages and a liquidity trap were facts of life) while not contesting that in a frictionless realm of theory the neo-classical postulate of equilibrium still held good.

In the last generation this peaceful co-existence has broken down, notably as a result of the work of Leijonhufvud.[5] It has become commonplace to distinguish between Keynesian economics and the economics of Keynes. But such distinctions mask sharp disagreements in a fierce struggle for legitimacy. It is, at one level, a variant of the parlour game played about all great thinkers: What Keynes Really Meant. Coddington proposed a taxonomy for this debate, between 'fundamentalism', 'hydraulicism' and 'reconstituted reductionism'.[6] In the first camp stood those like Shackle and Joan Robinson whose fundamentalism comprised not so much a reverence for the authority of 'the texts' as a frontal assault upon the whole idea of a reduction of market phenomena to individual choices, and hence upon the notion of equilibrium. Instead, Keynes's revolution centred upon the role of expectations founded upon uncertainty. His 'ultimate meaning' was accordingly to be found in the article he published in 1937 in the *Quarterly Journal of Economics*, which highlights these factors.[7] Under hydraulicism, by contrast, can be classified various models specifying determinate relations between macroeconomic aggregates. The neo-classical synthesis is included here, but its theoretical premise, that unemployment is a symptom of disequilibrium, is in turn contested by more radical versions of hydraulicism, like that expounded by Milgate.[8] Finally, reconstituted reductionism, as in Leijonhufvud's work, implies an effort to identify the flaw in the derivation of market outcomes from individual choices. The crucial imperfection is located in the deficient information available to individuals, so that their response to price incentives in maximising their utilities may not produce equilibrium.[9] It follows that the position of unemployment which results is one of disequilibrium.

One of the main theoretical issues, therefore, concerns the role of equilibrium in Keynes's analysis, and the significance of the various imperfections in the working of market forces.[10] There are versions of Keynesian economics pointing in all directions here. Just as Joan Robinson characterized the neo-classical synthesis as 'bastard Keynesianism', so the views of post-war Cambridge economists, notably herself and Kahn, have been analysed by Hutchison in terms of 'Keynes versus the "Keynesians"'. Hutchison professed his 'main and primary concern' as being 'with the history of economic thought',[11] but in general economists have acknowledged that their interest stems primarily from the relevance of such problems to their current preoccupations. Leijonhufvud, for example, warns that the 'doctrine-historical objective is strictly secondary' in his work.[12] Likewise, the fruitful adoption of 'an historical method of approach' by Milgate is, as he explains, 'in order to reveal analytical rather than historical conclusions and insights'.[13]

The historical literature, by contrast, often seems innocent of this debate. To be sure, professional economists who have studied the inception of policy proposals in this period have asked what role was played by ostensible differences in theory. Hutchison's earlier studies of Pigou's policy advice, which he rescued from the enormous condescension of post-war Keynesians, led him to imply that the novelty and practical importance of the *General Theory* had been much overrated.[14] Winch, on the other hand, has taken theoretical disputes more seriously, and, in his work with Howson, concludes that their impact upon the advice offered to government was not negligible.[15] Durbin's study of Labour economic thinking has also displayed an assured grasp upon the theoretical issues debated in the 1930s.[16] With the increasing availability of private papers and public records, government policy has been successively illuminated in major books by Skidelsky, Moggridge, Howson, Peden and Middleton.[17] The putative effects of a Keynesian alternative have in turn been assessed by economic historians concerned with the nature and causes of unemployment in the inter-war years.[18] Yet there remains, so far as the *General Theory* is concerned, a hole in the middle of the picture. Historians with ideological and political interests in the period have been too readily content with a tacit acknowledgement that something important was going on rather than attempting further explication.[19] Knowing allusions are thus common in the historical literature, though as historical explanation they hardly amount to more than saying 'with one bound Jack was free'. Serious historiographical concern with Keynesian economic theory has informed the work of Winch and Moggridge,[20] which is accessible to all, but otherwise it has been severely confined to the history of economic doctrine. It may be the impressive professionalism of writers like Patinkin and Milgate which has made it difficult for their work to be assimilated into ordinary historical discourse.

What is attempted here is not a rival contribution to the doctrine-historical literature: it is a resolutely historical account of Keynes's thinking on economic matters rather than a pedigree of his professional economic thought. It proposes a somewhat revised chronology for the making of the *General Theory*, using newly available sources, and building upon the existing work of Robinson, Klein, Harrod, Lambert, Moggridge, Milgate and Patinkin.[21] It recognizes that the question of when Keynes's ideas took shape is inextricably bound up with the issue of what those ideas were. One conclusion will be that Keynes's own account of the stages of his thinking raises implications in which logical and chronological aspects are not only intertwined but interdependent.

2

Keynes stated on the opening page of the *General Theory* that it should be contrasted with 'the classical theory of the subject, upon which I was brought up and which dominates the economic thought, both practical and theoretical, of the governing and academic classes of this generation, as it has for a hundred years past'. There is a footnote to explain his 'solecism' in describing here as classical the neo-classical successors of Ricardo, 'including (for example) J.S. Mill, Marshall, Edgeworth and Prof. Pigou'.[22] The final elaboration of general equilibrium analysis is often associated with the name of Walras, but so far as Keynes was concerned his target was the system expounded by Marshall and Pigou – the authors, as he put it to a German audience in 1933, of 'those English works on which I have been brought up and with which I am most familiar'.[23] This was the tradition to which he referred in the preface to the French edition of the *General Theory*. 'In that orthodoxy, in that continuous transition, I was brought up. I learnt it, I taught it, I wrote it.'[24]

In effect, the *General Theory* denied that we live in a Marshallian world where economic fluctuations are accommodated by price adjustments, and depicted instead a Keynesian world where changes in the level of output take the strain. Since the world sometimes looks arguably Marshallian and at other times plausibly Keynesian, the issue arises as to which vision of it has the more general application. Keynes was quite clear in the claim he made, 'that the postulates of the classical theory are applicable to a special case only and not to the general case'.[25] Despite the wealth of economic literature debating the validity of this assertion, the historical point, that such a claim represented Keynes's paramount intention, is beyond doubt. Those who contend that Keynes only succeeded in outlining a neglected special case, which the prevailing theory could in principle assimilate, must be saying that he did so inadvertently.

When Keynes gave his 'private evidence' before the Macmillan Committee on Finance and Industry in February 1930, he had been able to base his policy advice upon a singularly coherent theoretical foundation. His *Treatise on Money* was to appear only a few months later and the effort of composition made him the master – or perhaps the prisoner – of an integrated and consistent theory. There were certainly novel twists in Keynes's exposition, and in stating his case he made it distinctively his own; in particular, he turned the argument from more than one direction towards his favoured policy expedients, with public works to the fore. It should be observed, however, that the *Treatise*, with its sharp distinction between saving and investment, formed the acknowledged framework of this discussion. He was challenged on this point by the banker Brand: 'I suppose you would agree that the whole of your case depends upon whether this relationship that you said existed between savings and investment is actually true, that the losses and profits do occur according to your theory?' Keynes simply answered: 'Yes'.[26] To be sure, he was inclined to stress the innovative force of the *Treatise*'s analysis. 'I think it makes a revolution in the mind', he told Gregory, 'when you think clearly of the distinction between saving and investment'.[27] Yet Gregory had reasonable grounds for his sceptical pragmatism at this juncture, commenting: 'Although I have not seen Mr Keynes's full *exposé* there is not a very wide margin of difference between him and myself on some of the analytical points he has raised.'[28] For what Keynes had been expounding was, as he acknowledged, 'the essence of the classical theory' on how Bank Rate maintained monetary equilibrium. It was 'not a doctrine peculiar to myself' but 'the historic doctrine of Bank rate policy as it was evolved during the nineteenth century'; and Keynes took a delight in his mastery of its inner workings. 'I have told you', said the impresario, 'the whole story of how the traditionally sound financier thinks that he can make the adjustments required from time to time in our economic system, and I think – when one sees the way in which one part dovetails into another – there is no need to wonder why two generations, both of theorists and of practical men, should have been entranced by it.' While the rest of the committee piled on the compliments – 'An extraordinarily clear exposition'; 'An extraordinarily clear exposition, and thoroughly understood by us' – it was left to Gregory to introduce a note of caution. 'I accept everything that Mr Keynes has said', he interjected, 'but I should like to emphasise that this is not only a beautiful series of assumptions, but assumptions which translated into action have worked.'

It was at this point, and at this point only, that the author of the Treatise departed from orthodoxy, proposing next to confront 'the limitations and imperfections of the operation of this method in present-day conditions'.[29] The mechanism, as he went on to explain, was jammed or hitched – a grave and complex problem so far as policy was concerned, but not one with fundamental implications for economic theory. For the novelty of the *Treatise* lay in raising the question of *whether*, not *how*, saving and investment were brought into equilibrium. It was orthodox neo-classical doctrine that interest rate was a supply-and-demand mechanism which equilibrated saving and investment. Hence, it argued, full employment of all factors of production. This role for interest rate is not challenged in the *Treatise*. Indeed, Keynes's contention that saving need not be equal to investment – because they are different activities carried out by different people – can be seen as a rhetorical device for showing that the economy is in disequilibrium when they are unequal, so stressing the need to bring them together. The only reason why such a disequilibrium could persist in the real world, leading to waste of resources and unemployment, was that interest rate was thwarted in its assigned role.

3

In theory, then, Keynes agreed that interest rate would tend to restore equilibrium in a world of price flexibility. This was the general case. In practice, however, policy might have to be framed in terms of a special case governed by immediate circumstances – rigidities of an intractable kind which pragmatists could hardly ignore. The price of labour was a central issue here (though one which Keynes often evaded). He gave a clear statement of the relation of theory and policy in a public exchange with Robbins in March 1931, acknowledging that 'free trade, combined with great mobility of wage rates, is a tenable intellectual position' – in effect, though he did not mention it, the position stated in the *Treatise*. 'The practical reason against it', he continued, 'which must suffice for the moment, whether we like it or not, is that it is not one of the alternatives between which we are in a position to choose. We are not offered it, it does not exist outside the field of pure hypothesis.'[30]

It should not be supposed that Keynes was unique in taking up this position. Pigou, in his evidence before the Macmillan Committee, avoided urging wage cuts as a practical remedy,[31] though, like Keynes at this time, he was bound to admit that they offered a theoretical solution. Theory indicated the logical possibilities but policy options within this framework had to take account of broader considerations of expediency. Policy can be seen as departing from theory in a negative sense by refusing to endorse wage cuts. Advocacy of public works, by contrast, represented a positive departure. The starting point was again a recognition of the apparent impotence of self-righting forces within the economy. It took a strongminded doctrinaire like Robbins to stand out consistently against any palliative measures. In practice Pigou was ready to lend his support to proposals for public works, though it is fair to add that it was usually left to Keynes to make the running on this issue. Howson and Winch have summed up the position of the older members of the EAC committee of economists, like Pigou and Stamp: 'In order not to damage the chances of useful economic policies being adopted, they were prepared to minimise their disagreements over economic theory.'[32] That such disagreements remained, however, is inescapable, and they were to become sharper as the *General Theory* took shape. It is not enough, therefore, to look at the fair measure of consensus among academic economists on policy and imply that Keynes should have called his new book *Much Ado About Nothing*. Economists like Pigou, by supporting reflationary policies to counter the Slump, had not thereby become Keynesians. They were pin-and-tuck Marshallians coping with an anomaly.

Keynes himself, it should be reiterated, was in much the same position in 1929–31. The *Treatise* explained that there could be a disequilibrium between saving and investment, manifesting itself in depression and unemployment. It indicated cheap money as the cure. There has been a longstanding puzzle as to why Keynes simultaneously put forward a different cure, public works, notably in *Can Lloyd George Do It?* One suggestion has been that 'this incongruity is a manifestation of the simple fact that Keynes – like all of us – wrote and acted in different ways in the different roles that he played in life'.[33] There is something in this, especially if the respective criteria for theoretical explanation and remedial measures are distinguished. Yet it opens the door to a perception of Keynes as merely fluctuating in his views, whereas the inner consistency of both his policy advice and intellectual argument can withstand close examination. There is, in fact, a resolution of this difficulty, which has rightly won acceptance in the recent literature. This is to identify public works as a special case in terms of the *Treatise*, when defence of the currency at an internationally fixed parity prevented interest rates from falling efficiently to restore domestic equilibrium. Given Britain's adherence to the Gold Standard, Moggridge and Howson conclude: 'The *Treatise*'s special case formed the basis for Keynes's British policy advice throughout 1930 and the first nine months of 1931.'[34]

The verisimilitude of this point, however, is logical not chronological. If the return to Gold is advanced as the reason why Keynes began advocating public works, it is demonstrably misleading. Keynes himself propagated this legend, claiming in April 1929 that 'I began advocating schemes of National Development as a cure for unemployment four years or more ago – indeed, as soon as I realised that, the effect of the return to gold having been to put our money rates of wages too high relatively to our foreign competitors we could not, for a considerable time, hope to employ as much labour as formerly in the export industries'.[35] But Keynes had in fact begun his campaign not in 1925, after the return to Gold, but nearly twelve months previously, in May 1924.[36]

Just as Britain's return to Gold did not mark the beginning of Keynes's advocacy of public works, nor did the abandonment of Gold in September 1931 signal the end. The problem was complicated by the fact that Keynes had meanwhile adopted a further expedient to offset the effects of an overvalued currency – tariffs. He formally withdrew this proposal when the end of the link with Gold removed the special case, but in February 1932 was 'still not prepared to oppose it today with any heat of conviction'.[37] On public works, moreover, he was increasingly able to mount a general case as his own mind moved towards the *General Theory*. It was this which distanced him from Pigou and Robertson, of whom he later remarked that 'when it comes to practice, there is really extremely little between us. Why do they insist on maintaining theories from which their own practical conclusions cannot possibly follow?[38]

4

In making a theoretical case for public investment, Keynes was countering a theoretical objection, which the *General Theory* was to identify as Say's Law: the doctrine that supply creates its own demand. But it would be wrong to suppose that Say's Law was forever on the lips of contemporary neo-classical economists. Keynes's point was that, since the time of Say and Ricardo, full employment had become an unspoken assumption of theoretical analysis. Recent economists had 'conducted a line of argument which requires Say's Law or something of the kind in support, without ever giving the matter the slightest discussion'.[39] In the policy arguments, however, the gist of it had been blurted out. Churchill's statement of 'orthodox Treasury dogma, steadfastly held' was seized upon in *Can Lloyd George Do It?* as the crucial objection against public works.[40]

The 'Treasury View' is a Humpty-Dumpty phrase which needs definition. It can be used to describe actual Treasury policy – really a Whitehall view – upon unemployment in the inter-war period, in which case the conclusion of the best recent work is that practical and administrative considerations bulked large in the minds of civil servants like Sir Richard Hopkins.[41] When Hopkins appeared before the Macmillan Committee, the chairman spoke of 'a document which has come to be known as The Treasury View'.[42] This usage specifically referred to the memorandum produced in 1929 as the official riposte to the Liberal public works proposals. What Keynes meant by the Treasury View was a *proposition*, restated in the 1929 White Paper, and influential with the Chancellor of the Exchequer, but turning essentially upon a theoretical issue. The proposition, as he understood it, was: 'that any additional home investment which we could artificially stimulate would not in fact be any net addition at all, that it would be in fact diverted from other investments either at home or abroad'.[43] In short,

Archimedes could not have a bath without the water he displaced spilling over the side.

Keynes's main objection was that it followed 'too obediently the teaching of the economics of equilibrium'. It rested on a full employment assumption – not surprisingly, he thought, 'because practically all economic treatises do assume in most of their chapters that unemployment, except of a merely transitory character of which one need take no serious account, is an impossibility'.[44] Two qualifications need to be made here. First, Middleton has recently argued that the theoretical basis of the Treasury View has been misconstrued. It was not, he suggests, a Ricardian postulate about public investment 'crowding out' a comparable amount of private investment, but rather a sophisticated appraisal of the distortions involved and of the disruptive effect upon confidence.[45] In economic terms, this makes for a more coherent account of the conditions under which 'crowding out' becomes relevant. In historical terms, however, this reading is vulnerably dependent upon inference for support since it is admitted that 'the textual evidence is far from conclusive'.[46] Keynes, at any rate, saw the theoretical issue at stake as more fundamental in its simplicity. But, secondly, he did not accuse his fellow economists of subscribing to the Treasury View. Indeed, *Can Lloyd George Do It?* made the point that Pigou 'expressly declares it to be fallacious', and that he was not alone in so doing.[47] In the Macmillan Committee Keynes asked for the question to be put to all the expert economic witnesses – a sure sign that he was confident of what their verdict would be. He doubtless expected other economists to dwell upon the peculiarities of disequilibrium in sanctioning reflationary expedients.

At this stage Keynes believed that the *Treatise* supplied the best answer, by pointing to a potential discrepancy between saving and investment. This showed how unemployment could arise in a disequilibrium position (though Keynes was still, of course, assuming that full employment was axiomatic once equilibrium was reached). When Keynes faced Hopkins he thought he had a good hand to play, if only he could debate the central proposition. Hopkins, not unnaturally, refused to follow suit, and countered Keynes's court cards of economic theory with the low trumps of administrative pragmatism. Keynes was thrown back upon speaking of his 'misunderstanding' of the Treasury View, which he had conceived as 'a theoretical view, that the objection to these schemes was that they caused diversion on theoretical grounds'. Hopkins kept blandly maintaining that everything turned upon practical criteria. 'It bends so much that I find difficulty in getting hold of it?' asked Keynes. 'Yes', agreed Hopkins; 'I do not think these views are capable of being put in the rigid form of a theoretical doctrine.'[48] It would surely be naive to take these exchanges at face value in indicating not only Hopkins's pragmatism but also Keynes's acceptance 'that the Treasury View has been gravely misjudged'.[49] True, on one subsequent occasion he claimed that 'the main opposition to the public works remedy is based on the practical difficulties of devising a reasonable programme, not on the principle'.[50] It is also true that Keynes could not afford to dismiss administrative difficulties, acknowledging their reality if not their *centrality*. In this way he continually sought to find common ground with the Treasury on public works proposals, and was sometimes glad to find the views of the Treasury more flexible than the Treasury View.

It was the implicit proposition, however, which Keynes continued to regard as the crux of the argument. As he put it in 1933, he could only think of one reason for the rooted resistance to expansionary measures: 'the fact that all our ideas about economics, instilled into us by education and atmosphere and tradition are, whether we are conscious of it or not, soaked with theoretical presuppositions which are only properly applicable to a society which is in equilibrium, with all its productive resources already employed'.[51]

Two conclusions are germane at this stage. First, Keynes had not reached the coherent position which he defended before the Macmillan Committee in 1930 through patient intellectual advance. Instead, his policy intuitions, fuelled by his political commitments, often outran the justifying theory, which it dragged along behind until ultimately they were reconciled. More specifically, Keynes's own account of the origin of his ideas in the 1920s is crucially flawed by chronology. In turning to the making of the *General Theory* in the 1930s, therefore, similar questions must be posed about the nature of Keynes's enterprise and his own reliability as a source.

Keynes gave at least three retrospective accounts of the stages by which he reached the *General Theory*.[52] All three are mutually consistent, but it is his letter to Harrod of August 1936 which is clearest on chronology. The status this document has acquired can be inferred from the fact that it has been so often quoted in recent years and never challenged. It is fair to say that it has been analysed primarily in terms of its conceptual coherence and it remains to scrutinize it more closely as a historical record. If the paragraph numbered 2, which was composed with some care, is approached in this way, it can be broken down into four distinct stages, to which subsequent reference will be made.

5

At the time of its publication, Keynes set a high value on the *Treatise*, as can be seen from the confidence of his references to it before the Macmillan Committee. The proofs had, he explained, 'been read now by some of the principal economists of Cambridge, who did not all start sympathetic to it, but they are now satisfied, I think, that it is accurate'.[53] Of the accuracy of its central proposition – the saving/investment disequilibrium – he was himself more than satisfied, telling Montagu Norman, 'I can only say that I am ready to have my head chopped off if it is false!'[54] Yet if anyone supposed that this would be Keynes's last word, he was to be disillusioned. Hayek has recalled that, when he was asked to review the *Treatise*, he 'put a great deal of work into two long articles on it', which appeared in *Economica* in August 1931 and February 1932. 'Great was my disappointment', claimed Hayek, 'when all this effort seemed wasted because after the appearance of the second part of my article he told me that he had in the meantime changed his mind and no longer believed what he had said in that work.' To Hayek the subsequent moral was clear, in that the *General Theory* belied its name by being 'a tract for the times' and in this respect characteristic of a man who was 'more of an artist and politician than a scholar or student'.[55]

This raises a question put even more sharply by Johnson. Was Keynes 'an opportunist and an operator', whose brilliance as an applied theorist only meant that 'the theory was applied when it was useful in supporting a proposal that might win current political acceptance, and dropped along with the proposal when the immediate purpose had been served or had failed'? There is nothing inherently implausible in this view, as Keynes's activities in the 1920s serve to demonstrate. By extension, then, the *General Theory* has been depicted as 'the apotheosis of opportunism', on the grounds that 'a new theory' would be 'virtually certain to sell', if it satisfied the proviso that 'to be a new theory it had to set up and knock down an orthodox theory'.[56] Pursuing this hypothesis, one might expect the shift from the *Treatise* position to be signalled by some more obvious external ideological purchase available to the *General Theory*. Conversely, one would not expect to find the process inaugurated by a fundamental transformation in the internal structure of its logic.

The *Treatise* was, as Keynes had fully expected, 'exposed to the hostile criticism of the world for an appreciable time',[57] but he was less happy in arguing out its propositions than he had anticipated. A major difficulty was the ambiguity which developed over the role of hoarding. This controversy was joined not only by Hayek, whom Keynes privately identified as lacking 'that measure of "good will" which an author is entitled to expect of a reader', but by Robertson, who was broadly in sympathy with Keynes's endeavour.[58] Both attributed to Keynes the view that the excess of saving over investment could be measured by inactive deposits in banks.

In order to clarify his meaning, Keynes put forward a new elucidation of how the prices of liquid and non-liquid assets were determined. His object was to show that 'hoarding' was important in his system not as an actual *process* but as a psychological *motive* which price changes had to offset. He told Robertson in May 1931 that the price of investment goods would 'have to rise sufficiently to induce the existing holders, given their degree of bearishness, to part with non-liquid assets... Presumably this will mean some increase in the price of non-liquid assets, how much depending on the shape of the curve.' In redrafting this passage for publication, he described this sort of reluctance to hold non-liquid assets not as 'bearishness' (the *Treatise* term) but as the 'propensity to hoard'.

Keynes also summarized the argument afresh: 'What the state of mind of the public towards holding money, and the changes in this state of mind, determine is the price of non-liquid assets', which amounted to 'the propensity to hoard'.[59] In defending and explicating the *Treatise*, Keynes had been pushed into saying more than is to be found there in its discussion of the bearishness of the public.[60] It would, however, be wrong to jog his elbow at this point and simply write 'liquidity preference', which, as will be seen, did not emerge as a proper concept until there was a proper job of work for it to do.

Keynes acknowledged that since Hayek was not alone 'in falling into this misapprehension (or into some more subtle variant of it) it must be my own fault at least in part'.[61] The difficulty was that he did not have concepts that were at once rigorous and persuasive in formulating his central insight, viz. that the dynamics of the economy stem from the extent to which expectations (of entrepreneurs) are cheated or enhanced (in outcome). One way of formulating this was, as in the *Treatise*, to say that saving and investment might be unequal. This depended upon a definition of income which excluded 'windfall' gains or losses. If saving exceeded investment the excess was spilt upon the ground and the result was equilibrium at lower income levels. The advantage of putting it this way was the clear distinction between these activities, as in the fine passage on thrift and enterprise.[62] The disadvantage, however, was an ambiguity over what happened to excess savings (which, going to finance losses, did not constitute part of net savings at all). This is why Keynes was misunderstood to maintain that 'hoarding' was the explanation.

6

There was a second and more subversive line of attack on the *Treatise* – more subversive because it came from quarters whose approval of Keynes's objectives was unquestionable. This arose from the discussions of the *Treatise* by the younger economists at Cambridge ('the Circus'). Joan and Austin Robinson, Piero Sraffa, Richard Kahn and James Meade were the core of this group, which met chiefly in the early months of 1931. There are virtually no contemporary records of the thinking of the Circus, because of its closely informal operation, and the chief sources are subsequent recollections, with their attendant frailties. The most obvious hazard is that memory may have telescoped and antedated what took place. The position of Meade, however, who was visiting for the year from Oxford, offers some external control in that he was physically extracted at a known moment. Meade, moreover, made the surprising statement that, when he returned for the new academic year in the autumn of 1931, he was 'cautiously confident that he took with him back to Oxford most of the essential ingredients of the subsequent system of the *General Theory*'.[63]

What Meade understood by this can be gauged from a striking apophthegm in one of his essays, which has been widely quoted since its publication in 1975:

'Keynes's intellectual revolution was to shift economists from thinking normally in terms of a model of economic reality in which a dog called *savings* wagged his tail labelled *investment* to thinking in terms of a model in which a dog called *investment* wagged his tail labelled *savings*.'[64] Unknown to Meade, he was in fact repeating a metaphor employed by Keynes himself, which adds further authority to the phrase and may, through a subconscious echo, be the origin of it.

A digression may help to explain the senses in which Keynes was thinking of saving and investment after the publication of the *Treatise*, with its emphasis upon their potential disparity. 'In the past', Keynes proclaimed in June 1931, 'it has been usual to believe that there was some preordained harmony by which saving and investment were necessarily equal. . . .' [65] It was the *presumption* that they were the same which led both him and Robertson to look for definitions which made the matter problematic, as their correspondence illustrates.[66]

Keynes to Robertson. March 1932

The old 'common-sense' view not only held that savings and investment are necessarily equal (as – we have seen – *in a sense* they are), but inferred from this that therefore one need not bother.

Robertson to Keynes. 19 May 1933

But the

$$\text{'Savings} \left\{ \begin{array}{l} \text{exceeding} \\ \text{falling short of} \end{array} \right\} \text{Investment'}$$

phrase is so attractive for expressing what we both want to convey that one longs to find some definition of the words which will enable one to use it without straining the meaning of either word unbearably.

What common sense said was that realized savings and investment must be the same. What Keynes was contending was that this outcome need not correspond with what had been intended. The Swedish distinction between *ex ante* (the viewpoint of intention) and *ex post* (the viewpoint of accomplishment) would have cut through much of this ambiguity. When Keynes later became aware of it, he told Bertil Ohlin: 'This is in fact almost precisely on the lines that I was thinking and lecturing somewhere about 1931 and 1932, and subsequently abandoned.' Even in 1937 he acknowledged that 'from the point of view of exposition, there is a great deal to be said for it'.[67] It is only a trivial anachronism, therefore, to interpret Keynes's earlier exchange as defining saving *ex ante* as S but saving *ex post* as S'. It was the latter which provided 'the justification for the old-fashioned "common-sense" view that savings and investment are, necessarily and at all times, equal . . .' Keynes continued (using *I* for investment):[68]

> On the other hand the implications of this use of language are decidedly different from what 'common-sense' supposes. For *S'* always and necessarily accommodates itself to *I*. Whether *I* consists in housing schemes or in war finance, there need be nothing to hold us back, because *I* always drags *S'* along with it at an equal pace. *S'* is not the voluntary result of virtuous decisions. In fact *S'* is no longer the dog, which common sense believes it to be, but the tail.

7

The influence of the Circus can hardly be ignored in explaining why Keynes was thinking in this way as early as March 1932. Its most notable monument was the article which Kahn published in the *Economic Journal* in June 1931 on 'The relation of home investment to unemployment'. Its central message was that public investment could create not only an initial amount of employment but also secondary employment through its repercussions on spending. Keynes publicized this conclusion in 1933 under the irresistible title 'The Multiplier', but this name may give a misleading impression of the concept in the original article which, as Kahn has observed, 'is often cited but apparently little read'.[69] The importance of the multiplier (in Kahn's formulation) stems from the questions it was designed to answer; and to some extent its implications were for the time being restricted by those questions. Politically it followed up the proposals for public works in *Can Lloyd George Do It?* Thus Kahn at the outset twice referred to the 'beneficial repercussions' which were notoriously invoked by the (unnamed) advocates of public works. His purpose was to evaluate them in concrete arithmetical terms. Kahn was preoccupied with two questions. First, obviously, what are the dynamic effects on unemployment of a public works programme? Second – equally inescapable for anyone challenging the Treasury View – how to pay for it? The first draft of his paper, described as 'a very early version',[70] was seen by the committee of economists in September 1930, and seems to have been solely concerned with the relation of primary to secondary employment. It was naturally seized upon by Keynes in his policy advice as 'an argument, which seems to me convincing for supposing that in present conditions in Great Britain a given amount of primary employment gives rise to an approximately equal amount of secondary employment'.[71]

So far, so good. The significance of Kahn's multiplier, however, does not reside in an airy wave of the hand towards the infinite possibilities of cumulative prosperity but in specifying the finite limits to such an impact. Colin Clark had prepared a paper for the EAC referring to 'an infinite series of beneficial repercussions'. With no leakages, indeed, the multiplier would be infinity. Did Clark mean this? Or did he, as a trained physical scientist, appreciate that the sum of an infinite series may well be finite?[72] Hints about cumulative prosperity were commonplace but Kahn's achievement was to specify a finite relationship. As Keynes later put it to Clark: 'One must distinguish here between some sort of formal statement such as was given in Kahn's *Economic Journal* article and the general notion of there being such a thing as secondary employment.'[73]

What Kahn incorporated into the final draft of his article, as a result of the Circus, was 'Mr Meade's Relation'. Meade focused on the cost of investment and showed that it would be equal to: saving on the dole + increased imports + the increase in unspent profits. What Meade was doing was adding up all the parts of the initial investment which were not passed on via consumption and must therefore have lodged in some pocket of savings. These were necessarily exactly equal to the original outlay because 'money paid out by the Government to the builders of roads continues to be passed on from hand to hand until it reaches one of the *culs-de-sac*'. Here was the answer 'to those who are worried about the monetary sources that are available to meet the cost of the roads', since these turned out to be 'available to precisely the right extent'.[74] While Kahn demonstrated the leverage of the multiplier via its consumption effects, the article was, as he has affirmed, 'far more important for a quite different contribution',[75] viz., Meade's identification of the inversely proportional residues of saving which summed to unity.

Kahn comments: 'Of course what we had done – but failed completely to realise – was, by a very roundabout method, to establish the identity of saving and investment – if saving is defined on commonsense lines rather than those of the *Treatise*.'[76] There is some disagreement over whether the multiplier formula is logically equivalent to the theory of effective demand (defined as the 'formal proposition that *saving and investment are brought into equality by variations in the level of income (output)*'. Milgate contends that Kahn's multiplier argument fell short of the *General Theory*'s contention that an increase in expenditure on investment *generates* savings of exactly the required amount.[77] But this is surely the point established by Mr Meade's Relation. Patinkin, by contrast, accepts that there is a logical but not a chronological equivalence: 'the fact that A implies B does not in turn imply that at the time scholars understood A they also understood B.'[78] As a general caution, this point is well taken, but in this respect too it may be proper to distinguish between Kahn and Meade. It is not unnatural that Mr Meade's Relation should have bulked largest in the mind of its begetter.

It should not be forgotten that, as befits a seminal article, we are dealing with a seed[79] not a flower. Its present importance is as an indication of the thinking of the Circus in their discussions of the *Treatise* during the period November 1930 to March 1931. In these deliberations Meade was, according to Robinson, 'more active than any of us',[80] with the advantages of a man on academic leave.

The ideas which became the common property of the group were usually transmitted through Kahn, as 'angel-messenger', to Keynes himself,[81] who less frequently met the others face to face. It is recalled that Keynes, puzzled, looked around the room for 'Mr Meade's Relation' on first acquaintance.

If there is a theme to the activities of the Circus, it is to identify fixed output as the hidden assumption in the *Treatise* and to establish the bearings of this point for a full-employment equilibrium. As Robinson has put it, 'we learned to distinguish very clearly in those months between those propositions that are universally true and those propositions that are only true in conditions of full employment.'[82] The Treasury View was a clear target here, and the immediate butt of the multiplier article. Of course Archimedes could have a bath, without spilling the water, *if the bath was half empty*. The Circus contribution was thus to press the *Treatise* model hard, and to flush out the inconsistencies and special assumptions implied by its logical structure.

There was a subsequent refinement of the multiplier doctrine to which attention has recently been drawn. In June 1932 Jens Warming, in a sympathetic comment, sought to add one point to Kahn's analysis. He questioned the supposition 'that the new income (or rather the profit) is devoted to consumption in its entirety' and maintained that 'the saving from this income is a very important by-product to the secondary employment, and is just as capable of financing the activity'.[83] In short, Warming pointed to the lack of a general savings function – except insofar as it was indicated by references to 'unspent profits', as Kahn did not fail to point out.[84] Kahn's short riposte, in fact, took up the theme as its own ('When people's incomes are increased, the amount that they save will increase.') His further assertion that, since Warming was not defining 'savings' as in the *Treatise*, 'in this simple-minded sense of the term, savings are always and necessarily equal to investment', was doubly barbed. Ostensibly patronizing towards Warming, it concealed an unflattering appraisal of the adequacy of the *Treatise*.[85] The substantial point about personal savings was swiftly assimilated. When Meade published a popular exposition of the economics of public works in January 1933, it introduced 'individual savings' as the first of the ways in which additional expenditure was 'held up'.[86] By this time, in preparing *The Means to Prosperity*, Keynes had likewise made personal savings into the prime form of what he now called 'leakages' in explaining 'the multiplier'.[87]

8

In the summer of 1931, however, it was by no means clear that the Circus had moved Keynes from the ground of the *Treatise*. Joan Robinson's notorious remark, 'that there were moments when we had some trouble in getting Maynard to see what the point of his revolution really was', has some pertinence at this stage.[88] It is hardly surprising that Keynes stood by the *Treatise*, less than a year from its publication, with reviews still coming in. He seems, however, to have cancelled the university lectures which he was due to give in May 1931 because he wanted time for reappraisal. When he went to Chicago in June 1931 for the Harris Lectures, he spoke, it is true, of the possibility of 'a kind of spurious equilibrium', at less than full employment, and made references to adjustments of output as well as prices. But Patinkin's judgement that the lectures were 'first and foremost a song of praise to his Treatise' seems well-founded.[89] As in the *Treatise*, Keynes vehemently rejected the postulate that saving and investment were necessarily equal, saying, 'this is not so. I venture to say with certainty that it is not so.'[90] This marked, in fact, the finale of the euphoric period in which he was ready to have his head chopped off in defence of the *Treatise*.

There is no real puzzle over Keynes's apparent imperviousness to the arguments of the Circus up to this point. He sailed for the USA on 30 May 1931. The previous day he had written to Kahn: 'By a miracle I finished the work of the Macmillan Committee by 2 p.m. today, after going at it practically continuously since I left Cambridge.'[91] Drafting the Report and its Addendum had pressed hard upon him during April and May. It was only after he returned to England in July 1931 that he had, even by his standards, adequate time to consider criticisms which, after all, went to the root of his proclaimed doctrines. The remarkable thing is not that this process took so long but that Keynes was ready to enter into it at all.

The so-called Fundamental Equations of the *Treatise* were themselves a barrier to fresh thinking. It is notable that Kahn got bogged down in his multiplier article precisely at the point where he loyally attempted to formulate it in terms of the *Treatise*. Keynes was likewise constrained by his own formal apparatus, especially when it became mathematical.[92] He had considerable respect for the discipline and rigour of formal argument. But his insights were not translations into words of what he glimpsed in the equations: he implied the reverse when he spoke of equations as truisms which helped clear the mind.[93] Those who knew him all speak of his mind jumping ahead intuitively to conclusions which he could only later fully substantiate. It follows that there are two reputable schemes on which the chronology of the making of the *General Theory* can be founded. One is to set rigorous criteria for the consistent exposition of the doctrine in a form accessible to a professional readership. The other is that adopted here: to look for indications of developments in his thinking which represented his initial insights – the 'particles of light seen in escaping from a tunnel', of which he told Harrod.[94]

It is my contention that Keynes's statement in March 1932 that saving was no longer the dog but the tail is just such an indication rather than a chance verbal curiosity. It is all of a piece with the response which he was by then prepared to make to the contributions offered by the members of the Circus. In April 1932 he told Joan Robinson that 'of course my treatment is obscure and sometimes inaccurate, and always incomplete, since I was tackling completely unfamiliar ground, and had not got my mind by any means clear on all sorts of points. But the real point is not whether all this is so, as of course it is, but whether this sort of thinking and arguing about the subject is right.' On 1 June 1932 he concluded the protracted discussion of the *Treatise* with Hawtrey by telling him, 'I am working it out all over again.' Instead of savings, increments of expenditure would now be at the centre of the picture. 'This is,' he explained, 'so to speak, the inverse of saving, since saving is the excess of income or earnings over expenditure. . . .'[95]

9

Keynes's letter to Harrod now comes into close focus. Stage One in that account came 'after I had enunciated to myself the psychological law that, when income increases, the gap between income and consumption will increase, – a conclusion of vast importance to my own thinking but not apparently, expressed just like this, to anyone else's'. Expressed *just* like this, the formula does not appear before the second proof of the *General Theory* in the summer of 1935.[96] The nub of it, however, is surely there in the notes from which Keynes gave his first university lectures for three years on 2 May 1932: 'whenever there is a change in income, there will be a change in expenditure the same in direction but less in amount.'[97] On this basis, it seems that Keynes reached Stage One during the early months of 1932. He was, however, unsure how to handle this insight in *Treatise* terms and his lecture led to a series of criticisms in a manifesto from Kahn and the Robinsons. Keynes responded that their objections were insufficient 'to induce me to scrap all my present half-forged weapons.'[98]

At this stage Keynes simply did not have the tools to do the job. He had stepped out of the *Treatise* – but only with one foot. Milgate writes of a 'half way house' and Patinkin similarly characterises the drafts which survive from 1932: 'The voice is that of the *General Theory*: but the analytical framework is still largely that of the *Treatise*.'[99] The controversial point comes with Keynes's university lectures for 1932–3, given during the Michaelmas Term from 10 October to 28 November 1932. Keynes's own fragmentary notes for two of these lectures only came to light when a laundry basket full of additional papers was discovered at Tilton in 1976; but these are now complemented and elaborated in the available sets of lecture notes taken by his students, notably R.B. Bryce and Lorie Tarshis.[100]

In an impressive exegesis of the 'laundry-basket' notes, Milgate demonstrates that Keynes was unable to make his assertions theoretically watertight. True, Keynes now claimed that 'there is no reason to suppose that positions of long-period equilibrium have an inherent tendency or likelihood to be positions of optimum output'.[101] But Milgate's point is that 'this conclusion does not follow from the *Treatise*-type analysis Keynes had presented in the same lecture', because by that analysis an 'equilibrium' always implied full employment. Milgate may well be correct in thinking that his extension of Keynes's argument, so as to reveal its inconsistency, 'follows from the *Treatise* framework'.[102] But surely it *only* follows if the *Treatise* framework is explicitly worked through with more rigour than Keynes himself supplied, in which case one might conclude that Keynes seriously intended to maintain his proposition about sub-optimal equilibrium and lapsed from consistency in simultaneously invoking the *Treatise*.

Patinkin drew upon Bryce's notes, before the discovery of the laundry basket, to argue that implicit *Treatise* definitions vitiate Keynes's analysis. He goes on to cite what he identifies as 'further evidence that Keynes formulated his theory of effective demand after 1932'.[103] This evidence comprises the rough notes for Keynes's university lectures in the Easter Term of 1937, surveying his own ideas. 'I reached the conception of effective demand comparatively late on', he then confessed. 'Those who are old enough and attended in 1931–1932 may remember a contraption of formulas of process of all sorts of lengths depending on technical factors with income emerging at a given date corresponding to input at an earlier date.' This was the time when *ex ante/ex post* would have been useful, as also in the correspondence of March 1932. But it must be remarked that Keynes deliberately restricts his statement to the 1931–2 academic year.[104] The obvious implication is surely that things had changed by the time Keynes began the following year's lectures in October 1932.

Given that Stage One of the Harrod letter had been reached by May 1932, when did Stage Two come therefore? To anticipate slightly, it can be shown that Stage Three, which came 'appreciably later', had been reached by October 1932. It seems overwhelmingly likely, therefore, that it was in the summer of 1932 that Keynes believed himself to have grasped the principle of effective demand. His longstanding concern with the relation between saving and investment thereby found new expression. As he put it later: 'The novelty in my treatment of saving and investment consists, not in my maintaining their necessary aggregate equality, but in the proposition that it is, not the rate of interest, but the level of incomes which (in conjunction with certain other factors) ensures their equality.[105] Thus output had to be envisaged not as fixed or unique or optimal but as an equilibrator with many different possible positions.

Having experienced this revelation, Keynes recalled, 'the result of it was to leave the rate of interest in the air. If the rate of interest is not determined by saving and investment in the same way in which price is determined by supply and demand, how is it determined?'[106] In his letter to Harrod, Keynes described how the answer struck him: 'Then, appreciably later, came the notion of interest as being the measure of liquidity-preference, which became quite clear in my mind the moment I thought of it.' It was like a ripe apple falling off the tree – the fruit of his stale controversy with Robertson over hoarding and bearishness – and immediately fell into place with a wholly new importance. In Keynes's university lecture of 31 October 1932 the new theory of interest was unveiled. As Bryce recorded it, Keynes's exposition led up to a triumphant conclusion: 'in itself the rate of interest is an expression of liquidity preference.[107]

This story has a bearing on two contested points in Keynesian scholarship. The first is that it reinforces Milgate's convincing arguments for seeing liquidity preference as a positive new suggestion rather than part of a negative critique of the classical theory of the rate of interest. Neither Keynes's rejection of the classical theory, therefore, nor his advocacy of the new theory of effective demand, depended crucially upon liquidity preference being true.[108] Secondly, however, there is an anomaly in Patinkin's persistence in dating the inception of the theory of effective demand to 1933. His reading of the Bryce and Tarshis notes has led him to conclude that in October and November 1932 'Keynes's thinking was still largely in the mold of the *Treatise*'.[109] As has been acknowledged, from a doctrine-historical point of view the exposition of effective demand may still leave something to be desired at this point. But whatever the arguable shortcomings in this respect, the proclamation of the liquidity preference concept seems unambiguous. And since this constitutes Stage Three, it can hardly be denied that Stage Two must already have been reached. Denying this, in short, involves impugning what Patinkin himself describes as 'that most revealing letter to Roy Harrod'.[110]

10

When Tarshis arrived in Cambridge as a graduate student he had already received a thorough drilling in the *Treatise*, in which he had become a devout believer. He has testified that when he 'heard Keynes's first lectures in the autumn of 1932, along lines that seemed to differ from the *Treatise*, I wondered what he was talking about'.[111] The notes which he and Bryce took show why.

Keynes's lectures were now called 'The Monetary Theory of Production' and he began by pointing out that the change of title from 'The Pure Theory of Money' indicated a change of attitude. A monetary economy, he claimed, was different from Marshall's world where, with completely fluid wages, prices not output would change. Instead he argued that 'so long as there is a deficiency [of] disbursement, entrepreneurs as a body will incur a loss whatever fluidity of adjustment and hence will throw men out of work'.[112] What, then, determined the volume of output in a monetary economy? The 'supply curve of output as a whole', Tarshis noted, was conceived 'as being a function of profit rather than cost'. Profit in turn depended on aggregate demand. Changes in volume of output were how adjustments took place, and since income was equal to spending on current output, any curtailment of disbursement must be reflected in a contraction of income.[113]

This is really Keynes's first exposition of 'the theory of the demand and supply for output as a whole' (as in Stage Two of the Harrod letter). He was attempting to give an academic justification for his vernacular comment that 'one man's expenditure is another man's income'.[114] He had assured Hawtrey in advance: 'The whole thing comes out just as conveniently in terms of expenditure.[115] But in the effort to make good this claim, his propositions about 'disbursement' were still rather cumbersome.

It was when he came to define savings that Keynes looked back to the *Treatise* rather than forward to the *General Theory*. In writing, 'S' = I – under all circumstances', he was defining S' as 'Surplus'.[116] It was still possible in this scheme for saving to be in excess of investment, albeit with no reference to a full-employment equilibrium.[117]

For Keynes explicitly challenged the orthodox notion of a unique position of equilibrium. 'If this is right, it is true that there is no long-period tendency to an optimum position, i.e. to destroy unemployment.'[118] It followed that traditional theory was dealing with a special assumption – that of full employment – rather than a general case. In attempting to summarize the parameters of his new theory, Keynes suggested: 'Difficulty with all this is particularly in the language rather than the ideas.' He advised that the 'way to get all this is not to try to learn "the Russian" – the language but struggle through it and after that get the ideas then put them and use them in your own language'.[119]

In his final lecture (28 November 1932), Keynes offered a historical commentary on his conclusion that the volume of output was dependent upon the volume of investment, pointing out that it was only in the past century that this view had come to be regarded as eccentric. No sooner had he stumbled upon his new theory than he sought to establish a distinguished if unsuspected ancestry for it. The significant conjuncture is with the work which Sraffa had been doing for his edition of Ricardo, notably the discovery of Malthus's side of the correspondence between them. Keynes had written a paper on Malthus in 1922, which he was currently revising for publication in *Essays in Biography*. It is likely that his copy was ready for the printers in November 1932 – certainly the proofs were sent out in mid-December. There are two major interpolations into the 1922 text, which cannot be later than November 1932 (with a further short emendation in page proof a few weeks later). It was a new Malthus who emerged, one whose major discovery was 'something which might be described, though none too clearly, as "effective demand"'.[120] Compared with Ricardo, Malthus was found to have 'a firmer hold on what may be expected to happen in the real world'. It was Ricardo, by contrast, who had fathered the quantity theory of money. 'When one has painfully escaped from the intellectual domination of these pseudo-arithmetical doctrines', Keynes wrote, 'one is able, perhaps for the first time in a hundred years, to comprehend the real significance of the vaguer intuitions of Malthus.'[121]

Keynes used the correspondence which Sraffa made available to him to draw his own picture of Ricardo as 'investigating the theory of the distribution of the product in conditions of equilibrium', while Malthus was 'concerned with what determines the volume of output day by day in the real world'. At this point Keynes added an afterthought: 'Malthus is dealing with the monetary economy in which we happen to live: Ricardo with the abstraction of a neutral money economy.'[122] These were, of course, exactly the lines along which he had been lecturing that term. Keynes suddenly discovered in Malthus just what he was looking for. The retrieval of the lost correspondence by Sraffa ('from whom nothing is hid') enabled Keynes 'to show Malthus's complete comprehension of the effects of excessive saving on output via its effects on profits'. But the crucial letter, in which Malthus explained 'that the *effective* demand is diminished',[123] had not in fact remained hid until unearthed by Sraffa. It had been published in the *Economic Journal* in 1907, but was ignored by Keynes in preparing his 1922 paper. Only ten years later did it speak to his concerns and give him a name for his new concept – effective demand.

11

If this evidence is accepted, the inception of the *General Theory* must be placed firmly in 1932. Keynes's subsequent toils were chiefly in making its exposition fit for his professional colleagues. In this, as in other ways, what he wrote of Malthus – 'The words and the ideas are simple'[124] – had application to himself. When Keynes gave a lecture in Stockholm after the publication of the *General Theory* he began (according to his notes),[125]

> What I have to say intrinsically easy
> Difficulty lies in its running against our habitual modes of thought
> It is only to an audience of economists that it is difficult

This was, of course, precisely the audience ('my fellow economists') he chose to address in the *General Theory*, which he intended to be 'on extremely academic lines'. [126] Likewise, he responded to Robertson's comment, that a large part of the theoretical structure was to him 'almost complete mumbo-jumbo' by stating that 'this book is a purely theoretical work, not a collection of wisecracks'.[127] By his own conception of economics as a branch of logic, he was committed to a rigorous formal presentation. In this respect his university lecture course in the Michaelmas Term of 1933 gave a more cogent account of the theory of effective demand according to the criteria of professional economists. It is easy to see why it was this account which reconciled Tarshis at the time and which has subsequently persuaded Patinkin to place the formulation of the theory in 1933.[128] Yet Keynes also paused to reflect in his lecture of 6 November upon a distinction between original thought, on the one hand, and what he called scholasticism on the other. He saw these as two necessary stages. His remarks made a considerable impression upon both Bryce and Tarshis; but the fullest version is given by a newcomer, Marvin Faligatter:[129]

> Even in mathematics, when it is a matter of original work, you do not think always in precise terms. The precise use of language comes at a late stage in the development of one's thoughts You can think accurately and effectively long before you can so to speak photograph your thought. A not quite perfect epitome of this would be to say that when you adopt perfectly precise language you are trying to express yourself for the benefit of those who are incapable of thought.

Though he put the point somewhat differently on different occasions, Keynes continually adverted to a distinction of this kind. It followed that progress in his chosen field depended on a double process: 'Economics is a science of thinking in terms of models joined to the art of choosing models which are relevant to the contemporary world.'[130] The claims Keynes made for the *General Theory* were accordingly at once immodest and humble. 'If the simple basic ideas can become familiar and acceptable', he wrote in 1937, 'time and experience and the collaboration of a number of minds will discover the best way of expressing them.'[131]

12

There has been no lack of economists ready to take up this invitation. Some of their efforts in elaborating widely differing versions of Keynesian economics will be mentioned later. But Keynes's remark also poses a problem for historians, not in projecting his work forwards in time but in tracing it backwards. The task here is to identify the essential paradigm or message as Keynes apprehended it – the general theory behind the *General Theory*. What simple conception impressed itself upon Keynes's mind during 1932, allowing him to make sense in a new way of the relation between income and expenditure and between saving and investment?

The structure of his lecture course in the Michaelmas Term of 1932 points to the answer. After preparing the ground in his first lecture, Keynes stated his theme in the second. It was the distinction between what was true for the individual and what was true for the community as a whole which constituted the linchpin of the analysis. 'For [the] community as a whole disbursements must equal income, but this is not necessary for an individual. How are these compatible[?] – this is what people find difficult.[132] How could individual liberty in decision-making be reconciled with the necessity for an aggregate equality? Keynes's answer was that aggregate income would change so as to bring about this reconciliation. In the third lecture he introduced his variations in the form of 'two fundamental propositions'. One was familiar: that the harmony between individual choice in holding money and the necessity for total holdings to be what the banks create was brought about by changes in prices and income. The other he claimed as less familiar: 'while every individual has liberty to settle his own dispersals, the aggregate disbursements must be equal to total income.[133]

It is part of what every school child knows about Keynesian economics that it shifted attention to aggregates and established a macroeconomic approach to the analysis of the system as a whole. In doing so it identified as fallacious the claim, for example, that because individuals might benefit from cutting wages, everyone could beneficially do so at once. This 'fallacy of composition', however, plays a larger part than has been recognized in the structure of the *General Theory*. It is built into the architecture of the work as a whole. Book I, 'Introduction', concludes with a rejection of the direction taken by classical theory since Malthus. The last words of Book II, 'Definitions and Ideas', point to 'the vital difference between the theory of the economic behaviour of the aggregate and the theory of the behaviour of the individual unit, in which we assume that changes in the individual's own demand do not affect his income'.[134] Book III, 'The Propensity to Consume' likewise concludes with the sentence identifying unemployment as 'an inevitable result of applying to the conduct of the State the maxims which are best calculated to "enrich" an individual by enabling him to pile up claims to enjoyment which he does not intend to exercise at any definite time'.[135]

The first time the idea is introduced it is a *paradox*: 'It is natural to suppose that the act of an individual, by which he enriches himself without apparently taking anything from anyone else, must also enrich the community as a whole.'[136] This ultimately forms the basis for a *distinction* between 'the theory of the individual industry or firm and of the rewards and the distribution between different uses of a given quantity of resources on the one hand, and the theory of output and employment as a whole on the other hand'.[137] Keynes's great *coup*, however, was to provide an *explanation*. The reconciliation of the identity of aggregate saving and investment depended 'on saving being, like spending, a two-sided affair', with consequences for the incomes of others.[138] 'The mere act of saving by one individual, being *two-sided* as we have shown above, forces some other individual to transfer to him some article of wealth, old or new.'[139]

In the *Treatise*, Keynes had emphasized the potential disparity between saving and investment from the point of view of the individual decision-makers. In the *General Theory* he insisted on their aggregate equality and showed how the double aspect of every transaction accounted for this identity, requiring changes in prices, output, and employment in the process. This followed 'merely from the fact that there cannot be a buyer without a seller or a seller without a buyer'.[140] This conception informed all his thinking by the end of 1932. 'The course of exchange, as we all know, moves round a closed circle', he wrote in the *New Statesman*. 'When we transmit the tension, which is beyond our own endurance, to our neighbour, it is only a question of a little time before it reaches ourselves again travelling round the circle.[141]

What prompted Keynes to take up this idea? At a formal level the fallacy of composition must have been familiar to him The standard modern treatment was in Book III of J.S. Mill's *System of Logic*, which he had utilized for his own purposes in his work on probability.[142] The general notion enters prominently into his writings from the early months of 1931. In February 1931 he suggested that 'each individual is impelled by his paper losses or profits to do precisely the opposite of what is desirable in the general interest'.[143] When advocating a tariff in the next month, he cited the advantage each employer saw in wage cuts when he ignored the consequent reduction in his customers' incomes. This point was reiterated in the summer in the Addendum to the Macmillan Report, which also stressed the 'false analogy between the position of a particular firm and that of the community as a whole' in another respect, viz. that each, but not all, could increase liquid resources.[144] Almost an identical proposition was to reappear in the *General Theory*.[145]

One further possible influence on Keynes's thinking deserves mention at this point, namely the work of J.A. Hobson, to whom the *General Theory* paid a generous if belated tribute. Although often regarded simply as an underconsumptionist, Hobson gave his insight about unlimited saving more general bearing: 'It is at root a very simple fallacy, viz. the contention that what anyone can do, all can do.'[146] He called this the individualist fallacy and it runs as a leitmotif through his numerous publications. The evidence, however, is fairly conclusive that Keynes took very little directly from Hobson. Only when the *General Theory* was already in draft did he appreciate the sense in which his own ideas had been foreshadowed in these heretical writings. Afterwards he told Hobson, 'I am ashamed how blind I was for many years to your essential contentions as to the insufficiency of effective demand.'[147]

13

In November 1934 Keynes gave a radio broadcast which placed his current thinking in the context of what other economists were saying. He spoke of a gulf between two groups. 'On the one side are those who believe that the existing economic system is, in the long run, a self-adjusting system, though with creaks and groans and jerks, and interrupted by time lags, outside interference and mistakes.' This was a formidable position, buttressed by a century of economic analysis. But Keynes now chose to range himself, by contrast, with the heretics, like Hobson, believing that 'their flair and their instinct move them towards the right conclusions'.[148]

Although given to a popular audience, Keynes's talk focused on differences of fundamental theory rather than immediate policy, and he explicitly rejected the postulate of a full-employment equilibrium, even when qualified by imperfections. This marked the distance he had moved since the *Treatise*, where the analysis is basically imperfectionist. It may also account for a striking difference which has often been observed between the *Treatise*, with its concern for international considerations, and the *General Theory*, with its model of a closed economy. The theory of the *Treatise* was premised upon equilibrium, with market forces tending towards it; but the policies appropriate for Britain at the time of its composition were those which would tackle an actual disequilibrium. If wages or interest rates displayed a rigidity inappropriate for domestic harmony, it could all be blamed upon the Gold Standard – in short, the special case.

After September 1931, however, there was no such external constraint. Nor does the *General Theory* depend upon any assumption about the rigidity of wages. On the contrary, it was the 'classical' theory which was 'accustomed to rest the supposedly self-adjusting character of the economic system on an assumed fluidity of money-wages; and, when there is rigidity, to lay on this rigidity the blame of maladjustment'.[149] As for interest rate, where Keynes of the *Treatise* had supplemented 'creaks and groans and jerks' with deleterious 'outside interference' in keeping Bank Rate too high, its significance was now conceived quite differently. Interest rate might well be higher than the rate of return on the marginal investments needed to sustain full employment; but since liquidity preference determined the one and effective demand the other, there was no supply-and-demand mechanism tending to bring them together. Keynes therefore wrote that 'the weight of my criticism is directed against the inadequacy of the *theoretical* foundations of the *laissez-faire* doctrine upon which I was brought up and which for many years I taught. . . .'[150] The lack of self-adjusting forces was the real meaning of the new emphasis upon a sub-optimal equilibrium. The author of the *Treatise*, one might say, recognized unemployment as a condition of disequilibrium, because the economy was not *in balance*. The author of the *General Theory* saw the enormity of unemployment at equilibrium because the economy was *at rest*.[151]

Why, then, has Keynes been interpreted otherwise? The assimilation of the *General Theory* to neo-classical analysis received a strong impetus from Hicks's influential review in 1937, 'Mr Keynes and the Classics'. This was the origin of the ISLM diagram as a simplification of the relationship between saving and investment, income and interest. Hicks, contending that the liquidity preference doctrine was vital, showed how this new device might be incorporated into the neo-classical model where saving and investment were equilibrated via interest rate. 'With this revision', he claimed, 'Mr Keynes takes a big step back to Marshallian orthodoxy. . . .'[152] For liquidity preference was now only another imperfection, like sticky wages, thwarting the tendency of the system towards equilibrium. Unemployment, however intractable in the real world, was thus in theory a symptom of disequilibrium.

As the progenitor of the 'neo-classical synthesis', Hicks has sometimes been portrayed as the bad fairy in a changeling story, visiting the cradle of the *General Theory*, and, while nobody was looking closely enough, substituting for it 'Mr Keynes's special theory'. Yet Hicks had reasonable grounds for maintaining 'that Keynes accepted the ISLM diagram as a fair statement of his position – of the nucleus, that is, of his position'. At any rate, he told Hicks at the time that he had 'next to nothing to say by way of criticism'.[153] If Keynes was tacitly accepting ISLM as one possible application of his theory, however, he was hardly endorsing it as the authorized version; and here, as elsewhere, he did not insist on others 'learning the Russian'.[154] It is notable that Keynes's closest colleagues and successors in Cambridge did not countenance the neo-classical synthesis, either at the time or subsequently. There may be a further reason why Keynes did not make his own position crystal clear: that it was not. In fact, almost 60 per cent of the final text of chapter 14, 'The classical theory of the rate of interest', had been added at proof stage in 1935, as a direct result of Harrod's rooted defence of the supply-and-demand conception of interest. Milgate has persuasively argued that it was these changes which opened the door for assimilation to a Marshallian account; and he opts for reconstructing Keynes's critique on the basis of the drafts rather than the final published text.[155] From an economist's viewpoint this procedure is legitimate; from a historian's, it obviously does violence to the *General Theory* as it left Keynes's hands. If the historical Keynes argued himself into a muddle on the rate of interest, as some believe,[156] this cannot retrospectively be put right on his behalf. It is interesting, however, that Keynes seems to have been clearer in his own mind when drafting in 1934 than he was when revising a year later.

14

In 1933 Keynes gave a general presentation of his ideas in *The Means to Prosperity*. It was heavily dependent on the idea of the multiplier and used it to bolster the arguments for loan-financed public works. In this sense it was a better-mounted case along the lines of *Can Lloyd George Do It?*, now that Keynes had a convincing answer to his critics of 1929. It followed through the effect of public (or other new) expenditure; it dealt with the relief to the Exchequer via savings on the dole; it pointed to the revenue benefit from raising national income. The suggestion was also made at one point that tax cuts could be used to the same ends, with the implication of unbalancing the Budget (or leaving it unbalanced) by suspending the Sinking Fund and resorting to loans on capital projects. All this is plainly in the mainstream of 'Keynesian' policy proposals with an obvious cutting edge for political action.

The change in political context since 1929, however, was striking. The National Government stood immoveable. 'There is probably no practical good sense in any efforts except those deliberately aimed at ousting them', Keynes told Harold Macmillan in September 1932.[157] Yet the prospects of doing so were bleak. 'My own aim is economic reform by the methods of political liberalism', Keynes affirmed in 1934,[158] but he could no longer look confidently to the Liberal party, which lay in ruins. Relations with Lloyd George had become frosty. The notorious portrait of him as the 'goat-footed bard' in *Essays in Biography* created a minor sensation. *The Daily Mail* carried a headline:

MR LL. GEORGE – 'THIS SYREN'
MR J.M. KEYNES'S ATTACK

When its reporter asked Lloyd George for a comment, he replied scornfully, 'That was written in 1919.'[159] In 1933–4, when he took to authorship himself, he was less magnanimous and declared that Keynes was 'an entertaining economist whose bright but shallow dissertations on finance and political economy, when not taken seriously, always provide a source of innocent merriment to his readers'.[160] Readers of *Can Lloyd George Do It?*, of course, had been spared this advice in 1929.

Keynes was throughout his life a political animal. His view of the state was, in Harrod's classic phrase, imbued with one of 'the presuppositions of Harvey Road' – 'the idea that the government of Britain was and would continue to be in the hands of an intellectual aristocracy using the method of persuasion'.[161] Yet though Keynes attached great importance to the formation of expert opinion, his conception of politics also involved a wider constituency. Many Liberal intellectuals, from the 1860s onward, were beguiled by the notion of an alliance between 'brains and numbers' against the inert forces of conservatism. Keynes's commitment to the New Liberalism in his formative years before the First World War was founded upon the forms of 'progressive' politics – an intellectual reconciliation of liberalism with socialism and a practical working agreement between the Liberal party and Labour.[162] It was this conception which resurfaced as the political thrust behind Keynes's unemployment proposals from 1924 and led him to seek an answer that did not turn upon wage rigidities.[163] The *Treatise* was a *tour de force* in squaring this sort of policy advice and political action with neo-classical orthodoxy. Keynes's lack of party affiliations after 1931 provides a striking contrast with the late 1920s. In October 1935 Herbert Samuel, as leader of the Liberal Party, sent out the usual pre-election appeal. Keynes's generosity for public objects is well attested and his personal assets were in a very healthy state (between a quarter and half a million pounds). Yet he turned Samuel down flat, primarily 'because I do not really agree with what you quite properly stress in your letter, namely, the question of maintaining the separate identity of the Liberal Party'.[164] In claiming to stand somewhere between Liberal and Labour, he was at one with colleagues from a younger generation, like Austin

Robinson and James Meade; Joan Robinson stood further to the left, with Richard Kahn somewhere in between. This was the spectrum of Keynes's instinctive political affinities. In 1938 he told the incoming Liberal leader, Sinclair: 'The Liberal Party is the centre of gravity and ought to be the focus of a new alignment of the progressive forces. In practice, of course, the Labour Party has to be the predominant member.'[165] Here was a pipe dream of the revival of the progressive movement of his youth under new conditions – and one which, unexpectedly quickly, the political revolution of 1940 was to fulfil, bringing Keynes into the crux of a new consensus.[166] In the years in which he was writing the *General Theory*, however, Keynes showed peculiar detachment from immediate political objectives. He refused to endorse the manifesto of the (eminently congenial) Next Five Years Group in 1935, saying: 'whilst I thought that the proposal and the sort of ideas which your book contains was my job two years ago, and I daresay it was, I now consider my job is rather different.'[167]

Keynes seems to have believed that 'we are . . . at one of those uncommon junctures of human affairs where we can be saved by the solution of an intellectual problem, and in no other way'.[168] Hence the claim to Shaw that it was 'a book on economic theory' which had to revolutionize 'the way the world thinks about economic problems'. It was a revolution in economic theory which he purposed, no doubt in the confidence that changes in policy would follow. In 1934 he wrote that, while he had not yet convinced either the expert or the ordinary man that he was right, 'it is, I feel certain, only a matter of time before I convince both; and when both are convinced, economic policy will, with the usual time lag, follow suit.'[169] But there is almost nothing in the *General Theory* that speaks directly to the 'Keynesian' policy agenda – barely a mention of emergency public works, nothing on fiscal means of demand management, nor on deficit budgeting. The final passage of the book, with its theme that 'soon or late, it is ideas, not vested interests, which are dangerous for good or evil',[170] should be read as acknowledging the problem of ideology, not dismissing it. Keynes's letter to Shaw, often cited as an example of callow rationalism, continues: 'When my new theory has been duly assimilated and mixed with politics and feelings and passions, I can't predict what the final upshot will be in its effects on action and affairs.'[171]

In writing the *General Theory*, Keynes sought to grapple with economic theory in a fundamental way. His project can only be understood as a rigorous inquiry, in which certain directions were set, but one crucially determined thereafter by the unfolding of an immanent logic of discovery. Joan Robinson recalled of this period: 'I don't really agree with the idea of who influenced whom. Logic is the same for everybody. Keynes opened up a whole subject – we helped to clear up some connections which we saw – discovered – not invented.'[172] The move away from the *Treatise* was determined in this way. The searching critique from the Circus pointed towards new concepts; their significance took time to sink in; at least one fruitful contribution fed in from outside Cambridge; and the sharp minds of Robertson, Hawtrey, Harrod and others helped shape the book in draft. It may not be perfect in exposition but it can fairly be taken as a considered expression of its author's central convictions.

Those convictions, as he recognized, had been formed in his own mind in several stages. What organized them was a view of market transactions in which the random disparities of individual behaviour were contained by the requirement that all such transactions were double-sided. So in aggregate they were reconciled – not through a unique market-clearing adjustment of prices but through output and income changes. In equilibrium the economy was 'at rest' but might well not be 'in balance'. It followed that economic theory could not postulate market tendencies of a self-righting nature. To do so was to lapse into the fallacy that what one could do, all could do. Such were the relatively simple ideas, linked by a strong sense of logical necessity, which, by the close of the year 1932, guided Keynes's thinking. Whether Keynesian economics can be considered a viable economic model may be a problem for economists, as their avidity in debating it suggests. But the nature of Keynes's *General Theory* (1936) is a problem for historians – and one which needs addressing.

Notes

1. *JMK*, vol. 28, p. 42 (Keynes to Shaw, 1 Jan. 1935). This essay was read in draft by Stefan Collini, Ewen Green, Geoff Harcourt, Don Moggridge, Thomas K. Rymes, Mary Short, Barry Supple, Duncan Tanner and John Thompson, all of whom made useful suggestions, as did Neville Cain, Selwyn Cornish and Murray Milgate at an earlier stage; and I also benefited from interviews with the late Lord Kahn, Sir Austin Robinson and (most notably) Professor James Meade.

2. *JMK*, vol. 13, p. 548 (Keynes to Harrod, 27 Aug. 1935). Roy Harrod (1900–78), Student of Christ Church, Oxford, from 1924; author of *The Life of John Maynard Keynes* (1951).

3. It would be unfair to set up the first edition of Michael Stewart's widely read Penguin, *Keynes and After* (Harmondsworth, 1967) as a straw man of triumphalism, but it bears characteristic marks of the period in which it was written.

4. John Hicks (1904–89), lecturer in economics at the London School of Economics, 1926–35, and at Cambridge, 1935–8. The textbook diagram plotting the Investment-Saving curve against Liquidity Preference (and Money) is derived from 'Mr Keynes and the Classics', *Econometrica*, v (1937), reprinted in John Hicks, *Critical Essays in Monetary Theory* (1967), pp. 126–42. On the influence of this model see Hyman P. Minsky, *John Maynard Keynes* (1975), chs. 1 and 2.

5. Axel Leijonhufvud, *On Keynesian Economics and the Economics of Keynes* (1968); also *Keynes and the Classics*, Institute of Economic Affairs, Occasional Paper No. 30 (1969).

6. Alan Coddington, *Keynesian Economics: The Search for First Principles* (1983), esp. pp. 92–114. A new perspective, bringing out some recent convergences, is given in G.C. Harcourt and T.J. O'Shaughnessy, 'Keynes's unemployment equilibrium', in G.C. Harcourt (ed.), *Keynes and His Contemporaries*, Sixth and Centennial Keynes Seminar (1985), pp. 3–41.

7. 'The general theory of employment', *JMK*, vol. 14, pp. 109–23. The exegesis in ch. 11 of G.L.S. Shackle, *The Years of High Theory: Invention and Tradition in Economic Thought, 1926–39* (1967), is subtitled 'Keynes's ultimate meaning'.

8. Murray Milgate, *Capital and Employment: A Study of Keynes's Economics* (1982); cf. John Eatwell and Murray Milgate, *Keynes's Economics and the Theory of Value and Distribution* (1983), esp. pp. 93–128, 203–13, 247–80.
9. Leijonhufvud, *On Keynesian Economics*, p. 390.
10. Eatwell and Milgate, indeed, make this the hub of their alternative taxonomy, contending that a wide variety of 'imperfectionists' assume that the market is *inhibited* in its otherwise implicit tendency towards full employment, and identify the reason in a string of frictions, rigidities and misapprehensions – 'any factor which causes the market to work imperfectly will do.' Eatwell and Milgate, *Keynes's Economics*, p. 3.
11. T.W. Hutchison, *Keynes v. the Keynesians. . . ?*, Institute of Economic Affairs (1977); cf. Joan Robinson, 'What has become of the Keynesian revolution?', in Milo Keynes (ed.), *Essays on John Maynard Keynes* (1975), p. 127.
12. Leijonhufvud, *On Keynesian Economics*, p. 9. This was a prudent restriction. His identification of the 'revolutionary' element in the *General Theory* as a reversal in the adjustment speeds of the Marshallian ranking of price as against quantity changes (p. 52), has been rebutted by Richard Jackman on doctrine-historical grounds. 'There is, of course, no support whatsoever in any of Keynes's writings for such an interpretation.' See 'Keynes and Leijonhufvud', *Econ. Jnl.*, n.s., xxvi (1974), p. 265.
13. Milgate, *Capital and Employment*, p. 6.
14. T.W. Hutchison, *Economics and Economic Policy in Britain, 1946–66* (1968), App., 'Pigou and Keynes on employment policy', esp. pp. 294–5. A.C. Pigou (1877–1959), succeeded Marshall as Professor of Political Economy at Cambridge in 1908; Fellow of King's College.
15. Donald Winch, *Economics and Policy: A Historical Study* (revised edn, 1972); Susan Howson and Donald Winch, *The Economic Advisory Council, 1930–39* (1977), esp. pp. 47–9, 51–5, 128–31, 137–9, 162–4.
16. Elizabeth Durbin, *New Jerusalems: The Labour Party and the Economics of Democratic Socialism* (1985).
17. Robert Skidelsky, *Politicians and the Slump: The Labour Government of 1929–31* (1967); D.E. Moggridge, *British Monetary Policy, 1924–1931: The Norman Conquest of $4.86* (1972); Susan Howson, *Domestic Monetary Management in Britain, 1919–38* (1975); G.C. Peden, *British Rearmament and the Treasury, 1932–39* (1979); Roger Middleton, *Towards the Managed Economy: Keynes, the Treasury and the Fiscal Policy Debate of the 1930s* (1985). See also the useful articles concerned with the 'Treasury view', n. 41 below.
18. This literature is surveyed in Sean Glynn and Alan Booth, 'Unemployment in interwar Britain: a case for re-learning the lessons ofthe 1930s?', *Econ. Hist. Rev.*, 2nd ser., xxxvi (1983), pp. 329–48. See also two chapters in vol. 2 of Roderick Floud and Donald McCloskey, *The Economic History of Britain since 1700* (1981): Susan Howson, 'Slump and unemployment', pp. 265–85, and T. Thomas, 'Aggregate demand in the United Kingdom, 1918–45', pp. 332–46.
19. See the brisk conclusion: 'Keynes went off and wrote the *General Theory*.' P.F. Clarke, 'The Progressive Movement in England', *Trans. Roy. Hist Soc.*, 5th ser., xxiv (1974), p. 181. This citation is not uniquely culpable in its question-begging circumspection but is humbly offered as an illustration of the sort of thing historians say when they are not quite sure what they are talking about.
20. Winch, *Economics and Policy* remains the most illuminating introduction to the whole subject. D.E. Moggridge, *Keynes* (2nd edn, 1980) is an authoritative distillation of the author's unrivalled knowledge of the Keynes papers.
21. E.A.G. Robinson, 'John Maynard Keynes, 1883–1946', *Econ. Jnl.*, lvii (1947), esp. pp. 39–46; Lawrence R. Klein, *The Keynesian Revolution* (1947; 1952), esp. ch. 2; Harrod, *Life*, ch. 11; Paul Lambert, 'The evolution of Keynes's thought from the *Treatise on Money* to the *General Theory*', *Annals of Public and Cooperative Economy*, xl (1969), pp. 243–63; D.E. Moggridge, 'From the *Treatise* to the *General Theory*: an exercise in chronology', *Hist. of Pol. Econ.*, vol. 5 (1973), pp. 72–88, and reformulated to some extent in the 2nd edn. of *Keynes*, pp. 91–119; Milgate, *Capital and Employment*, and 'The "new" Keynes papers', in Eatwell and Milgate, *Keynes's Economics*, pp. 187–99; Don Patinkin, *Keynes's Monetary*

Thought: A Study of Its Development (1976), chs 7–9, and Anticipations of the General Theory? (1982), Pt I; see also Don Patinkin and J. Clark Leith (eds), Keynes. Cambridge and the General Theory (1977), pp. 3–25.

22. JMK, vol. 7, p. 3 and n. 1.
23. JMK, vol. 13, p. 409 ('A monetary theory of production', 1933). Patinkin at one point advanced the contention, firstly that Keynes did not draw a sharp distinction between Marshallian (partial equilibrium) and Walrasian (general equilibrium) approaches, and secondly that 'he effectively made use of both of them in the General Theory': Keynes's Monetary Thought, p. 101. The first but not the second point is accepted here.
24. JMK, vol. 7, p. xxxi.
25. JMK, vol. 7, p. 3.
26. JMK, vol. 20, p. 133 (evidence, 6 March 1930). R.H. Brand (1878–1963), managing director of the merchant bankers, Lazard Brothers, and director of Lloyds Bank.
27. JMK, vol. 20, p. 87 (evidence, 21 Feb. 1930). T.E. Gregory (1890–1970), Sir E. Cassel Professor of Banking at the London School of Economics and noted for his orthodox views.
28. JMK, vol. 20, p. 87.
29. JMK, vol. 20, pp. 51–4 (evidence, 20 Feb. 1930).
30. JMK, vol. 20, pp. 496–7 (New Statesman & Nation, 16 Mar. 1931); cf. JMK, vol. 5, p. 165 (Treatise). Lionel Robbins (1898–1984), Professor of Economics at the LSE since 1929 and the youngest member of the committee of economists of the EAC
31. See Hutchison, Economics and Economic Policy, esp. pp. 282–4.
32. Howson and Winch, Economic Advisory Council, p. 63; cf. pp. 61–3 for Robbins's dissent and pp. 64–6 for a lucid analysis of Pigou's 'second-best' assumptions in his policy advice. Milgate demonstrates that, whatever their policy divergences in the 1920s, 'there was never any ultimate theoretical principle at stake in the Keynes-Pigou debates' until after 1931: 'Keynes and Pigou on the gold standard and monetary theory', Contribs to Pol. Econ. (1983), pp. 39–48, at p. 40.
33. Patinkin, Keynes's Monetary Thought, p. 132.
34. D.E. Moggridge and Susan Howson, 'Keynes on monetary policy, 1910–1946', Oxford Econ. Papers, n.s., xxvi (1974), p. 236; cf. Moggridge, Keynes, pp. 85–8. My own study of Keynes's writings in this period fully endorses Moggridge's defence of his consistency: Peter Clarke, 'The politics of Keynesian economics, 1924–31', ch. 3 above. One phrase about 'the somewhat fluctuating views of J.M. Keynes' originated with Reginald Bassett, Nineteen-Thirty-One: Political Crisis (1958), p. 339, and was well met by Winch, Economics and Policy, pp. 151–2.
35. JMK, vol. 19, pp. 812–13 (letter to the Evening Standard, 30 April 1929). Robert Skidelsky follows this line in making 1925 the watershed in Keynes's analysis of unemployment: 'Keynes and the Treasury View: the case for and against an active unemployment policy 1920–1939', in W.J. Mommsen (ed.), The Emergence of the Welfare State in Britain and Germany, 1850–1950 (1981), pp. 178–80. This misconception may originate in E.A.G. Robinson, 'John Maynard Keynes', pp. 34–6; though Harrod is firmly on the right track: Life, p. 350.
36. Ch. 3 above, 'The Politics of Keynesian economics', seeks to bring home this point. It may be objected that the interest rate structure already anticipated the return to Gold, as a declared policy aim, which is partly true. But the key point concerns Keynes's perceptions at the time, which, although generally fearful of deflation, also manifested surprising 'inflationary expectations' of the pound rising above parity. See Moggridge, British Monetary Policy, p. 96; cf. p. 43 n. 6; also Milgate, 'Keynes and Pigou', pp. 41–5. In the June 1924 issue of the Economic Journal Keynes commented that 'it is certainly possible that we shall return to our former parity of exchange without resorting to deflation' (JMK, vol. 19, p. 213). In May 1924, when this must have been written, Keynes simultaneously broached his 'drastic remedy' for unemployment.
37. JMK, vol. 21, p. 57 (Halley-Stewart lecture).
38. JMK, vol. 14, p. 259 (Keynes to Kahn, 20 Oct. 1937).

39. *JMK*, vol. 14, p. 123 ('The general theory of employment', Feb. 1937); cf. *JMK*, vol. 29, p. 215 (Keynes to Lerner, 16 June 1936). Keynes wrote to G. Haberler, 3 April 1938: 'I mean by a "classical economist" one who, whether he knows it or not, requires for his conclusions the assumption of something in the nature of Say's Law.' *JMK*, vol. 29, p. 270.

40. *JMK*, vol. 9, p. 115, quoting Churchill from *Hansard*, 15 Apr. 1929. This is the *locus classicus*, but by no means an isolated statement. See Howson and Winch, *Economic Advisory Council*, p. 27, tracing its theoretical pedigree back to R.G. Hawtrey. Neville Cain, 'Hawtrey and multiplier theory', *Australian Econ. Hist. Rev.*, xxii (1982), pp. 68–77, makes it clear that Hawtrey's views were more sophisticated and actually anticipated some of the later insights of Keynes and Kahn.

41. G.C. Peden, 'The "Treasury View" on public works and employment in the interwar period', *Econ. Hist. Rev.*, 2nd ser., xxxvii (1984), pp. 167–81; idem, 'Sir Richard Hopkins and the "Keynesian revolution" in employment policy, 1929–45', *Econ. Hist. Rev.*, xxvi (1982), pp. 281–96; Jim Tomlinson, *Problems of British Economic policy, 1870–1945* (1981), pp. 76–91; Alan Booth, 'The "Keynesian revolution" in economic policy-making', *Econ. Hist Rev.*, 2nd ser., xxxvi (1983), pp. 103–23, and his exchange with J.D. Tomlinson, ibid., xxxviii (1984), pp. 258–67; Roger Middleton, 'The Treasury in the 1930s: political and administrative constraints to acceptance of the "new" economics', *Oxford Econ. Papers*, n.s., xxxiv (1982), pp. 48–77, and *Towards the Managed Economy*, chs 5 and 8.

42. *JMK*, vol. 20, p. 166 (evidence, 22 May 1930).

43. *JMK*, vol. 20, p. 129 (evidence, 6 March 1930). Keynes was clearly referring to the unsigned Treasury memorandum in *Memoranda on Certain Proposals relating to Unemployment*, Cmd 3331 (1929), pp. 43–55. This proposition is affirmed at pp. 50–1, 53. According to Kahn, 'Sir Richard Hopkins was warned and the "Treasury View" no longer appeared in the White Paper as fundamental and decisive, taken by itself, as Winston Churchill had made it appear in his Budget statement.' Richard F. Kahn, *The Making of Keynes' General Theory* (1984), p. 81.

44. *JMK*, vol. 20, p. 130 (evidence, 6 March 1930).

45. Middleton, *Towards the Managed Economy*, pp. 149, 153–65, 171.

46. Middleton, *Towards the Managed Economy*, p. 155.

47. *JMK*, vol. 9, p. 121.

48. Q. 5603, 5624, 5625, *JMK*, vol. 20, pp. 169–70, 172 (evidence, 22 May 1930).

49. Q. 5689, *JMK*, vol. 20, p. 179. Peden seems to me to accept this comment too literally, with insufficient sensitivity to the kind of game Hopkins and Keynes had been playing. In this respect Harrod's account (*Life*, pp. 420–2) is still more successful in capturing the essence of the encounter.

50. *JMK*, vol. 9, p. 143 (*New Statesman & Nation*, 15 Aug. 1931). One other example is that cited by Peden ('The "Treasury View"', p. 174 n. 31), viz. an aside in Keynes's open letter to President Roosevelt, 30 Dec. 1933, where Keynes acknowledged that there were real practical obstacles to be overcome in improvising public works. *JMK*, vol. 21, p. 293.

51. *JMK*, vol. 9, p. 350 (*Means to Prosperity*).

52. Keynes to A.P. Lerner, 16 June 1936 (*JMK*, vol. 29, pp. 214–16); Keynes to Harrod, 30 Aug. 1936 (*JMK*, vol. 14, pp. 84–6); 'The general theory of employment', published *Quarterly Jnl of Econ.*, Feb. 1937, but drafted late 1936 (*JMK*, vol. 14, esp. pp. 119–23). The original draft of the letter to Harrod is printed as an Appendix below.

53. *JMK*, vol. 20, p. 86 (evidence, 21 Feb. 1930). Harry Johnson's comment that Keynes 'was struggling to get the *Treatise on Money* off his hands in order to clear the way for the *General Theory*' is puzzling. Elizabeth S. Johnson and Harry G. Johnson, *The Shadow of Keynes* (Oxford, 1978), p. 69.

54. *JMK*, vol. 20, p. 351 (Keynes to Norman, 22 May 1930).

55. F.A. Hayek, *A Tiger by the Tail*, ed. Sudha R. Shenoy, Institute of Economic Affairs (1972), pp. 100, 103–4. F.A. von Hayek (1899–1992), Tooke Professor at the LSE from 1931.

56. Harry Johnson, 'Keynes and British economics', in Milo Keynes (ed.), *Essays on John Maynard Keynes*, pp. 115–16; reprinted in Johnson and Johnson, *Shadow of Keynes*,

pp. 211–12; cf. p. 27 for Elizabeth Johnson's variant view that the *General Theory* was required by Keynes's 'intellectual honesty and concern for economic science'.

57. *JMK*, vol. 20, p. 87 (evidence, 21 Feb. 1930).

58. Keynes's comment on Hayek was noted on his copy of *Economica*, *JMK*, vol. 13, p. 243. D.H. Robertson (1890–1963), Fellow of Trinity College, Cambridge, and Reader in Economics since 1930.

59. *JMK*, vol. 13, pp. 228–9, 230–1 (variorum of Keynes to Robertson, 5 May 1931, and his rejoinder, *Econ. Jnl*, Sept. 1931).

60. *JMK*, vol. 5, pp. 128–31.

61. *JMK*, vol. 13, p. 246 ('The pure theory of money: a reply to Dr Hayek', *Economica*, Nov. 1931).

62. 'It is enterprise which builds and improves the world's possessions. . . . If enterprise is afoot, wealth accumulates whatever may be happening to thrift; and if enterprise is asleep, wealth decays whatever thrift may be doing.' *JMK*, vol. 6, p. 132.

63. *JMK*, vol. 13, p. 342. Joan Robinson (1903–83), Fellow of Newnham College and Assistant Lecturer in Economics at Cambridge from 1931. E.A.G. Robinson (1897–1993), Fellow of Sidney Sussex College, Cambridge, from 1931; University Lecturer in Economics from 1929. Piero Sraffa (1898–1983), a member of King's College, Cambridge, and from 1930 Librarian of the Marshall Library. Richard Kahn (1905–89), Fellow of King's College, Cambridge, from 1930 and University Lecturer in Economics from 1933. James Meade (1907–95), Fellow and Lecturer in Economics at Hertford College, Oxford, from 1930. A first-hand account of the Circus, by Kahn and Robinson, is in the proceedings of the Sixth Keynes Seminar, G.C. Harcourt (ed.), *Keynes and His Contemporaries*. It gives a list (p. 50) of earlier published accounts, to which the article by Lambert, 'The evolution of Keynes's thought', should be added.

64. James Meade, 'The Keynesian Revolution', in Milo Keynes (ed.), *Essays*, p. 82.

65. *JMK*, vol. 13, p. 355 (Harris Lectures, June 1931).

66. *JMK*, vol. 13, p. 278; *JMK*, vol. 29, p. 25.

67. *JMK*, vol. 14, p. 184 (Keynes to Ohlin, 27 Jan. 1937). Shackle calls Myrdal's concept 'a suggestion of utter simplicity yet of transforming power' (*Years of High Theory*, p. 94).

68. *JMK*, vol. 13, p. 276 ('Notes on the definition of saving', sent to Robertson, 22 March 1932).

69. Richard Kahn, *Selected Essays on Employment and Growth* (1972), p. vii, reprinting 'The relation of home investment to unemployment,' pp. 1–27.

70. Ibid., p. vii.

71. *JMK*, vol. 13, p. 188 (Memorandum to the committee of economists, 21 Sept. 1930). This draft is described by Moggridge (*JMK*, vol. 13, p. 340 n. 3) and by Howson and Winch, *Economic Advisory Council*, p. 49. Both cite the copy in the Keynes Papers, file EA/4. This cannot now be found. No copy exists in the Public Record Office, nor in the Hubert Henderson Papers, Nuffield College, Oxford; and neither Kahn nor Meade kept a copy. [This footnote as drafted in 1985; but see also comments in the introduction above.]

72. See Howson and Winch, *Economic Advisory Council*, p. 36n., and Don Patinkin, 'Keynes and the multiplier', *Manchester School*, xlvi (1978), pp. 216–17. Patinkin noted (p. 217n.) – but was not convinced by – the interesting suggestion which had been put to him by John Flemming, that Clark may have had in mind a finite magnitude. Four years later, in the revised version of Patinkin's article in *Anticipations*, he added that he had since asked Clark which interpretation, 'mine or Flemming's, was correct – and he unhesitatingly replied that Flemming's was' (p. 197, addendum to n. 10). Kahn has now claimed: 'I cannot recall any doubt on his part that the sum of an infinite convergent series is finite' (*Making of General Theory*, p. 96). Patinkin's scepticism still seems justified.

73. *JMK*, vol. 14, p. 806 (Keynes to Clark, 31 May 1938).

74. Kahn, *Selected Essays*, p. 18.

75. Kahn, *Making of General Theory*, p. 98, reinforcing what Kahn wrote at the time of Keynes's death: 'John Maynard Keynes', *Proc Brit. Acad.*, xxxii (1946), p. 409.

76. Kahn, *Making of General Theory*, p. 99.

77. Milgate, *Capital and Employment*, pp. 78–82.

78. Patinkin, *Anticipations*, pp. 30–1.

79. Or an egg, as Klein called it in his early statement of the view that it was Kahn who took 'the necessary step': *Keynesian Revolution*, p. 38.
80. Austin Robinson, 'Keynes and his Cambridge colleagues', in Patinkin and Leith, *Keynes*, p. 33.
81. The image of Kahn as 'angel-messenger' (to Keynes's God in a miracle play) derived from Mrs Meade. *JMK*,vol. 13, pp. 338–9. Kahn's role has provoked intermittent speculation. Joseph A. Schumpeter, *History of Economic Analysis* (1954), advanced the claim that his share 'cannot have fallen very far short of co-authorship' (p. 1172). Schumpeter's contemporary contacts with members of the Circus were mentioned by Robinson as a possible source of misapprehension in a discussion with Paul Samuelson, who was acting as devil's advocate for Kahn as 'actually the creator'. See Patinkin and Leith, *Keynes*, pp. 79–81; cf. Lambert, 'Evolution of Keynes's thought', p. 245. Luigi Pasinetti has also put this case in his remarks in Kahn, *Making of General Theory*, pp. 223–4, to which Kahn retorts: 'Why does Luigi Pasinetti regard it as extraordinary that Keynes preferred not to work in a vacuum?': ibid., p. 240.
82. Austin Robinson, 'The Cambridge Circus', in Harcourt (ed.), *Keynes and His Contemporaries*, p. 55. Milgate points out that others, notably Pigou, had observed to Keynes that the *Treatise* assumed fixed output, and concludes that 'orthodox "classical" economists found no difficulty in allowing for output changes in a disequilibrium process' ('Keynes and Pigou', pp. 46–7).
83. Jens Warming, 'International difficulties arising out of the financing of public works during depression', *Econ. Jnl*, xlii (1932), pp. 211–24, at p. 214. Moggridge carved out a small niche for Warming in the 1980 edition of *Keynes*, p. 94 and n. 4 on p. 182. Kahn also came to recognize his significant contribution: *Making of General Theory*, pp. 100–1. But the credit for rediscovering Warming belongs to the important article by Neville Cain, 'Cambridge and its revolution: a perspective on the multiplier and effective demand', *Economic Record* (1979), pp. 108–17, which also has some pregnant observations on Meade and the multiplier. Since Keynes was editor of the *Economic Journal*, it would be interesting to know when he saw Warming's submission and what he made of it. Unfortunately there is nothing in the relevant files in the Keynes Papers bearing upon this point.
84. In a subsequent amendment to his 1978 article on the multiplier, Patinkin claims that Cain's point about Kahn's lack of a general savings function is 'unwarranted': *Anticipations*, p. 198 n. 17. But Kahn's lack of attention to personal savings in his concentration on unspent profits surely provides the necessary warrant.
85. R.F. Kahn, 'The financing of public works – a note', *Econ. Jnl*, xlii (1932), p. 494. I read Kahn's response as more accommodating than does Cain: 'Cambridge and its revolution', p. 114. I am reinforced in this interpretation by Kahn's recent gloss: 'Dennis Robertson deduced from my use of the adjective 'simple-minded' that I was opposed to these sensible definitions rather than strongly in favour': *Making of General Theory*, p. 101.
86. J.E. Meade, *Public Works in their International Aspect*, New Fabian Research Bureau (1933), pp. 14–15. It is interesting that Evan Durbin had told Meade in February 1932 that, compared to Keynes, 'you are an immense advance on him in lucidity and precision'. Quoted in Durbin, *New Jerusalems*, p. 139.
87. *JMK*, vol. 9, p. 340. Kahn, who was in the USA, told Keynes that he 'had been grappling for something of the same sort . . ., even going so far as to use the word "leakage" '.) Kahn to Keynes, 30 March 1933, *JMK*, vol. 13, p. 414.
88. Joan Robinson, 'What has become of the Keynesian revolution?', in Milo Keynes (ed.), *Essays*, p. 125.
89. Patinkin, *Anticipations*, pp. 23–6. Kahn's interpretation, however, is quite different: 'that the members of the Circus could claim that their influence was beginning to be revealed': *Making of General Theory*, pp. 109–10. Moggridge is much more tentative than this: '*Treatise* to *General Theory*', p. 79.
90. *JMK*, vol. 13, p. 355.
91. *JMK*, vol. 20, p. 310.

92. Even after the *General Theory* was published, Keynes wrote of one passage: 'I have got bogged in an attempt to bring my own terms into rather closer conformity with the algebra of others than the case really permits.' Keynes to H. Townshend, 23 April 1936, *JMK*, vol. 29, p. 246.

93. See R.B. Bryce's lecture notes, 24 Oct. 1932: 'These equations are mere truisms arising out of the analysis. Hence the dilemma that things must be either truisms or unimportant. Whole of mathematics is a truism. But truisms help to clear up one's mind.' For this source see n. 100 below.

94. See Appendix below for all subsequent references to the letter to Harrod. The first alternative is that specified by Patinkin, *Anticipations*, esp. pp. 11, 16, 85.

95. *JMK*, vol. 13, p. 270 (Keynes to J. Robinson, 14 April 1932) and p. 172 (Keynes to Hawtrey, 1 June 1932).

96. Compare *JMK*, vol. 14, p. 446 with the *General Theory*, *JMK*, vol. 7, p. 96. This passage was a reworking of the mid-1934 draft of the chapter on 'The propensity to spend': *JMK*, vol. 13, p. 445.

97. *JMK*, vol. 29, p. 39. Keynes would certainly have been aware by this time of Warming's contribution, which must have been in the press.

98. *JMK*, vol. 13, p. 378 (Keynes to J. Robinson, 9 May 1932); cf. the memorandum, *JMK*, vol. 29, pp. 42–7. Patinkin sees Keynes's reversion to the definitions of the Treatise in his mid-1932 drafts as clear evidence that he had not apprehended the 'fundamental psychological law': *Anticipations*, pp. 19–20.

99. Milgate, *Capital and Employment*, p. 81; Patinkin, *Keynes's Monetary Thought*, p. 72.

100. Bryce and Tarshis were both Canadian graduates (Bryce in Engineering) who came to Cambridge in 1932, took the BA in 1934, and worked as graduate students thereafter. Professor T.K. Rymes has made transcripts from the original notes: those of Bryce held by Carleton University, Ottawa, and of Tarshis, now held with these transcripts in the Marshall Library, Cambridge. I have relied upon Rymes's editorial work throughout. The citations given below from either set are corroborated in the other set for the same date except where specified to the contrary.

101. *JMK*, vol. 29, p. 55 (Keynes's notes for 14 Nov. 1932); this part of the fragment is corroborated in both Bryce's and Tarshis's notes of that date.

102. Milgate, 'The "new" Keynes papers', p. 194. It is quite possible that the *Treatise*-like part of this fragment was not actually delivered; see n. 117 below.

103. See *Keynes's Monetary Thought*, pp. 72–3, for Patinkin's pioneering use of an early transcript of Bryce's notes; citation at p. 73 n. 11.

104. *JMK*, vol. 13, p. 180 (notes, 'Ex Post and Ex Ante'). The reference cannot be to the calendar years (hence including the Michaelmas Term of 1932) because, as has been seen above, Keynes did not lecture in 1931. The 1931–2 lectures were those of the Easter Term, 1932.

105. *JMK*, vol. 14, p. 211 ('Alternative theories of the rate of interest,' *Econ. Jnl*, June 1937).

106. Ibid., p. 212.

107. The concept had been introduced as 'somewhat analogous to the state of bearishness' but was now simplified down to the public's 'preference for holding money and holding debts'. Bryce notes, 31 Oct. 1932. Robertson later recalled a passage from the Macmillan Committee evidence of 1930 in which he spoke (in effect) about liquidity preference, and commented to Keynes: 'This train of thought woke no response in you whatever . . .'. *JMK*, vol. 29, p. 167 (Robertson to Keynes, 1 Jan. 1938). Two years after the Macmillan Committee, when Keynes saw where Robertson's train was going, he caught it.

108. See Milgate, 'Keynes on the "classical" theory of interest', in Eatwell and Milgate (eds), *Keynes's Economics*, pp. 79–89, and Milgate, *Capital and Employment*, pp. 111–22. It is notable that Joan Robinson had no love for the liquidity preference concept: see Joan Robinson and Frank Wilkinson, 'Ideology and logic', in Fausto Vicarelli (ed.), *Keynes's Relevance Today* (1985), p. 88.

109. Patinkin, *Anticipations*, p. 21; cf. pp. 22–3.

110. Patinkin, *Keynes's Monetary Thought*, p. 80. The explanation seems to lie in Patinkin's view of liquidity preference as 'a theory . . . whose basic features had already been presented in

the *Treatise'*, ibid., pp. 37–40; reaffirmed in *Anticipations*, p. 9. But not, of course, as a theory of the interest rate.

111. Lorie Tarshis, 'Keynes as seen by his students in the 1930s', Patinkin and Leith, *Keynes*. p. 49.
112. Bryce notes, 10 Oct. 1932; cf. *JMK*, vol. 29, pp. 51–2 (Keynes's notes for 10 Oct. 1932).
113. Tarshis notes, 17 Oct. 1932.
114. *JMK*, vol. 21, p. 53 (Halley-Stewart lecture, Feb. 1932). The phrase was still in Keynes's mind in the winter of 1932–3. He repeated it in a letter to his mother, 11 Dec. 1932 (Keynes Papers, King's College, Cambridge); and in a radio broadcast, 4 Jan. 1933 (*JMK*, vol. 21, p. 145).
115. *JMK*, vol. 13, p. 172 (Keynes to Hawtrey, 1 June 1932).
116. Bryce notes, 24 Oct. 1932.
117. This is suggested in the fragment reproduced in *JMK*, vol. 14, pp. 55–6 – an argument which Kahn later found 'disconcerting': *Making of General Theory*, p. 113. Patinkin, however, has pointed out that the absence of such a passage in either Bryce's or Tarshis's notes means that 'there is no direct evidence that this description was actually included in the lecture of that date': *Anticipations*, p. 21 n. 18.
118. Bryce notes, 14 Oct. 1932.
119. Bryce notes, 21 Nov. 1932. Tarshis has nothing on these concluding comments in the lecture.
120. From the text in the Keynes Papers, Marshall Library. When Keynes corrected the proofs, he changed 'might be described' to 'he described': *JMK*, vol. 10, p. 88 (*Essays in Biography*). The stages of emendation can be dated from the manuscript and correspondence in file B/1. They are helpfully summarized by Moggridge in *JMK*, vol. 10, p. 71n., except the misleading impression is created that it is the major changes which date from early 1933, instead of just the short passage on pp. 101–3. Everything quoted above must have been written before the end of Keynes's lecture course on 28 Nov. 1932.
121. *JMK*, vol. 10, p. 88.
122. Ink insertion into the text, printed in *JMK*, vol. 10, p. 97.
123. *JMK*, vol. 10, p. 99; cf. p. 97.
124. *JMK*, vol. 10, p. 89.
125. *JMK*, vol. 14, p. 100.
126. *JMK*, vol. 21, p. 344 (Keynes to Brand, 29 Nov. 1934).
127. *JMK*, vol. 13, p. 520 (Keynes to Robertson, 20 Feb. 1935).
128. Tarshis, 'Keynes as seen by his students in the 1930s', Patinkin and Leith, *Keynes*, p. 49; Patinkin, *Anticipations*, pp. 22–3.
129. Fallgatter was a graduate student in Physics who took these notes in shorthand for his friend James S. Earley. A copy of Earley's transcript is in the Marshall Library. For Bryce's impression see his notes and Bryce, 'Keynes as seen by his students', Patinkin and Leith, *Keynes*, p. 41.
130. *JMK*, vol. 14, p. 296 (Keynes to Harrod, 4 July 1938).
131. *JMK*, vol. 14, p. 111 ('The general theory of employment').
132. Bryce notes, 17 Oct. 1932.
133. Ibid., 24 Oct. 1932.
134. *JMK*, vol. 7, p. 85. In identifying Keynes's paradigm, Josef Steindi hammers home the general point I am stressing here: 'J.M. Keynes: society and the economist', in Vicarelli (ed.), *Keynes's Relevance Today* pp. 99ff. Harcourt and O'Shaughnessy also bring out the salience of the fallacy of composition; Harcourt (ed.), *Keynes and His Contemporaries*.
135. *JMK*, vol. 7, p. 131.
136. Ibid., p. 20.
137. Ibid., p. 293.
138. Ibid., p. 84.
139. Ibid., p. 212.
140. Ibid., p. 85.
141. *JMK*, vol. 21, p. 213 (*New Statesman & Nation*, 24 Dec. 1932).

142. Admittedly, Keynes wrote in his *Treatise on Probability*, 'treatment of this topic in the *System of Logic* is exceedingly bad'. *JMK*, vol. 8, p. 298n.

143. *JMK*, vol. 20, p. 480 (Royal Institution lecture, Feb. 1931).

144. *JMK*, vol. 20, p. 289, cf. *JMK*, vol. 9, p. 235 (*New Statesman & Nation*, 7 Mar. 1931).

145. *JMK*, vol. 7, p. 160.

146. J.A. Hobson, *Confessions of an Economic Heretic* (1938), p. 34.

147. *JMK*, vol. 29, p. 211 (Keynes to Hobson, 14 Feb. 1936). For Hobson's work and its relation to Keynes see Peter Clarke, *Liberals and Social Democrats* (1978), esp. pp. 46–54, 125–7, 226–42, 268–74. Keynes's copy of A.F. Mummery and J.A. Hobson, *The Physiology of Industry* (1889) is in the Marshall Library – the only such of Hobson's works. The marked passages in it are broadly as cited in the *General Theory* (*JMK*, vol. 7, 367–70). It is likely that these date no earlier than July 1935.

148. *JMK*, vol. 13, pp. 486–7, 489 ('Poverty in plenty', Nov. 1934).

149. *JMK*, vol. 7, p. 257.

150. Ibid., p. 339.

151. In mounting his argument that there was 'no long-period tendency to an optimum position', Keynes distinguished two senses of 'long period': '(A) – one towards which short period moves (1) if no other forces arise (2) the stable position it would arrive at. (B) – or is the period when the optimum disposition of production would be achieved.' Bryce notes, 14 Nov. 1932.

152. Hicks, *Critical Essays*, p. 134. For a 'brief account of a bizarre episode in intellectual history' from a fundamentalist viewpoint see Charles H. Hession, *John Maynard Keynes* (1984), pp. 368–9.

153. John Hicks, *Economic Perspectives* (1977), p. 146; *JMK*, vol. 14, p. 79 (Keynes to Hicks, 31 March 1937). See Alan Coddington, 'Hicks's contribution', *Keynesian Economics*, pp. 64–91, for a sympathetic account.

154. Keynes wrote to Joan Robinson, 2 Dec. 1936: 'So far as I myself am concerned, I am trying to prevent my mind from crystallising too much on the precise lines of the *General Theory*. I am attentive to criticisms and to what raises difficulties and catches people's attention – in which there are a good many surprises'. *JMK*, vol. 29, p. 185.

155. Milgate, *Capital and Employment*, pp. 118–23.

156. For example, Coddington, *Keynesian Economics*, p. 78.

157. *JMK*, vol. 21, p. 127.

158. *JMK*, vol. 28, p. 29 (letter to the *New Statesman & Nation*, 11 Aug. 1934).

159. *Daily Mail*, 14 Mar. 1933. It is possible that Lloyd George, not having seen the book, supposed it to be a re-issue of material in *The Economic Consequences of the Peace*.

160. David Lloyd George, *War Memoirs*, 2-vol. edn (1938), i, p. 410.

161. Harrod, *Life*, pp. 192–3. Harvey Road, Cambridge, was Keynes's parental home.

162. See Clarke, *Liberals and Social Democrats*, esp. pp. 131–2. I am naturally disappointed that Robert Skidelsky finds the evidence which I adduced 'extremely flimsy': *John Maynard Keynes: Hopes Betrayed. 1883–1920* (1983), p. 241. Readers must judge whether 'political indifference' (pp. 229, 232) is a more plausible assessment than Sir Austin Robinson's: 'Keynes's absorbing interest at this stage of his life was politics.' 'John Maynard Keynes', p. 10.

163. Clarke, *Liberals and Social Democrats*, pp. 226–42; idem, 'Politics of Keynesian economics', ch. 3 above.

164. *JMK*, vol. 21, p. 373 (Keynes to Samuel, 23 Oct. 1935); cf. *JMK*, vol. 12, p. 11, table 3. Keynes's only political donation appears to be £25 to the Labour Party in South Norfolk where Colin Clark was the candidate.

165. *JMK*, vol. 28, p. 107 (Keynes to Sinclair, 4 April 1938). On Keynes's general sympathy for the left in the 1930s, Winch provides an excellent corrective to Harrod's 'establishment' view: *Economics and Politics*, pp. 350–60. In the 1930s Harrod had himself been ready to work with the New Fabian Research Bureau: Durbin, *New Jerusalems*, esp. pp. 98, 105–6, 162. By 1951, however, Keynes's official biographer was seeking to become Conservative

candidate for Bournemouth: see Harold Nicolson, *Diaries and Letters, 1945–62* (London, 1968), p. 214.
166. This is well conveyed by Paul Addison, *The Road to 1945: British Politics and the Second World War* (1975), esp. pp. 18, 21, 277.
167. *JMK*, vol. 21, p. 355 (Keynes to Arthur Salter, 10 July 1935).
168. *JMK*, vol. 13, p. 492 ('Poverty in plenty', Nov. 1934).
169. *JMK*, vol. 28, p. 35 (letter to the *New Statesman & Nation*, 21 Nov. 1934).
170. *JMK* vol. 7, pp. 383–4.
171. *JMK*, vol. 28, p. 42; cf. *JMK*, vol. 21, p. 348, for a similar statement in a letter to Susan Lawrence, 15 Jan. 1935.
172. Quoted in Lambert, 'The evolution of Keynes's thought', p. 256.

Appendix
The text of the central section of Keynes's letter to Harrod, printed below, is taken from the original pencil draft, dated 27 Aug. 1936, in the Marshall Library. There are a few variant readings compared with the version dated 30 Aug. 1936 printed in *JMK*, vol. 14, pp. 84–6 (corrected in *JMK*, vol. 29, p. 298). The letter as despatched is now in the Harrod Papers in Japan. I have added in square brackets the chronological stages referred to in my essay.

1. I have been much pre-occupied with the causation, so to speak, of my own progress of mind from the classical position to my present views, – with the order in which the problem developed in my mind. What some people treat as an unnecessarily controversial tone is really due to the importance in my own mind of what I used to believe, and of the moments of transition which were for me personally moments of illumination. You don't feel the weight of the past as I do. One cannot shake off a pack one has never properly worn. And probably your ignoring all this is a better plan than mine. For experience seems to show that people are divided between the old ones whom nothing will shift and are merely annoyed by my attempts to underline the points of transition so vital in my own progress, and the young ones who have not been properly brought up and believe nothing in particular. The particles of light seen in escaping from a tunnel are interesting neither to those who mean to stay there nor to those who have never been there! I have no companions, it seems, in my own generation, either of earliest teachers or of earliest pupils; I cannot in thought help being somewhat bound to them, – which they find exceedingly irritating!

    My second point is, perhaps, part of my first.

2. You don't mention *effective demand* or, more precisely, the demand schedule for output as a whole, except in so far as it is implicit in the multiplier. To me, regarded historically, the most extraordinary thing is the complete disappearance of the theory of the demand and supply for output as a whole, i.e. the theory of employment, *after* it had been for a quarter of a century the most discussed thing in economics. One of the most important transitions for me, after my *Treatise on Money* had been published, was suddenly realising this [STAGE TWO]. It only came after I had enunciated to myself the psychological law that, when income increases, the gap between income and consumption will increase, – a conclusion of vast importance to my own thinking but not apparently, expressed just like that, to anyone else's [STAGE ONE]. Then, appreciably later, came the notion of interest as being the measure of liquidity-preference, which became quite clear in my mind the moment I thought of it [STAGE THREE]. And last of all, after an immense lot of muddling and many drafts, the proper definition of the marginal efficiency of capital linked up one thing with another [STAGE FOUR].

5   Hobson and Keynes as economic heretics

1

In his old age, J.A. Hobson professed himself gratified that 'Mr J.M. Keynes, though not in full agreement with my analysis, has paid a handsome tribute to my early form of the over-saving heresy.'[1] This tribute, extending to seven pages, printed in a prominent position in the twentieth century's most famous book on economics, has in itself guaranteed Hobson's reputation a measure of continued professional recognition. The result has been that students of economics almost invariably know his name – but often little more than his name. Whether Hobson's work in this field deserves to be remembered as more than an extended footnote to the *General Theory* is a question which has, from time to time, provoked sympathetic economists into making stronger claims on his behalf. The most far-reaching, and also the most influential in left-wing circles, was that advanced by G.D.H. Cole: 'For me at any rate, what is commonly known as the Keynesian was much more the Hobsonian revolution in economic and social thought.'[2]

Cole's declaration may, however, tell us more about his own ideological affinities than about Hobson's intellectual achievements. D.J. Coppock's scrupulous attempt to argue that Keynes was 'ungenerous in the account he gave of Hobson's theory' carries more scholarly authority.[3] From a close study of half-a-dozen of Hobson's economic treatises it shows that, while his theoretical formulations may have been crude, they contain passages which are pregnant with insight. Supplied with the appropriate distinctions – 'several suppressed assumptions must be made explicit' – a good deal more can be squeezed out of Hobson than might have been expected; and it accordingly becomes 'hard to understand how Keynes could have overlooked such statements'.[4] If only he had, on the basis of his presumed acquaintance with Hobson's writings, put together this paragraph from *The Economics of Unemployment* (1922) with that paragraph from the second edition of *The Industrial System* (1910) and the other paragraph from *Rationalisation and Unemployment* (1930), Keynes could have discovered an altogether fuller and more suggestive anticipation of his own central conceptions! In particular, Coppock suggested that the admittedly unsystematic Hobson – 'his argument lacks rigour'[5] – can nonetheless be read as pointing towards contraction of total income as the means by which excess saving is eliminated, which begins to sound very much like the equilibration process of the theory of effective demand. Further exegesis along these lines, scrutinizing possible analytical anticipations, seems unnecessary. But this whole issue can be put into historical perspective by seeking to establish what actual, direct, demonstrable influence (if any) Hobson exerted upon the development of Keynes's thought.

2

Hobson's heresy was, in the first place, underconsumption. In maintaining that a general process of over-saving was possible – and that it was the root cause of economic depression – he put himself beyond the pale of orthodox economics. He first took up this position in the book he wrote with A.F. Mummery, *The Physiology of Industry* (1889), published at just the time when, under the guidance of Alfred Marshall, economics was seeking to establish its claims to academic respectability. The defensive mentality of the emergent profession partly explains the prickly exclusiveness which Hobson thereafter encountered. 'This was the first open step in my heretical career', he later recalled, 'and I did not in the least realize its momentous consequences.'[6] Faced with little alternative, Hobson made the best of his career as a self-conscious outsider.[7]

Keynes, by contrast, could hardly have been more of an insider. Born in Cambridge, the son of a don who had done respected work in logic and economics, the winner of scholarships to Eton and to King's – here was a gilded youth selected by that old family friend, Alfred Marshall, as fit to bear the torch of Cambridge economics. Keynes was to admit: 'I was brought up in the citadel and I recognise its power and might.'[8] Now it was against this same Marshallian school that Hobson directed some of his characteristic shafts, notably in the two books in which he turned towards problems of economic methodology. This was the field in which John Neville Keynes had published a standard work, which Hobson subjected to sustained criticism on the grounds that its positivist approach excluded ethical considerations and value judgements. 'Like Professor Marshall', Hobson commented in 1901, 'Dr Keynes wants to simplify by falsification.'[9] The same charge against 'the Cambridge doctrine' was repeated and developed in the mid 1920s, largely by reference to Marshall and his successor as Professor of Political Economy at Cambridge, A.C. Pigou – with a passing reprimand for a junior figure, H.D. Henderson.[10] Marshall and Pigou had been pre-eminent among Maynard Keynes's teachers; Henderson was currently his close colleague and collaborator.

Filial loyalties alone, then, might suggest that, from the time he began his studies in economics in 1905, Keynes would be disposed to distrust this persistent critic, from whom he considered one had to expect, along with some stimulating ideas, also 'much sophistry, misunderstanding, and perverse thought'.[11] For nearly a quarter of a century, the star pupil of the Cambridge Economics Faculty remained sceptically impervious to anything that the underconsumptionist Hobson might be trying to tell him.

There was another Hobson, however, with whose temperament and outlook Keynes developed an ambivalent sympathy. For Hobson comprehended his insight about the impossibility of unlimited saving within a more general formulation: 'It is at root a very simple fallacy, viz. the contention that what anyone can do, all can do.'[12] It is, in short, the fallacy of composition, or what Hobson preferred to call the individualist fallacy. It is a recurrent theme in many of his writings and one which he was fond of illustrating by saying that though any one boy might go from a log cabin to the White House, all boys could not simultaneously become President of the United States. When Hobson seized upon the term heretic to describe himself it was in the broader sense: subsuming the underconsumptionist doctrine under the individualist fallacy, thereby casting doubt upon the adequacy of laissez-faire economics in general. Moreover, he located the root of his own unorthodoxy in psychological predisposition as well as in logical analysis. In his autobiography, he insisted that he had not taken the name heretic in a spirit of bravado; but he recognized that the 'break-away disposition', which he prized as a means to progress, might itself be suspect as 'a pugnacious self-assertion of superiority over the accepted thought or faith of others'.[13]

Thus for Hobson the doctrine of underconsumption, though neither trivial nor incidental, was 'a narrower economic heresy'.[14] Intellectually, it was an inference from a fundamental logical distinction; temperamentally, it was the product of a particular cast of mind. In both respects, Keynes manifested significant affinities with Hobson's general approach appreciably before he was prepared to acknowledge any force in Hobson's most notorious economic contention. This is literally apparent in the language which Keynes began to use about the limitations of the free market in the 1920s. When he first proposed public works in 1924, he claimed that in considering this abridgement of laissez-faire, 'we are brought to my heresy – if it is a heresy'.[15] Keynes's thirst for originality and his readiness to shock made him susceptible to the temptations of striking an iconoclastic pose. Once doubtful of an orthodox proposition, he was not the man to dissimulate conformity. He began toying with the imagery of himself as a heretic a decade before Hobson – apparently prompted by Keynes's usage – arrogated the term.[16] Certainly Keynes became fascinated by this metaphor as applied to himself, asking after the *General Theory* was completed: 'how can one brought up a Catholic in English economics, indeed a priest of that faith, avoid some controversial emphasis, when he first becomes a Protestant?'[17] Here I stand, he now told his German readers: I can do no other.

3

Similarity of language, however, though it might indicate general temperamental congruence, may turn out to be misleadingly superficial when it comes to specific intellectual influence. Though in Keynes's *Treatise on Money* (1930) the analysis can be described in terms of over-saving, its provenance remains basically neo-classical. If Keynes was impelled to acknowledge, for the first time, a possible theoretical convergence with underconsumption, it was one which he substantially repudiated. The word 'over-saving', in fact, could mean two things. When Hobson used it, he meant under-consumption; but when Keynes used it in the *Treatise* he meant under-investment. Unlike Hobson, who saw saving and investment as two names for the same process, Keynes now sought to make a distinction between them in order to emphasize that a problem existed over how they were brought into equilibrium He maintained that it was attempted over-saving which left investment deficient, whereas Hobson held that it was actual over-saving which resulted in actual over-investment. As Keynes put it, any reconciliation of such a theory with his own would only be 'at a later stage in the course of events'[18] – meaning, presumably, that a deficiency in consumption ('Hobsonian over-saving') might in due course, through its erosion of profitability, depress the level of investment ('Keynesian over-saving').

That these difficulties were substantial, not simply terminological, can be seen by considering the appropriate remedy for each condition. 'Keynesian over-saving' could best be remedied by stimulating investment; 'Hobsonian over-saving' only by stimulating consumption. Thus, while Keynes was prepared to consider a whole range of possible expedients, he called his proposals for home investment 'my own favourite remedy – the one to which I attach the greatest importance'.[19] Hobson, conversely, remained lukewarm about schemes for public works. His own plans for redistribution of income aimed to boost consumption, but also candidly avowed their rationale as a means of reducing the saving – or over-saving – which he regarded as the other side of the same coin. A decrease in saving, however, had little attraction for Keynes. 'If we can find *no* outlet for our savings, then it would be better to save less', he conceded. 'But this would be a counsel of despair.'[20]

Yet the *Treatise* showed Keynes adopting a rhetoric about thrift which had long been Hobson's trademark. *The Physiology of Industry* had opened with an assault on Mill's proposition that 'saving enriches and spending impoverishes the community along with the individual'.[21] Its own demonstration of the consequences of over-saving led up to the conclusion: 'The labourers, therefore, are the chief sufferers from the saving habits of the rich, and, in so far as evil proceeds from poverty, the highly-extolled virtues of thrift, parsimony, and saving are the cause.'[22] In the *Treatise* Keynes did not disparage the utility of saving; but when he insisted that it only had this utility in so far as it permitted investment to take place, he challenged a conventional preconception. 'It has been usual', he wrote, 'to think of the accumulated wealth of the world as having been painfully built up out of that voluntary abstinence of individuals from the immediate enjoyment of consumption which we call thrift.' In extolling enterprise instead, he suggested that 'not only may thrift exist without enterprise, but as soon as thrift gets ahead of enterprise, it positively discourages the recovery of enterprise and sets up a vicious circle by its adverse effect on profits'.[23]

It was at this point, already sidling up to the church door with his own theses stuffed in his pocket, that Keynes seems to have glimpsed the old heretic in a new light. Writing to Hobson apropos of a draft article recapitulating his views, Keynes admitted that

> reading it has brought home to me how very near together you and I are on this matter. You have done all the pioneer work and the essential truth has been in you. But logically I have always felt your standpoint to be unsatisfactory. Now that I have worked out a point of view of my own which, to me at any rate, is logically satisfactory, I see how very near it comes to your view.[24]

Keynes's description of his new book as 'a synthesis of orthodox economics with your own unorthodoxy' was no doubt ingratiating but not misplaced. For the *Treatise* is indeed a synthesis between, on the one hand, new notions of saving, and, on the other, a fundamentally neo-classical concept of equilibrium.[25] 'Keynesian over-saving', which was merely another name for under-investment, was a condition of disequilibrium, when interest rate was thwarted in its normal function of establishing equilibrium between saving and investment. Interpreted in these terms, 'Hobsonian over-saving' could be recognized as a special case under the analysis of the *Treatise*, albeit one which had been misleadingly specified by underconsumptionists like Hobson, who had not 'succeeded in linking up their conclusions with the theory of money or with the part played by the rate of interest'.[26]

The very interesting correspondence which took place between Keynes and Hobson in 1931 fastened upon this point. Keynes sought to disabuse Hobson of the misapprehension that 'there must be a body of real capital corresponding to the uninvestable savings' by referring him to the Banana Parable in the *Treatise*. In the banana republic, bananas were the only item of production or consumption. A thrift campaign, by increasing the proportion of income saved, obviously withheld that part of income from consumption – but did not necessarily divert it into investment. What happened? The same amount of production took place, and it was all sold (for bananas do not keep), but at reduced prices. The general public pocketed the gains through consumption at lower prices; but the entrepreneurs made equivalent losses which ultimately had to be covered from the excess of savings. The thrift campaign had not increased the wealth of the community through higher investment; it had only transferred wealth from producers to consumers.[27]

Hobson's response was that these unfavourable consequences of a fall in prices could in principle be offset by maintaining the proportion of income devoted to consumption; and that the trouble arose in practice when there was a refusal to raise consumption in this way. Keynes had no quarrel with this; he recognized that it brought them closer together; but he reiterated that there was 'also another way out besides the way of increased consumption, namely through a fall in the rate of interest'. For, by opening up new market opportunities at more attractive prices, this would stimulate investment so as to absorb the excessive savings. 'If you could accept this other side of the shield which I offer', Keynes wrote, 'as well as the face which you have stamped with your imprint, we should be at peace.'[28]

Hobson's reply has not survived. But it was such as to provoke Keynes to reaffirm that the Hobsonian analysis only held so long as interest rate failed to fall fast enough to stimulate investment. He acknowledged a limiting case where the interest rate, having already fallen to zero, was obviously incapable of falling further – 'at which point I would agree with you that my alternative exit is closed, and that your exit of more spending and less saving is the only one left'. But this was only a hypothetical possibility, not an approximation to the real position. Hence Keynes's reiterated contention: 'It is the failure of the rate of interest to fall fast enough which is the root of much evil.'[29] In saying this, Keynes showed his continued confidence in the equilibrating mechanism of interest rate.

4

All of this was perfectly consistent with the analysis of the *Treatise*. Yet by the time Keynes concluded his correspondence with Hobson, the *Treatise* had been subjected to a searching critique which ultimately led to the reformulation of Keynes's theories. In particular, the *Treatise* was discussed at length by the 'Circus' of younger economists at Cambridge; and Richard Kahn, largely as a result, put forward the concept which we know as the multiplier. Through successive increments of consumption, passed from hand to hand, aggregate income was multiplied in a determinate way until it produced a level of saving sufficient to match the initial investment. The essence of the multiplier mechanism was thus that an equilibrium between investment and saving was achieved, not through variations in interest rate but through variations in output. What the Circus was concerned with was the crucial role of changes in *output* (given that the economy was at less than full capacity) rather than changes in *price*, on which Keynes had focused in the *Treatise*.[30]

One of Keynes's illustrative set pieces, at the time of the *Treatise*'s publication, was the paradox which he called after the widow's cruse (which was continually replenished with oil; see 1 Kings 17:12–16). An example of it, as he explained to the Macmillan Committee, was when consumers on fixed incomes sought to increase their rate of saving: 'prices will fall still further, so that they can both save and consume as much as before, and however much they save they can always consume as much as before. It is the widow's cruse.' Their position was thus analogous to that of the consumers in the Banana Parable. Moreover, because the entrepreneurs would lose and would be forced to dispose of their assets at knock-down prices, 'gradually the whole wealth of the community will pass into the hands of those savers, and those savers can go on consuming all the time just as much as they did before'.[31]

But *what* would they be consuming? How *could* it go on? In the Banana Parable, whereas consumers initially made a killing for similar reasons, retribution nonetheless lay around the corner. Indeed it can be read as implying a primitive multiplier process which worked through reduced consumption to contract incomes, output and employment, and thus presumably established a new (and sub-optimal) equilibrium position.[32] In November 1930, however, when Keynes explained the widow's cruse to the Macmillan Committee, his delight in it seems to have closed his perceptions to such implications. It took the deliberations of the Circus during the following months to discover that there was a fallacy here: a concealed assumption of fixed output.

How soon Keynes's eyes were fully opened to this fallacy is not clear. For in November 1931, when he might conceivably have been twelve months the wiser, he still reverted, in effect, to the analysis of the widow's cruse, in order to make a point which he did not feel that Hobson had grasped, in the concluding shot of their exchanges:

> The point is that when savings exceed investment prices fall, so that that part of income which is spent buys just as much goods as would have been purchased by the whole of the income if nothing had been saved. The paradox is that saving in excess of investment involves in itself no sacrifice whatever to the standard of life of the consuming and saving class.

Although there would be a transfer of wealth, there would be 'no change in the aggregate of wealth and no change in the rate of consumption' – which surely implies no change in output either. The only consolation for Hobson, on the receiving end of this disquisition, was a final caveat: 'Obviously this cannot go on long without the producers seeking to protect themselves from such losses. Hence unemployment etc. etc.'[33]

It is not surprising, in the light of this correspondence, to find that it ran into the sand at this point. Keynes's attempt to patch up the widow's cruse, or simply to ignore the fact that it was fatally cracked, did nothing to make it serviceable. Judging from his apologetic closing comment – 'I must be at pains to expound the whole matter again from the bottom upwards' – he seems to have sensed as much himself. This can be read as an early hint that the *Treatise* was not to be the last word. It may indeed be the earliest indication that Keynes was proposing a major reformulation of his theory.[34]

Whatever their other differences about the concept, Keynes and Hobson were in agreement upon one crucial aspect of 'over-saving': it might be dysfunctional for the community as a whole but it was not irrational for the individual savers. Hobson had spent much of his life trying to dispel misconceptions on this score. 'There is no limit to efficacious thrift on the part of an individual', his first book had emphatically stated. It identified the root of the difficulty in 'the fundamental fallacy which underlies the Economist's view of Saving, the assumption that the interests of the Community must always be identical with the interests of its several members.'[35] This crucial distinction – one of Hobson's most characteristically trenchant ideas – was, of course, the individualist fallacy or the fallacy of composition.

What role, then, did this conception come to play in Keynes's thought? Analytically, this constitutes the most important question concerning the relationship between Hobson and Keynes. The answer, moreover, is highly provoking. For there is, I believe, strong reason to regard the fallacy of composition as integral to the conception and development of the theory of effective demand in the early 1930s. Though the concept was hardly new to the author of the *Treatise on Probability* (1921), it was only a decade later that he seized upon it as a key which could turn in the lock of a door which he needed to open. Keynes himself made two repeated claims about his own thinking during this period: first, that it underwent a revolution, and secondly, that this rested upon ideas which were 'extremely simple and should be obvious'.[36] Whatever his subsequent toils in writing the *General Theory* so that it constituted a rigorous exposition, fit for his fellow economists, what he regarded as paramount was the simple basic conception at its heart. In this sense, the general theory behind the *General Theory* might be regarded more as an application of what later became game theory rather than a *tour de force* in technical economic analysis.

I hope to have succeeded in demonstrating elsewhere, moreover, that Keynes had seized upon his new theory of effective demand before the end of 1932.[37] When he explained it for the first time, in his university lectures in the Michaelmas Term of 1932, he did so by outlining 'two fundamental propositions', both distinguishing between the choices open to individuals and the outcome necessarily true in the aggregate.[38] This distinction was an analytical tool that could be applied to a variety of decisions: about holding money, about saving and spending, about cutting wages. Hence the structure of the *General Theory*, with its emphasis on 'the vital difference between the theory of the economic behaviour of the aggregate and the theory of the behaviour of the individual unit'.[39] It is hardly too much to say that Keynes's status as the major pioneer of macroeconomics rests upon this analysis.

If such an interpretation is accepted, it has a specific relevance here. From an analytical viewpoint, it presents a strong prima facie case for ascribing decisive significance to these characteristically Hobsonian insights in the making of the *General Theory*. From a historical viewpoint, however, there remains considerable difficulty in finding empirical evidence which would corroborate Hobson's direct influence. In fact, it seems that Keynes, not for the first time, progressed by a series of intuitive flashes towards an understanding which he only formalized into a coherent theory at a late stage. From the end of 1930, under the impact of the world slump, he was prompted, time and again, to ask whether competitive strategies – a flight into liquidity, implementation of wage cuts, a policy of tariffs, resort to devaluation – which were rational for one person, or for one firm, or for one country, were universally valid or viable: and by the end of 1932 he had generalized this distinction without ever acknowledging a specific debt to Hobson.[40]

5

Having stumbled upon his new theory, Keynes cast about for unsuspected predecessors, a number of whom, along with Hobson, receive their meed of praise in the *General Theory*. 'As is often the case with imperfectly analysed intuitions', Keynes wrote of Silvio Gesell, 'their significance only became apparent after I had reached my own conclusions in my own way.'[41] Some names on his list had suggested themselves almost immediately. Having given the first exposition of the theory of effective demand during the Michaelmas Term of 1932, Keynes teased his audience in the final lecture by references to the 'traditionally uncultured' outlook of the Economics Faculty, and alluded to his own 'habit of browsing among old books', which he promptly turned to advantage. He became discursive over how the classical economists had regarded usury; he spoke up in defence of the mercantilists; he commended Mandeville's *Fable of the Bees*; above all, he reminded his audience of the triumph of Ricardo's polished theoretical reasoning over Malthus's crude but firm grasp on reality, so that 'for a hundred years this primitive common sense has lived only in uneducated circles'.[42] Keynes's rediscovery of Malthus was a genuine catalyst in the crystallization of his own thought; though even here he posthumously attributed to Malthus a suspiciously cogent (and Keynesian) doctrine of 'effective demand'.[43]

   In his 1933 lectures Keynes found no time to hunt predecessors but in 1934 he reverted to this theme in the course of a discussion of Say's Law. This proposition – essentially that the process of supply must create a sufficient demand to purchase the whole of it – formed the basis of Ricardo's proposition that over-production was impossible. It is critically examined in chapter 4 of the *Physiology of Industry*, from which the *General Theory* was to cite, and endorse, a comment on Marshall.[44] In his lecture of 29 October 1934, however, Keynes seemed unaware that Marshall had written in this sense at all; and though the lecture repeated previous comments on Ricardo and Malthus, and now added references to Marx, Gesell and Major Douglas, there is no recorded mention of the name of Hobson.[45]

This is fully congruent with surviving drafts of the *General Theory*, from which it appears that Keynes was at this stage projecting two historical chapters on his antecedents.[46] The first of these, on mercantilism, was circulated in proof in the summer of 1935. When Roy Harrod read it, he acknowledged the 'age-long tradition of common sense' as worthy of note, but cautioned Keynes as being 'inclined to rationalise isolated pieces of common sense too much, and to suggest that they were part of a coherent system of thought'.[47] Keynes's gloss on his remarks – 'Roy strongly objects to chapter 26 as a tendentious attempt to glorify imbeciles' – should not be construed as covering Hobson, for whom Harrod subsequently evinced respect.[48] It was not this but the further chapter that was to deal with 'the notion of "effective demand"', presumably from Malthus (or Mandeville) onward. Only at a very late stage were the two conflated into what became chapter 23 of the *General Theory*.

The surviving evidence, in sum, suggests that Keynes did not seriously begin his study of Hobson's writings until the summer of 1935, by which time the preceding twenty-two chapters of his book, with their full exposition of the theory of effective demand, had already been set up in proof. It was in July 1935 that Keynes told Hobson that a section on his ideas was to be included in the *General Theory*, and Hobson accordingly supplied Keynes with an unpublished autobiographical paper from which substantial quotation was made.

Keynes worked from his own copy of the *Physiology of Industry*, which is annotated with his cryptic markings – the only such copy of Hobson's works to survive in Keynes's library. The marked passages are largely those cited in the *General Theory*: substantial sections of the preface, summarizing the argument, with supporting quotations drawn chiefly from the early chapters. Keynes lighted upon passages which argued that capital formation was not uniquely dependent upon an unchecked exercise of thrift, and that saving could not usefully be carried beyond a level limited by consumption.[49] The *Physiology of Industry* claimed that 'no more capital can economically exist at any point in the productive process than is required to furnish commodities for the current rate of consumption'. Keynes jotted down his own gloss: 'capital brought into existence not by saving but by the demand arising from actual and prospective consumption'.[50]

It is clear that Richard Kahn was asked to examine these materials, and the short but revealing letter he received from Keynes is worth quoting in full.

Thanks very much for taking so much trouble about the Mummery. Hobson never fully understood him and went off on a side-track after his death. But the book Hobson helped him to write, The *Physiology of Industry*, is a wonderful work. I am giving a full account

of it but old Hobson has had so much injustice done to him that I shan't say what I
think about M's contribution to it being, probably, outstanding.[51]

It was Mummery, forty years in his Himalayan grave, whom Keynes honoured
in coram as his intellectual ancestor; it was the publication of the one book which
Hobson had written in collaboration with him that was hailed as marking 'in a
sense, an epoch in economic thought'.[52] Keynes, however, can be called tactful
rather than insincere in privately offering Hobson 'the consolation of being
remembered as a pathbreaker in economic theory';[53] this was readily compatible
with the candid public qualification to the *General Theory*'s tribute, that 'Mr
Hobson laid too much emphasis (especially in his later books) on underconsumption leading to over-investment'.[54]

6

The spirit in which Keynes recognized the value of Hobson's insight is perhaps
best caught in a radio broadcast, part of a series in which both participated, which
went out at the end of 1934. Hobson had given a popular recapitulation of his
views on underconsumption. Although he started by taking 'the word "saving"
to mean paying people to make more plant or other capital goods' – that is, the
use made of saving in investment – he then turned his attention to the *lack of
use* often made of it, in the process mentioning idle bank deposits. The
approximation to Keynes's analysis was, at best, only rough and ready. Yet
Hobson firmly stressed, on the one hand, the inability of orthodox theory to
account for this position and, on the other, the helplessness of any individual
in effecting a remedy.[55]

Keynes, speaking a month later, pointed to a fundamental theoretical gulf
between those economists who believed the system to be self-adjusting and those,
like Hobson, who rejected such a view. It was in this context that Keynes
described them as 'heretics' – a reference adopted by Hobson in his autobiographical lecture, 'Confessions of an economic heretic', the following summer.
'The heretics of today', Keynes maintained, 'are the descendants of a long line
of heretics who, overwhelmed but never extinguished, have survived as isolated
groups of cranks.' Even when right, it was often because their flair, being
stronger than their logic, had preserved them from drawing otherwise inescapable
conclusions. So where did Keynes stand? 'Now *I* range myself with the heretics',
he proclaimed – he could do no other – but knowing them to be 'half-right, most
of them, and half-wrong'.[56]

Likewise, in the *General Theory*, Hobson was congratulated for putting
'one half of the matter, as it seems to me, with absolute precision'; while the
root of his mistake was identified as supposing excessive saving to cause an *actual*
over-supply of capital.[57] Even after reading Keynes's 'great book', Hobson still
found difficulty in accepting this conception, arguing that actual over-investment

was one stage in the cycle, and also hankering after idle savings as part of the explanation.[58] In either event, it still seemed to him a fairly straightforward case of underconsumption.

Keynes made a final effort to define their differences: 'The apparent failure of consumption in such circumstances is not really due to the consuming power being absent, but to the falling of incomes. This falling off of incomes is due to the decline in investment occasioned by the insufficiency of the return to new investment compared with the rate of interest.' In writing this, in February 1936, Keynes surely gave a fair account of 'the main points on which we have diverged at the later stages of the argument'.[59] He knew that Hobson was nearing eighty – 'my brain is getting feeble and unable to concentrate effectively'[60] – but Keynes paid him the implicit compliment of sustaining the sort of critical discussion which had opened between them in 1930. The explicit compliment with which their correspondence closed rendered Keynes's attitude nicely: 'I am ashamed how blind I was for many years to your essential contention as to the insufficiency of effective demand.'[61]

On the whole, then, the best authority on the relationship between Hobson and Keynes remains the account in the *General Theory*. In it Keynes stated the extent of his debt with generosity and defined their similarities with precision. On neither score did Hobson have any quarrel with him. In particular, Hobson remained unreceptive to the income-adjustment process which lay at the heart of the theory of effective demand; and efforts to read it back into his own work must falter accordingly. If this is the good reason why Keynes could not have taken such ideas from him, the bad reason is that Keynes was simply unfamiliar with the bulk of Hobson's oeuvre. It was a deficiency for which Keynes made belated and partial amends once he had independently arrived at conclusions which he recognized as speaking to Hobson's distinctive concerns.

Goodwill was not lacking from 1930 onward, but only in 1934–5 was Keynes's mind triggered into a full appreciation of the extent of their affinity. By that time, the theory of effective demand had already taken shape; and the pivotal notion around which its analysis revolves – the fallacy of composition – was a further parallel in the two men's work rather than a transmitted influence. Again, Keynes might have learnt more from Hobson had he shown himself as receptive to suggestion when it came from outsiders as when it came from Cambridge economists reared like himself in the Marshallian tradition. When he read the *General Theory*, Hobson undoubtedly felt that the individualist fallacy, which had long lain deep in the very arsenal of orthodox economics, had finally been exploded; and thereby the citadel hoist with its own petard. He hoped that Keynes's book would revolutionize economics, and had no grounds to suspect its author of grand larceny; but, in an innocent piece of petty pilfering of his own, he was content to appropriate the copyright of the label heretic as a badge of honour in his declining years. It was, by any reckoning, a fair division of the spoils.

Notes

1. J.A. Hobson, *Confessions of an Economic Heretic* (1938), ed. Michael Freeden (Brighton, 1976), 194. I am grateful to Stefan Collini, Donald Moggridge, Barry Supple and John Thompson for their comments on this essay.
2. *New Statesman*, 5 July 1958; for Cole's role as a filter of perceptions about Hobson and Keynes see Peter Clarke, *Liberals and Social Democrats* (Cambridge, 1978), pp. 272–3.
3. D.J. Coppock, 'A reconsideration of Hobson's theory of unemployment', *Manchester School*, xxi (1953), pp. 1–21, at p. 1; see also David Hamilton's interesting 'renovation', 'Hobson with a Keynesian twist', *American Journal of Economics and Sociology*, xiii (1953–4), pp. 273–82; and E.E. Nemmers, *Hobson and Underconsumption* (Amsterdam, 1956), esp. pp. 85–113.
4. Coppock, pp. 10, 16.
5. Coppock, p. 7.
6. Hobson, *Confessions*, p. 30; cf. the similar passage quoted by Keynes in the *General Theory* from Hobson's 1935 lecture of the same title: *JMK*, vol. 7, p. 365.
7. For useful studies of Hobson's work see Michael Freeden, *The New Liberalism* (Oxford, 1978) and John Allett, *New Liberalism: The Political Economy of J.A. Hobson* (Toronto, 1982).
8. *JMK*, vol. 13, p. 489 (*Listener*, 31 Nov. 1934).
9. Hobson, *The Social Problem* (1901), p. 69; ch. 6 of this book is mainly an attack upon Marshall and J.N. Keynes.
10. 'Neo-classical economics in Britain', *Political Science Quarterly*, xl (1925), pp. 337–83, at 341–8; this section reprinted in Hobson, *Free Thought in the Social Sciences* (1926), pp. 96–104.
11. *JMK*, vol. 12, p. 388 (*Econ. Jnl*, 1913); this was a review of Hobson's book, *Gold, Prices and Wages* (1913).
12. *Confessions*, p. 34; cf. *Social Problem*, p. 30, for a similar statement forty years previously.
13. *Confessions*, pp. 7, 91.
14. *Confessions*, p. 29.
15. *JMK*, vol. 19, p. 228; cf. p. 225 (*Nation*, 7 June 1924).
16. Even in the mid 1920s there is no invocation of the metaphor of heresy where one might expect it in Hobson's writings – that is, in the sort of context where it is invoked ten years later; compare Hobson in *Free Thought in the Social Sciences*, pp. 45–8, 52–3, with *Confessions*, pp. 88–92; for Keynes's introduction of the term see below at n. 56.
17. *JMK*, vol. 7, p. xxv (preface to the German edn of the *General Theory*).
18. *JMK*, vol. 5, p. 160 (*Treatise*, vol. i).
19. *JMK*, vol. 20, p. 126 (Macmillan Committee, 6 March 1930).
20. *JMK*, vol. 20, p. 353 (to Montagu Norman, 22 May 1930).
21. A.F. Mummery and J.A. Hobson, *The Physiology of Industry*, (1889), p. iii.
22. Ibid., p. 182.
23. *JMK*, vol. 6, p. 132 (*Treatise*, vol. 2).
24. Keynes to Hobson, 23 April 1930, Keynes Papers; these unpublished letters were first used in the late Alan Lee's pioneer work, 'A study of the social and economic thought of J.A. Hobson' (London PhD thesis, 1970), pp. 289–96.
25. It could perhaps be said that such views on saving and investment had been anticipated by Knut Wicksell and Dennis Robertson; but Keynes certainly gave them a new salience.
26. *JMK*, vol. 5, p. 161 (*Treatise*, vol. 1).
27. See *JMK*, vol. 5, pp. 158–60 (*Treatise*, vol. 1).
28. *JMK*, vol. 13, p. 333 (Keynes to Hobson, 28 Aug. 1930); cf. pp. 331–2 (Hobson's 'Notes on over-saving', 18 Aug. 1930).
29. *JMK*, vol. 23, pp. 333–4 (Keynes to Hobson, 2 Oct. 1930).
30. For the Circus see *JMK*, vol. 13, pp. 337–43 and the other sources listed in Peter Clarke, *The Keynesian Revolution in the Making, 1924–36* (Oxford, 1988), p. 244 n. 45.

31. Private minutes of the Macmillan Committee, 7 Nov. 1930, p. 13 (copy in the Public Record Office, T 200/5); cf. the Danaid Jar as explained in *JMK*, vol. 5, p. 125 (*Treatise*, vol. 1).
32. This sort of argument has recently been developed in B. Littleboy and G. Mehta, 'Patinkin on Keynes's theory of effective demand', *Hist. of Pol Econ.*, xix (1987), pp. 311–28, esp. pp. 313–16, 324–7; and I regret that I did not have the benefit of it when considering this point in *Keynesian Revolution in the Making*, p. 252. The contrary position, which I continue to find persuasive, has been elucidated with exemplary rigour in Don Patinkin, *Anticipations of the General Theory?* (Chicago, 1982), pp. 15–16.
33. *JMK*, vol. 13, pp. 335–6 (Keynes to Hobson, 1 Nov. 1931). It is interesting to compare this with what Keynes had written to R.G. Hawtrey, nearly a year previously, specifying the normal order of events as first involving a change in prices and only subsequently a change in output; see *JMK*, vol. 13, p. 143 (Keynes to Hawtrey, 28 Nov. 1930).
34. *JMK*, vol. 13, p. 336 (Keynes to Hobson, 1 Nov. 1931). A month later, on 9 Dec. 1931, he wrote to Nicholas Kaldor: 'Well, I must be more lucid next time. I am now endeavouring to express the whole thing over again more clearly and from a different angle; and in two years' time I may feel able to publish a revised and completer version.' *JMK*, vol. 13, p. 243.
35. *Physiology of Industry*, pp. 105, 108.
36. *JMK*, vol. 7, p. xxiii (preface to the *General Theory*).
37. See *Keynesian Revolution in the Making*, pp. 259–64, which in this respect modifies the standard accounts in D.E. Moggridge, 'From the *Treatise* to the *General Theory*: an exercise in chronology', *Hist. of Pol Econ.*, v (1973), pp. 72–88; Moggridge, *Keynes*, 2nd edn (1980), pp. 91–119; Don Patinkin, *Keynes's Monetary Thought* (Durham, N.C., 1976), chs 7–9; Patinkin, *Anticipations*, Pt 1.
38. Lecture notes of R.B. Bryce, 24 Oct. 1932; typescript edition by Thomas K. Rymes, A18 (Marshall Library, Cambridge).
39. *JMK*, vol. 7, p. 85 (*General Theory*).
40. See *Keynesian Revolution in the Making*, pp. 269–72.
41. *JMK*, vol. 7, p. 353
42. Bryce notes, 28 Nov. 1932, Rymes edition, A48–51.
43. *JMK*, vol. 10, pp. 88ff. (*Essays in Biography*); and see p. 71n. for Moggridge's helpful editorial note on the dating of these passages.
44. *JMK*, vol. 7, 19n., citing *Physiology of Industry*, p. 102.
45. See the notes by Bryce and by (Sir) Bryan Hopkin for 29 Oct. 1934, Rymes edition, C8 and H8–9.
46. Compare draft tables of contents, *JMK*, vol. 13, pp. 423–4, 525–6.
47. *JMK*, vol. 13, p. 555 (Harrod to Keynes, 30 Aug. 1935).
48. *JMK*, vol. 13, p. 650 (Keynes to Joan Robinson, 3 Sep. 1935). I have to confess that I myself construed it thus in *Liberals and Social Democrats*, p. 273, but, on closer inspection, now find this implausible (and uncharitable). Harrod was responsible for the publication of a (posthumous) 4th edn of Hobson's book, *The Science of Wealth* (Oxford, 1950).
49. For example, *Physiology of Industry* pp. 35–6.
50. *Physiology of Industry*, p. 63, with Keynes's pencilled note, Marshall Library.
51. *JMK*, vol. 13, p. 634 (Keynes to Kahn, 30 July 1935).
52. *JMK*, vol. 7, p. 365 (*General Theory*).
53. Keynes to Hobson, 31 July 1935 (copy), Keynes Papers.
54. *JMK*, vol. 7, p. 370.
55. Hobson, 'Underconsumption and its remedies', *Listener*, 31 Oct. 1934, pp. 735–6.
56. *JMK*, vol. 13, p. 488–9 ('Is the economic system self-adjusting?', *Listener*, 21 Nov. 1934); cf. *JMK*, vol. 7, p. 371 (*General Theory*).
57. *JMK*, vol. 7, pp. 367–8.
58. *JMK*, vol. 29, p. 209 (Hobson to Keynes, 10 Feb. 1936).
59. *JMK*, vol. 29, p. 210–11 (Keynes to Hobson, 14 Feb. 1936).
60. *JMK*, vol. 29, p. 208 (Hobson to Keynes, 3 Feb. 1936).
61. *JMK*, vol. 29, p. 211 (Keynes to Hobson, 14 Feb. 1936).

6 Keynes in history

1

'This book is primarily addressed to my fellow economists.'[1] The preface to the *General Theory* defined at the outset the scholarly community to whom it proposed to speak. Historians – historians of modern Britain, at any rate – have tended to take Keynes at his word. Undeniably important as a historical figure, the author of the *General Theory* has been approached at second-hand, via the supposed influence of Keynesianism, or through his own direct role in making economic policy, or through his fitful interventions in party politics. His significance was never minimized – perhaps at one time it was exaggerated – but it was not properly investigated. A.J.P. Taylor's laconic biographical note on Keynes – 'invented most of modern economics'[2] – nicely captures this sense that something important was going on, rather like a battle offstage, but something that historians were prepared to take on trust from the experts rather than to subject to their own scrutiny.

Three developments have modified this view in the course of the last twenty-five years. One was very general: Keynesianism was dethroned from its ascendancy as the political economy of a triumphant post-war consensus. Secondly, among historians as among other social scientists, a more sophisticated investigation of the process of policy-making on economic matters produced new lines of research. Thirdly, and most specific to historians, a concern with the context in which ideas are formed and become influential has been recognized as an illuminating type of inquiry. It is, I hope, no longer regarded as eccentric for a historian to grapple with Keynes's fundamental ideas, without being supposed to have 'gone native' among the doctrine-historical community, but instead with the firm intention of slipping back through the lines with a first-hand report which lay colleagues might find comprehensible. Such was my hope when I began the preface of my own book on Keynes with two plagiarized sentences: 'This book is addressed to my fellow historians. I hope that it will be intelligible to others.'[3] I hoped that historians would recognize the sentiment and that economists would recognize the plagiarism and that both would read on. As it has turned out, the response from economists, especially, of course, doctrine-historical specialists, has been the more notable.

The period of Keynesian triumphalism coincided with trends in British history which may have had little to do with economic theory but were – sometimes in subtle and pervasive ways – ideologically compatible with the received wisdom of Keynesianism. Thus Britain had apparently won the war,

128

with and through full employment of all resources in the economy.[4] The 1930s were retrospectively viewed as a devil's decade, at home and abroad, with slump sliding through appeasement into war, and all presided over by Conservative politicians of the stripe of Neville Chamberlain, first at the Treasury and then at 10 Downing Street. Guilty Men! Never Again! This was the spirit of 1945, when Labour achieved its great electoral landslide. The welfare state was widely perceived as the foundation of a post-war consensus, accepted as the framework within which the political parties chose to differ, with a fairly explicit Keynesian underpinning. Not only was there a commitment by government to maintain a high and stable level of employment: the redistribution of income to the working class received the sanction of economic theory as well as of social justice; and the enhanced position of the trade unions was applauded as working in the same direction. This was a social democratic vision for which the authority of Keynes could be claimed – and certainly was claimed by the guardians of the Keynesian tradition, centred on the Cambridge Economics Faculty.

Who were the historians to challenge this reading? For, although congenial to the liberal left, this was no partisan position, as was shown by the return to power of the Conservative governments of the 1950s. The Churchillian takeover of the Conservative Party was a standing repudiation of the Chamberlainite legacy. Though Munich remained the most damning epithet in Churchill's expansive vocabulary, as prime minister after 1951 his watchword in domestic policy was appeasement. Harold Macmillan emerged as the most stubborn and articulate defender of a commitment to Keynesianism, as befitted the great man's publisher, and in this he was abetted by the private advice of the great man's official biographer, Sir Roy Harrod. Now Macmillan, unusually, had been an opponent of the pre-war National Government in both its economic and foreign policies. The fact that Neville Chamberlain was painted as axiomatically wrong over Munich reinforced the view that he must have been equally benighted in his policy as Chancellor of the Exchequer. It was a historiographical landmark when the rise of a revisionist school on appeasement meant that the rationale of the National Government's foreign policy was first given a dispassionate hearing in the 1960s. It is notable that its record on unemployment had to wait longer for sympathetic reappraisal.

The foundations of a truly historical approach to Keynes were not laid until the 1960s, with two notable books which still rightly command attention. When Donald Winch began his major study of 'a lengthy period of interaction between professional economic thinking and policy questions',[5] he may have been a card-carrying economist, but his insights and his methodology were those of a historian, more concerned with a faithful reconstruction of developments over time than with current debates, theoretical or applied. Winch worked at a number of levels, from economic history through policy-formation to polemical arguments and issues of economic theory. The Keynes whom he discovered kept coming into this story: playing one role and then another, making up his mind and changing his mind, influencing events and failing to do so. The sense of a real argument going on was vividly conveyed, not least through Winch's backbreaking efforts in retrieving much of his documentation from the files of dusty periodicals and newspapers. Though this Keynes was unmistakeably the author of the *General Theory*, he was not its predestined author, still less was his magnum opus his only claim on our attention.

This was true *a fortiori* of the Keynes who first attracted his future biographer, Robert Skidelsky, in his study of the economic policy of the second Labour Government. With access now available to Keynes's private papers, Skidelsky gave an account of Keynes's policy arguments for a radical economic strategy in 1929–30. His overt political support for Lloyd George's pledge to reduce unemployment by means of large-scale public works was documented, as were the running battles with the Treasury, especially under the minority Labour Government which Ramsay MacDonald formed in 1929. Here was Keynes as publicist and policy adviser, rather than as economic theorist, making out a cogent case for action which was defeated by the inertia of the existing political system. Skidelsky's interpretative coup was to delineate an important political division – between economic radicals and economic conservatives – which cross-cut conventional party boundaries. The obstacles to a Keynesian solution comprised not only the hidebound Treasury and the reactionary Conservatives but also the Labour Party, with its dogmatic attachment to socialism giving it an alibi for its refusal to tinker with the existing capitalist system. Thus 'the Government rejected Conservative protection, the Liberal national development loan, the Keynesian and Mosleyite amalgams of both, preferring instead the advice of the least progressive sections of the "economic establishment".'[6] If the political dimension to this story was explicit, the implicit assumption was that the Keynesian case for tackling unemployment was simply common sense.

It was this assumption which naturally came into question once the Keynesian consensus had collapsed in the 1970s; and it was in this sceptical spirit that a number of historians of economic policy exploited the newly opened public records. The reduction of the period of restriction from fifty to thirty years meant that the market was glutted with a backlog of material covering virtually the whole period of Keynes's active influence. Donald Moggridge's reconstruction of the arguments over Britain's return to the Gold Standard in 1925 was a pioneer demonstration of the rich pickings that could be gleaned from the ostensibly uninviting Treasury files of this period.[7] Though there were incidental insights on the theoretical framework within which Keynes currently operated, the real historical gain here was a much fuller picture of him in action as a policy adviser and publicist.

If he emerged, on the whole, creditably from this episode, his subsequent stance on domestic expansion was to come under more severe scrutiny. What was at stake in both instances was Keynes's practical judgement. Over the Gold Standard his case about overvaluation and rigidities could easily have been integrated into a free-market analysis. A politically prudent Keynes or an intellectually modest Keynes might have achieved this limited goal, as Harry Johnson put it, 'if he had set himself to convince his professional colleagues that they were taking a theory designed for an economy in which wages and prices adjusted rapidly enough to maintain full employment and misapplying it to an economy in which severe monetary disturbance had made this assumption false, instead of setting out to demonstrate that that theory was wrong from the bottom up and that a new theory which he was providing was necessary for the understanding of reality'. In this might-have-been scenario, of course, 'there would have been no "Keynesian Revolution"'.[8] As it was, Keynes's further proposals for a counter-cyclical programme of public works raised contentious issues of theory as well as policy.

The question Keynes asked in the pamphlet which he wrote with Hubert Henderson in 1929 was *Can Lloyd George Do It?* An affirmative answer was much more readily forthcoming in retrospect so long as there was a general acceptance that the multiplier really worked and that increased state expenditure raised aggregate output rather than crowding out other economic activities in an inflationary spiral. Hence the double bonus which the historical Keynes of 1929 received, forty years on, from scholars who were slaves of this same defunct economist: in effect they appraised his practical judgement under rules which he had himself invented. Hence too the double penalty when a Keynesian analysis went abruptly out of fashion and the expedients of the historical Keynes were judged by more sceptical criteria. One welcome result has been to rescue the case mounted by the Treasury from the sort of dismissive scorn – 'Nowadays this seems merely laughable' – which Joan Robinson used to dispense so tellingly in the 1960s.[9] Recognizing the strength of the arguments which Keynes had to counter is the beginning of wisdom in understanding his own point of view. When he was making proposals of such a highly practical nature as in the 1929 road-building schemes, the caveats of able and experienced administrators like Sir Richard Hopkins deserve the sympathetic attention which they have belatedly received.[10] Likewise, the importance of confidence in constraining a radical programme is now better recognized.[11] What the administrative historians have succeeded in doing, in short, is to provide an empirical account of policy formation which underpins more ambitious conceptualization of 'bringing the state back in'.[12]

Has the author of the *General Theory* got lost in the corridors of Whitehall? Or is there an Ariadne thread which can retrieve him? It was the forte of Howson and Winch's book on the Economic Advisory Council that, apart from offering an institutional history of this first attempt to bring professional economists into the policy-making forum, it presented an integrated view of Keynes. The publicist and the Liberal politician are not lost sight of; but the real interest is in observing the changing tactics of the policy adviser against the background of the fermenting ideas of the economic theorist. In particular, the work of the committee of economists, which the EAC spawned in 1930, is analysed so as to bring out the relevance of Keynes's policy proposals both to the brute facts of the real world and to the analytical scheme of his *Treatise on Money*. By seeing Keynes at work in committee – chopping and changing, persuading and compromising, reordering his priorities when his own preferences could not prevail – a truly historical account is conveyed.[13]

2

Keynes's thinking, in short, needs to be contextualized; and this implies some methodological commitments, albeit of a generic rather than a doctrinaire kind.

Historians have become increasingly aware of the need to understand ideas not as discrete theories, suddenly disclosed, but in terms of the context in which they took shape. This postulates a complex interaction between a particular historical situation and the ideas formed in it – certainly more complex than all-or-nothing attributions of a single direction to causality. Naive intellectualism postulates the direct influence of great texts upon historical developments, whereas vulgar Marxism postulates the opposite: the production of ideas which reflect the underlying realities of social and economic relations. Neither model is currently very popular with historians, and, rather than a mix-and-match option, an altogether more subtle approach is required. A few propositions may serve to clarify this.

1. Great texts have to be seen in the context of lesser texts, which help constitute the intellectual environment in which they were produced. Recovering this context, as Quentin Skinner classically stated the point, is crucial to understanding their meaning.[14]

2. The argument in which authors were participating needs to be identified. 'The context of refutation' is an illuminating concept, introduced by Stefan Collini.[15] It offers an important key in understanding the extent to which an agenda was set and the terms of argument established by opponents whose acknowledged or ghostly influence leaves its own traces.

3. Conversely, texts cannot properly be made to speak on issues, however portentous, which lay outside the cognizance of the poor author at the time of writing, circumscribed by his or her own concerns. It is simply unhistorical to intuit undeclared doctrines from fragments and obiter dicta, and to father these constructs on unwitting historical figures, however eminent. Intellectual history ought not to be a bag of tricks which we play upon dead intellectuals.

4. It has to be recognized that the form in which influential ideas were conceived may well be different from that with which we have subsequently become familiar. The great eponymous 'isms' – Benthamism, Darwinism, Marxism, Freudianism, Keynesianism – have been particularly vulnerable. Indeed such distortions, which I would call ideological, may have been a condition of their influence, through the social purchase which they were thereby enabled to exert. In this sense, the ideological purchase of ideas raises a quite separate issue from whether they are true or false; instead it focuses on the selectivity in the reception of ideas by the social groups to whom they appeal.[16] Their ideological consequences, working out in a complex historical process, may be impossible to foresee – they can fitly be described as opaque.

5. The next proposition is the converse: if ideas sometimes have opaque consequences, neither are their origins always transparent. They may have been prompted by influences which do not immediately strike us as relevant. For example, the classic liberal doctrines, both political and economic, which we associate with such names as Locke and Bentham, have often been seen as a rationalistic demystification of the world. Certainly they have subsequently been understood in secular terms. Yet John Dunn, as a historian of Locke's political thought, points to 'the intimate dependence of an extremely high proportion of Locke's arguments for their very intelligibility, let alone plausibility, on a series of theological commitments'.[17] Likewise, Boyd Hilton, in seeking to explain the historical significance of such characteristically Victorian precepts as free trade, laissez-faire, sound money and public retrenchment, came to think 'that I had not previously noticed the operation of ideological factors because I had been looking for the wrong ideology'. He invoked instead 'another model of free-trade individualism, one *not* based on classical economics or the prospects of growth, or the superiority of the industrial sector', but one 'deriving mainly from theology and eschatology'.[18] Sometimes the historical task is a matter of reading between the lines; sometimes it is a matter of restoring the lost lines ruthlessly edited out in the course of popular or scientific dissemination.

6. Vulgarization is not the only reason for discrepancies between the form in which historical ideas were conceived and the conventional form in which they have subsequently been understood: specialization, notably in academic communities, can lead to the same result. For scientific knowledge, in its broadest sense, is currently demarcated by disciplinary boundaries which may have had little relevance to thinkers of previous generations. The danger of reconstituting the past as a canonical teleology has been aptly identified: 'By implicitly assuming that the discipline has in some ideal sense long existed, though in ways that were only partially disclosed and understood in the past, the teleological history of disciplines superimposes the intellectual map of the present, or some version of it, on the usually significantly different ones

employed in earlier periods, often to the point of obliterating them entirely.'[19] This cuts both ways. One is that divisions which strike us as arbitrary may once have been real barriers to a meeting of minds between contemporaries whose mutual affinities strike us as obvious. Conversely, our own separate scholarly communities, who are sometimes literally not on speaking terms, may need introducing to the right people.

These six propositions help stake out a methodology within which *The Keynesian Revolution in the Making* can be located. Since talk of a school would be wholly misplaced, however, I will instead risk solipsism by broaching some interlocking issues of interpretation with direct reference to my own book. Its central section tells the story of Keynes's activities on the Macmillan Committee on Finance and Industry, offered as a parallel and complement to Howson and Winch on the EAC. This is prefaced by a study of the Treasury View and succeeded by an account of the composition of the *General Theory*. What is new about this? How does it relate to other productions of the Keynes industry? How does its interpretation reflect the fact that the author is a historian?

3

Let me take three specific claims to novelty, one in each substantive part of the book. The first is over the Treasury View, which in effect provides the context of refutation for the development of Keynes's policy agenda on public works. I was much indebted to the administrative historians who had documented the Treasury position on the different schemes which were proposed in this period. Moreover, the reminder 'that the conflict between Keynes and the Treasury, which has absorbed so much of the energy of historians, was but one aspect of a wide-ranging reappraisal of the role of the state in the economy'[20] was salutary in correcting a Keynes-centred view of the whole problem. It was not just that busy civil servants had more on their minds – and their desks – than thwarting the bright ideas of an academic economist. It was also the fact that Keynes was not the unique champion of the forces of light, as suggested in Keynesian myth and legend. Nor did 'the authorities' stand in for the forces of darkness with the requisite hardfaced ghoulishness. The expertise of the Treasury and the Bank of England, it could be agreed, lay in managing a bad situation, in an old country, in an imperfect world, with a pragmatic good sense and good faith which their later accommodation to parts of the Keynesian agenda testified. This revisionist reading, established in the late 1970s and early 1980s, served to put the Treasury, in particular, in a notably more flattering light, perhaps suspiciously so. For its openness to reasoned argument was proclaimed, notably in its evidence to the Macmillan Committee in 1930. Under questioning, Hopkins distanced himself from the dogmatic Treasury View which had been imputed to himself and his maligned colleagues by Keynes. The problem of historical interpretation was how much of this testimony to accept at face value. Could the Treasury View have been misunderstood all along? Could it have been a figment of Keynes's imagination? Could it have been a straw man, set up in *Can Lloyd George Do It?*, the better to be knocked down?

What convinced me otherwise was finding a long-lost document. Almost at the end of my research in the Public Record Office, I came across a previously unknown Treasury file (T172/2095), which had never been placed in the archive, documenting the formation of the Treasury View in the run-up to the 1929 General Election. It was the sort of archival discovery which historians are conventionally supposed to make and rarely do – altering their interpretation by altering the evidence on which it is based. This particular document popped out of the system at this particular time in a quite fortuitous way, and it would obviously have been noticed sooner or later by other researchers. So it was pure luck that I found it – but not simply chance that I was looking for it. The file contained documents which answered a number of hitherto inconclusive questions about Treasury policy on unemployment under Winston Churchill. It vindicated authors, like Howson and Winch, who had argued that there was a clear Treasury View, deriving its crowding-out doctrine from the theoretical writings of Ralph Hawtrey, and proclaimed in such terms by Churchill as Conservative policy in 1929.[21] Moreover the file demonstrated Churchill's amateur enthusiasm for economic theory in personally developing the policy, which provides not only an interesting sidelight on his methods in formulating policy but also a general reflection on the potential political influence of even quite abstract ideas.[22] Furthermore, it revealed that the origins of his declaration lay not in a partisan wish to thwart Lloyd George, and prove that he simply could *not* do it, but in a tactical dispute within the cabinet, where some Conservative ministers toyed with a public works scheme of their own as a possible spoiler.

The relevance of this account to Keynes is obviously that, when he debated the Treasury View in 1929, and tried to show how it was fallacious, he was engaged in a crucial task, not a sham battle. His identification of the fallacy as the full-employment assumption was of fundamental significance for both policy and theory. As to policy, it prompted an adroit retreat by the Treasury to the pragmatic arguments which Hopkins deployed in 1930. As to theory, it is hardly too much to say that attention had been directed to the issue of the elasticity of the supply curve for output as a whole. Seeing the story in this way partly depends on intellectual inferences from writings that have long since been published; but it also depends partly on finding a file that no one had looked at for half a century.

4

A second claim to novelty is less clear-cut. There were two connected limitations in the literature about Keynes which were particularly troubling for the years

1929–31 when he was simultaneously firing on all cylinders as publicist, expert and theorist. The trouble was that some of the best accounts of him in each role showed so little cognizance of him in the others.[23] Conversely, when the different roles in which he was speaking were not distinguished at all, the composite Keynes who emerged from an eclectic amalgam of diverse quotation was a bundle of confusion and contradiction. This was not a new problem. It is no coincidence that it is from exactly this period that a well-worn gibe originates: 'Where five economists are gathered together, there will be six conflicting opinions and two of them will be held by Keynes!'[24] Now Keynes was notoriously a man who changed his mind and set little store by maintaining a formal consistency. Yet a good deal of the inconsistency with which he has been charged is the result of misreading his theoretical analysis as expedient policy advice in a particular contingency (or vice versa). The links between the two in his own mind needed to be established by studying the man in all his relevant activities. Moggridge and Howson had long since resolved one apparent inconsistency: that between the argument of *Can Lloyd George Do It?* for public works and the contention of the *Treatise on Money* that cheap money was the answer. The resolution was the *Treatise*'s 'special case', which permitted government investment when the Gold Standard precluded the fall in Bank Rate necessary to stimulate private investment.[25] Here Keynes's policy advice flowed from his theory, as a second-best option in the real world. But was the link always in this direction? Did policy never prompt a theoretical response?

Economists are good at analysing Keynes's different ideas to show whether they are formally consistent, given this or that premise or application under specified conditions. Historians make do with a more old-fashioned heuristic device: telling stories. So I set out to tell 'the story of an argument' in which Keynes was involved at a number of levels – politics and policy and theory – and to pursue his activities at all of those levels. Like all Keynesian scholars these days, I was much assisted by the publication of the magnificent edition of Keynes's collected writings, volume 20 of which had made accessible Keynes's so-called 'private evidence' to the Macmillan Committee. What it offered was the spectacle of Keynes arguing out his ideas at a pregnant stage in their development, at a level pitched to the understanding of intelligent laymen, connecting up the theoretical analysis of the *Treatise* on one side with the practical application of his policy proposals on the other. The published double volume of evidence to the committee, given by witnesses whom Keynes questioned at length, together with other unpublished 'private evidence' in the Public Record Office, completed a virtually verbatim account of its proceedings. For a historian who had done enough homework in the economic literature to be able to understand the theoretical as well as policy issues at stake, this source was treasure trove. Harrod had long ago glimpsed the dramatic possibilities of the 'tense combat' between Keynes and Hopkins, where 'every muscle was taut' and 'displacement by an inch might give victory to one side or the other', in their 'drawn battle' over the Treasury View.[26] Yet the more cerebral tension of Keynes's chess games with Cambridge colleagues like A.C. Pigou and Dennis Robertson gave another dimension to the argument as it was played out, line by line, with the official shorthand-writers poised to catch every word.

Although Keynes appealed to the *Treatise* for theoretical support, it is surely plain that its analysis was likewise shaped in important ways by the policy argument which had surrounded the final stages of its composition. Not that the doctrines of the *Treatise*, with its peculiar definitions of saving and investment, were necessary to win acceptance for the policy options which Keynes put forward. His seven remedies drew support for many diverse reasons – political as well as economic – and his own preference among them for public works reflected his own predilections. All that Keynes claimed was that a consistent rationale underlay them. Moreover, he could count on pragmatic agreement from Pigou and Robertson, a fact which reinforces the historiographical rescue of their reputations from an earlier generation of Keynesian demonology.[27] One reason for this consensus was that the *Treatise* did not sever Keynes from the fundamentals of orthodox analysis, which identified unemployment as a symptom of the rigidities which had caused a departure from equilibrium. Such points emerge with unique verisimilitude in the context of the Macmillan Committee.

5

A third novelty is the dating which I proposed for the inception of the theory of effective demand. The source which permits this exercise is the record of what Keynes said (or is said to have said) in his university lectures in Cambridge from 1932 to 1935, which has become available in recent years through the efforts of Thomas K. Rymes.[28] Early accounts of the transition from the *Treatise* to the *General Theory* had been necessarily dependent upon heroic inferences from publication dates of relevant works.[29] This could be supplemented by Keynes's published drafts and correspondence, once the relevant volumes of the Collected Works were out; and the results were tempered by an uncertain oral tradition. Whatever their frailties or discrepancies, should not the common evidence of the students' notes be able to settle this issue? It now seems to have narrowed the range of possibilities, to a date sometime between the summer of 1932 and the end of 1933. The grounds for continuing disagreement are interesting – some would say more interesting than a pedantic disputation over a few months here or there. For the underlying issue over *when* Keynes came forth with his seminal theory concerns *how* that theory is defined.

Since readings of the *General Theory* have been notoriously diverse in recent years, it is natural that a particular view of what Keynes really meant in it will be used as the criterion for ascertaining the moment at which such a meaning can be attributed to him. One problem here concerns the role of uncertainty, which enters the book, in a systematic way, at a relatively late stage in its composition. There is, of course, a long-established view, associated with Shackle, that Keynes's 'ultimate meaning' is to be sought here, which implies an almost testamentary status for his 1937 article in the QJE.[30] In recent years, however, there has been a spate of studies suggesting that the *General Theory* itself hinges on uncertainty, in ways that have been traced back, via very different routes, to Keynes's concern with probability, the topic of his early research as a philosopher.[31] If, as Bateman now proposes, uncertainty is integral to the vision of the *General Theory*, then there is a lot to be said for his argument that it was not presented in these terms until the Michaelmas Term of 1933.[32]

My own account, written in ignorance of this impending deluge of publications, made an implicit distinction between the *General Theory*, as finally published, and the theory of effective demand, which was what I sought to date. It now seems prudent to draw attention to this distinction. The justification for making it lies in the evidence of Keynes's own view of his theory, notably in a letter to Harrod in August 1936, which has likewise been regarded as a most revealing source by Patinkin.[33] This much-quoted letter (see Appendix to chapter 4) is a product of Keynes's reflection on the process by which his ideas had developed. The central paragraph emphasizes 'effective demand', links it to 'the psychological law' about increases in income and consumption, mentions 'the notion of interest being the measure of liquidity preference', and concludes with the difficulty in defining the marginal efficiency of capital. Here are the building blocks of the theory which Patinkin and Moggridge, as well as myself, took to be the explanandum. Why, appealing to the same evidence, do our explanations of its chronology differ?

The answer, I am clear, is that, as economists, they were looking for the first exposition of effective demand by Keynes in terms which they regard as analytically rigorous. They differ between themselves over the degree of rigour in this test, and hence over exact chronology. But, as a historian, the significant point that struck me about the letter to Harrod was not just that it insisted on what the four analytical building blocks were but that it was equally clear on their chronological sequence. Keynes wrote that he was preoccupied 'with the order in which the problem developed in my mind'. Crucially ('one of the most important transitions for me') came the apprehension of effective demand; only after that ('appreciably later') did 'the notion of interest being the measure of liquidity preference' snap into place. Conversely, by the time this new salience for liquidity preference was apprehended, effective demand was already understood. Earlier adumbrations of liquidity preference in terms of 'bearishness' were clearly not the point. It was when Keynes needed a new theory of interest – because his new theory of effective demand now performed the equilibrating role in which he had previously conceived interest rates – and saw liquidity preference as the solution, that the moment had arrived. When? 31 October 1932, said the students' notes.

Essentially this was the proof – and a historian's proof – of a contention which obviously remains arguable but can only be disproved at the price of repudiating the integrity of Keynes's own account. Consistently enough, Moggridge has candidly declined to 'take *strictly* Keynes's retrospective view of the development of his ideas.'[34] This may well turn out to be Patinkin's preferred resolution of the matter; meanwhile there seemed to me to be an anomaly here which was worth noting. For the authority of Keynes's letter rests on the clarity and coherence of the view which it stated. It surely represents, at the very least, his own conception of what his new theory was and how he arrived at it.

This helps make sense of Keynes's actions in their particular historical context. For if Keynes believed himself to have hit upon a new explanation of unemployment during 1932, and had seen the pertinence of liquidity preference as a theory of interest by October 1932, and had purloined the concept of 'effective demand' from his creative reading of Malthus before Christmas 1932, then his first steps in the New Year of 1933 become wholly comprehensible. After a long period of silence on policy issues, he burst into print in the newspapers with confidently renewed advocacy of public works. *The Means to Prosperity* appeared in March and April. Seen in context, the sense that he was already seized with his big idea seems palpable. That this line of interpretation naturally appeals to political historians is shown by the fact that the recent volume of Robert Skidelsky's biography now endorses the essential steps in the same chronology. He maintains that 'the critical stages in refashioning the theory of the *Treatise* occurred in the early spring and summer of 1932', and contests Patinkin's claim that the lectures of Michaelmas 1932 did not show an understanding of the theory of effective demand. By the end of 1932, therefore, there was 'a preliminary sketch of the final picture, blurred and incomplete, but perfectly recognisable'. Skidelsky's next sentence, beginning a new section on the *Means to Prosperity*, completes the argument: 'With increasing confidence in his analysis, Keynes started to propound his policies for the 1930s.'[35]

What I would now add, drawing on the two new biographies of Keynes, is a restatement of how the final links were riveted into place. For Moggridge, whose actual chronology differs little from my own, accepts *The Means to Prosperity* as evidence that 'the penny had firmly dropped for the theory of effective demand'.[36] He bases this verdict on the exposition of what Keynes now called 'the multiplier'. This was, of course, the argument which Kahn and Meade had presented, in drab and scholarly guise, a couple of years previously, with its implication that there was an equilibrating mechanism between saving and investment through output changes. They specified this process tightly, but, in Kahn's recollection, half a century later, did not apprehend its general significance.[37] Whether Kahn and Meade – or Kahn alone – remained in the dark, and for how long, may be a moot point. But Keynes quickly grasped the point that 'Mr Meade's Relation' showed how an increase of output and income, by mobilizing unused resources, generated savings exactly equal to the initial increment of investment. This is shown by a hitherto unpublished letter of December 1931, now printed by Skidelsky.[38]

Looking back in 1936, Keynes's reproach to Harrod was: 'You don't mention *effective demand* or, more precisely, the demand schedule for output as a whole, except in so far as it is implicit in the multiplier.'[39] By the end of 1932 he found that Malthus spoke to this neglected problem. The difficulty presented by Keynes's lectures of Michaelmas 1932 stems from his insufficently rigorous proof of his intuition that variations in the volume of output as a whole served as an equilibrating mechanism. By March 1933, when he purloined the Kahn–Meade concept as his 'multiplier', he saw how to make the account watertight. It recalls the anecdote of Halley's challenge to Newton – 'Have you proved it?' – about one of his most fundamental discoveries. As the story goes: 'Newton was taken aback – "Why, I've known it for years," he replied. "If you give me a few days, I'll certainly find you a proof" – as in due course he did.' It is not only historians who tell stories; Keynes liked to tell this one.[40]

Notes

1.   *JMK*, vol. 7, p. xxi.
2.   A.J.P. Taylor, *English History, 1914–1945* (Oxford, 1965), p. 136n.
3.   Peter Clarke, *The Keynesian Revolution in the Making, 1924–36* (Oxford, 1988), p. vii.
4.   A story not explicitly challenged until Correlli Barnett's revisionist indictment of the endemic failures of British mobilization was published in the very different climate of the Thatcher era; see *The Audit of War* (1986). There is a useful discussion of the historiography in Philip Williamson, *National Crisis and National Government: British Politics, the Economy and Empire. 1926-32* (Cambridge, 1992), pp. 4–10.
5.   Donald Winch, *Economics and Policy: A Historical Study* (1969; Fontana paperback, 1972), p. 7.
6.   Robert Skidelsky, *Politicians and the Slump: The Labour Government of 1929–31* (1967), p. 388.
7.   D.E. Moggridge, *British Monetary Policy, 1924–1931* (Cambridge, 1972).
8.   Harry Johnson, 'The social and intellectual origins of the *General Theory*', in Elizabeth S. Johnson and Harry G. Johnson, *The Shadow of Keynes* (Oxford, 1978), p. 78.
9.   Joan Robinson, *Economic Philosophy* (1962; Penguin paperback, 1964), p. 71.
10. See J. Tomlinson, *Problems of British Economic Policy, 1870–1945* (1981), ch. 5; A. Booth and M. Pack, *Employment, Capital and Economic Policy* (Oxford, 1985), chs 2 and 8; G.C. Peden, 'Sir Richard Hopkins and the "Keynesian Revolution" in employment policy', *Econ. Hist. Rev.*, 2nd ser., xxxvi (1983), pp. 281–96; G.C. Peden, 'The "Treasury View" on public works and employment in the inter-war period', *Econ. Hist. Rev.* 2nd ser., xxxvii (1984), pp. 167–81.
11. See Roger Middleton, *Towards the Managed Economy* (1985), ch. 8, building on his article, 'The Treasury in the 1930s: political and administrative constraints to acceptance of the "new" economics', *Oxford Econ. Papers*, n.s., xxxiv (1982), pp. 48–77; Alan Booth, 'The "Keynesian revolution" in economic policy-making', *Econ. Hist. Rev.*, 2nd ser., xxxvi (1983), pp. 103–23.

12. See Peter B. Evans, Dietrich Rueschemeyer and Theda Skocpol (eds), *Bringing the State Back In* (Cambridge and New York, 1985), esp. ch. 4; Peter A. Hall, *The Political Power of Economic Ideas: Keynesianism across Nations* (Princeton, 1989).

13. Susan Howson and Donald Winch, *The Economic Advisory Council* (Cambridge, 1977).

14. Quentin Skinner, 'Meaning and understanding in the history of ideas', *History and Theory*, viii (1969), 3–53.

15. Stefan Collini, *Liberalism and Sociology: L.T. Hobhouse and Political Argument in England, 1880–1914* (Cambridge, 1979), p. 9.

16. Peter Clarke, *Liberals and Social Democrats* (Cambridge, 1978), pp. 3–4, was my first effort at formulating this way of understanding ideology, and developed in 'Political history in the 1980s: ideas and interests', *Journal of Interdisciplinary History*, xii (1981), 45–7, reprinted in Theodore K. Rabb and Robert I. Rotberg (eds), *The New History* (Princeton, 1982), pp. 45–7.

17. John Dunn, *The Political Thought of John Locke* (Cambridge, 1969), p. xi.

18. Boyd Hilton, *The Age of Atonement: The Influence of Evangelicalism on Social and Economic Thought, 1785–1865* (Oxford, 1988), pp. viii–ix.

19. Stefan Collini, Donald Winch and John Burrow, *That Noble Science of Politics* (Cambridge, 1983), p. 4.

20. A. Booth and M. Pack, *Employment, Capital and Economic Policy* (Oxford, 1985), p. 185.

21. Howson and Winch, p. 27.

22. Peter Clarke, 'Churchill's Economic Ideas, 1900–1930', in Robert Blake and Wm Roger Louis (eds), *Churchill* (Oxford, 1993), pp. 79–95, develops this point.

23. John Campbell, *Lloyd George: The Goat in the Wilderness* (1977), ch. 7, offers an excellent guide to Keynes's role in the Liberal Industrial Inquiry in the late 1920s; J.Tomlinson, *Problems of British Economic Policy, 1870–1945* (1981), ch. 5 is a trenchant study of the administrative debate over Keynes's 1929 proposals; Don Patinkin, *Keynes's Monetary Thought* (Durham, N.C., 1976), ch. 12, is a lucid account of theory and policy in the development of Keynes's monetary thinking in the same period. Instead of regretting that the common ground between these three accounts is negligible, one could, of course, commend the achievement of an economical division of labour – what Patinkin (p. 132) calls 'the simple fact that Keynes – like all of us – wrote and acted in different ways in the different roles that he played in life'.

24. Thomas Jones, *A Diary with Letters, 1931–50* (1954), p. 19 (entry for 20 October 1931).

25. D.E. Moggridge and Susan Howson, 'Keynes on monetary policy, 1910–46', *Oxford Econ. Papers*, n. s., xxvi (1974), p. 236. This is, so far as I can see, the first appreciation in print of a point that had, from its publication, been staring all readers of the *Treatise* in the face: *JMK*, vol. 6, pp. 337–8.

26. R.F. Harrod, *The Life of John Maynard Keynes* (1951), pp. 421–2.

27. T.W. Hutchison, *Economics and Economic Policy in Britain* (1968) was a pioneer work in rehabilitating Pigou.

28. The published text, *Keynes's Lectures, 1932–35: Notes of a Representative Student*, transcribed, edited and constructed by Thomas K. Rymes (London, 1989) is now an accessible guide to this source.

29. Lawrence R. Klein, *The Keynesian Revolution* (1952; first published New York, 1947), p. 39, innocently perpetrated a fallacious speculation, which has become notorious in the literature, by building on a chronology of publication, as between two articles by Joan Robinson, which in fact reversed their sequence of composition.

30. See the engagingly eschatological heading for ch. 11 in G.L.S. Shackle, *The Years of High Theory* (Cambridge, 1967) – 'To the *QJE* from Chapter 12 of the *General Theory*: Keynes's ultimate meaning.'

31. R.M. O'Donnell, *Keynes: Philosophy, Economics and Politics* (1989); Anna M. Carabelli, *On Keynes's Method* (1988); Bradley W. Bateman, 'Keynes's changing conception of probability', *Economics and Philosophy*, iii, (1987), pp. 97–120; idem, 'G.E. Moore and J.M. Keynes: a missing chapter in the history of the expected utility model', *American Economic Review*, lxxviii, pp. 1098–1106; Athol Fitzgibbons, *Keynes's Vision* (Oxford, 1988); Allan H. Meltzer, *Keynes's Monetary Theory: A Different Interpretation* (Cambridge, 1988).

32. [My reference was to an unpublished version of Bradley Bateman, *Keynes's Uncertain Revolution* (Ann Arbor, Michigan, 1996).]
33. Keynes to Harrod, 30 Aug. 1936, *JMK*, vol. 14, pp. 84–6; cf. Patinkin, *Keynes's Monetary Thought*, pp. 66, 80; and Moggridge, *Maynard Keynes*, pp. 558ff., building on his pioneer account, 'From the *Treatise* to the *The General Theory*: an exercise in chronology', *History of Political Economy*, 5 (1973), pp. 72–88.
34. Moggridge, *Maynard Keynes*, p. 562.
35. Robert Skidelsky, *John Maynard Keynes: The Economist as Saviour, 1920–1937* (London, 1992), pp. 459, 462 and n., 466–7.
36. Moggridge, *Maynard Keynes*, p. 564.
37. Richard Kahn, *The Making of Keynes's General Theory* (Cambridge, 1984), p. 99, commenting on his article. 'The relation of home investment to unemployment', *Econ. Jnl*, xli (1931), pp. 173–98.
38. Keynes to Harold Jeffreys, 18 Dec. 1931, Skidelsky, *Keynes*, p. 451.
39. *JMK*, vol. 14, p. 85.
40. *JMK*, vol. 10, p. 365.

7   The Treasury's analytical model of the British economy between the wars

1

The first question posed in this essay is concerned with 'practical knowledge' – how did Treasury officials understand the British economy to work in the 1920s and 1930s? A second question, however, is how far that understanding was influenced and modified over time by 'professional knowledge', on the one hand, and by 'general folklore' on the other.[1] One issue is thus highly general – about the role of ideas in the process of government. It has, no doubt, often been easy to form an exaggerated view of the importance of 'ideas', especially those expressed in 'classic texts' written by 'great thinkers'. Such an account, in fact, can serve as a retrospective rationalization which tidies up more messy and complex developments, gaining in intellectual coherence what it lacks in historical verisimilitude. There are possible sub-Hegelian overtones and variations here; but let us restrict attention to a rationalist model of purposive intellectual influence. Politics thus comprises little more than a unilinear logic of realized intentions – in this case the supposed intentions of an articulate elite who are assigned a unique, if vaguely specified, importance.[2] Nowadays it is easy to mock this view; yet it may be equally misguided to swing, in one irresistible sweep, to the conclusion that it must inevitably be wholly erroneous. If it implies a fallacious account of policy-making, its fallacy surely resides in supposing that a sufficient explanation can be derived from an examination of prevailing theories or doctrines. So a more inclusive, comprehensive, multi-causal account of policy is clearly required. But this still does not obviate the question, what sort of ideas are a *necessary* part of the explanation?

The specific topic with which my essay deals – British economic policy in the inter-war period – has seen fashion scuttle from one extreme interpretation to its opposite. The long wave of Keynesian triumphalism after the Second World War led to the great man's own view of the matter being accepted at face value. In 1929 Keynes had characterized existing Treasury policy as not just practically inadvisable but theoretically misconceived. 'Certainly this dogma is not derived from common sense', he wrote. 'On the contrary, it is a highly sophisticated theory.' He pilloried a leading Conservative cabinet minister for propagating it by saying that 'he half understands an ancient theory, the premises of which he has forgotten'.[3] An echo of the same charge is to be heard in the well-known final passage of the *General Theory*: 'Practical men, who believe themselves to be quite exempt from any intellectual influences, are usually the slaves of some defunct economist.'[4]

Some recent historians have reacted – or over-reacted – against what they see as Keynes's influentially misleading intellectualization of the problems faced by policy-makers in this period.[5] Indeed it may now seem tempting to return the flatly negative answer that the Treasury simply did not have anything that can be described as an analytical model of the economy as a whole. At any rate it needs to be asked whether British economic policy in the inter-war period should be seen in terms of a dichotomy between Treasury orthodoxy and an alternative Keynesian agenda, with the one eventually being overturned by the force of the other. Keynes's image of the Treasury mandarins – 'a few old gentlemen tightly buttoned-up in their frock coats, who only need to be treated with a little friendly disrespect and bowled over like ninepins'[6] – is indelible but blatantly partisan. The starting point must be how they saw themselves.

2

It is true that the Treasury remained fundamentally Gladstonian in outlook. It did not conceive its role in terms of general economic responsibilities but rather of particular tasks in the field of public finance. It saw itself as the national housekeeper not the national breadwinner. It had to balance the accounts, and do so in a way that did not prejudice the creation of wealth; but its responsibilities had conventionally been held to end there. The way the economy worked, in short, was not seen as a problem for the Treasury – one might say it was defined as a non-problem.[7] Indeed the role of 'the authorities' – the Treasury and the Bank of England – was seen as that of servicing a self-acting system. As long as the principles of sound finance were upheld, there was no need for the Treasury to become involved in a task of economic management for which it was unsuited. It maintained a self-denying ordinance against assuming the functions of an economic ministry.[8]

The self-acting system was founded upon three interlocking principles. The balanced budget convention defined the Treasury's essential task as that of raising sufficient revenue from the public to cover government expenditure – or rather of reining back public spending to a level which the long-suffering taxpayer felt he could afford. Any fiscal impact upon the economy was unintended – indeed it should be obviated so far as possible. The second principle was free trade, which merely extended the same precept to the international sphere, seeking to avoid distortion in the play of market forces. The third principle was the Gold Standard, envisaged as the pursuit of unimpeachable ends by inviolable means. The ends were those of sound money, riveting the parity of the pound to gold by a solemn and binding fiat (the obligation to convert sterling at a fixed value). The means were circumscribed by this prior commitment, leaving the Bank of England with only the barest margin of room for manoeuvre in operating a domestic credit policy dictated by its defence of sterling. Well might Sir John Bradbury, with the authority of a former Permanent Secretary to the Treasury (1913–19), commend this system on the ground that it was 'knave-proof' – a phrase embalmed for posterity by his disciple P.J. Grigg, who served as private secretary to successive Chancellors of the Exchequer for nearly ten years from 1921. The merit of a knave-proof system was precisely that it was self-acting and that government was insulated from its economic consequences.

That it nonetheless had economic consequences was in many ways the salient lesson of the 1920s; and learning this lesson was one way in which the economic knowledge of government grew. As Chancellor of the Exchequer in Baldwin's Conservative Government, Churchill recognized the decision on the Gold Standard as one which involved crucial choices, with no guarantee of an easy transition. His expert committee, under the successive chairmanship of Austen Chamberlain and Sir John Bradbury, and including the economist A.C. Pigou, was ultimately unanimous in favour of an early return. Grigg was later adamant that Churchill's advisers never concealed from him 'that a decision to return might involve adjustments which would be painful, and that it would certainly entail a more rigorous standard of public finance than any system of letting the exchanges go wherever the exigencies of a valetudinarian economic and financial policy took them'.[9] Churchill was to respond to the taunt 'that the gold standard will shackle us to the United States' by saying: 'For good or ill, it will shackle us to reality.'[10] But there was no doubt about the grand object of the policy, whatever its immediate side effects. In the long run it was surely designed to restore the health of the British economy and thus to cure unemployment.

The self-acting system had been legitimated by the object lesson of British prosperity in the pre-war era. Britain's return to the Gold Standard in 1925 can be seen as an attempt to re-enter the Garden of Eden, to recover and recapture a prelapsarian innocence compromised by the war and its aftermath. With the restoration of the Gold Standard, the circle of sound finance was virtually complete. Despite the burdens of the war debt, the balanced budget convention was not to be effectively challenged until the 1930s. Nor, once the Conservatives had burned their fingers over tariffs in the 1923 election, was free trade in immediate danger from governments of left or right. The late 1920s thus saw a consistent effort to re-create the conditions associated with pre-war prosperity. Because the medicine notoriously failed to effect the cure, it thereby provoked a natural scepticism over the diagnosis. In the 1880s, as Barry Supple has shown, foreign competition, declining profits and mounting unemployment promoted a more introspective mood;[11] likewise, in the 1920s, similar adverse changes in the real world led to a more searching economic analysis of the problem.

3

Questions of policy rested in very few hands. Without entering into a full account of the structure of the Treasury as it was until the internal reorganization of 1932, one can summarily identify two posts as crucial: the Controller of Finance and the Deputy Controller. The first post was occupied in the early 1920s by Sir Otto Niemeyer, who was succeeded in 1927 by Sir Richard Hopkins; and the post of deputy was filled by F.W. (later Sir Frederick) Leith-Ross from 1925 to 1932, when he was, in effect, succeeded by (Sir) Frederick Phillips.[12] The thinking of the Treasury between the return to Gold in 1925 and the outbreak of war in 1939 was thus dominated by these four Treasury knights. In the years up to 1931 their viewpoint was sympathetically interpreted to the Chancellor by Grigg, as his private secretary.

Grigg, like Leith-Ross, looked back on the era of Bradbury and Niemeyer as truly a golden age; and the changing of the guard may itself be significant. Churchill had rankled under the tutelage of the doctrinaire Niemeyer and shed no tears over his premature departure to the Bank of England. To Niemeyer's lieutenant Leith-Ross, who obviously nurtured his own expectations of the succession, the appointment of the outsider Hopkins to the top post in the Treasury (from the Board of Inland Revenue) was a heavy blow. While the accommodating temperament and political dexterity of 'Hoppy' made him many friends – including Keynes – it did not appease the testy 'Leithers', who took the opportunity to leave the Treasury at the beginning of 1932 for another post (nominally as Economic Adviser to H.M. Government). By this point, Bradbury's praetorian guard had been replaced; Hopkins and his taciturn adjutant Phillips were left to set their stamp upon the Treasury in the changed conditions of the 1930s.

None of these men was trained as an economist – but then, as President Reagan once reminded us, neither was John Maynard Keynes. Niemeyer got a First in Classics (Greats) at Balliol College, Oxford, and came top in the civil service examinations in 1906 (Keynes came second). Leith-Ross trod exactly the same path three years later. Hopkins read Classics in Part I of the Tripos at Emmanuel College, Cambridge, and History in Part II, with Firsts in both Parts. Phillips was also at Emmanuel, with Firsts in the Mathematical and Natural Sciences Triposes; he came top in the civil service examinations in 1908. Grigg was at St John's College, Cambridge: another mathematician, with Firsts in both Parts of the Tripos, and top of the civil service examinations in 1913. These men were part of a small self-conscious elite, largely self-taught in economics, but owning intellectual deference to nobody.

The nearest thing to a professional economist, in the modern sense, within the Treasury was the Director of Financial Inquiries – a post created to accommodate the peculiar talents of R.G. Hawtrey. Hawtrey read Mathematics at Trinity College, Cambridge (Nineteenth Wrangler in 1901; his friend Keynes

– fellow Etonian, fellow Apostle – was to be Twelfth Wrangler in 1905). In the Treasury Hawtrey was customarily regarded as rather a joke and there is a vivid oral tradition depreciating his role.[13] It is easy to see that the herbivorous Hawtrey was no match for fully-fledged carnivores like Niemeyer and Leith-Ross. But even Grigg's cameo of him can be read as a veiled acknowledgement that ultimately he could not be ignored.[14]

> Mr Churchill, when he became Chancellor, used to accuse us of giving Hawtrey too little scope. I remember his demanding from time to time that the learned man should be released from the dungeon in which we were said to have immured him, have the chains struck off and the straw brushed from his hair and clothes and be admitted to the light and warmth of an argument in the Treasury board room with the greatest living master of argument.

For in becoming their house economist, Hawtrey acquired an expertise which busy administrators lacked themselves; and I shall argue that in the late 1920s and 1930s this exerted a permeative influence which is masked by the heavy banter which Hawtrey had to endure from his colleagues. While his direct advice on policy was often discounted, his pattern of thought helped determine Treasury perceptions, and hence policy, in more indirectly pervasive ways.

4

In April 1925, when Britain returned to the Gold Standard, the official unemployment figure stood at 10.9 per cent. During the following twelve months the figure climbed above 12 per cent before dropping back to 9.1 per cent in April 1926. At this point there was a sudden jump upwards – over 14 per cent from May to August 1926 – which could satisfactorily be explained by the impact of the General Strike and the prolonged coal dispute. By the summer of 1927 the figure had dipped below 9 per cent – taking the most optimistic view of the trend, one could point to a reduction from 14.6 per cent to 8.7 per cent in the twelve months to May 1927. The government's story up to this point was thus fairly plausible: the return to Gold had laid the foundation for a return to prosperity which had been temporarily impeded by the industrial disputes of 1926.[15] From this point onward, however, the record no longer spoke for itself as an endorsement of sound finance. With a tendency for unemployment to rise rather than fall, so that it fluctuated around 10 or 11 per cent throughout 1928 and 1929, the situation cried out for explanation, if not action. Moreover, the Treasury was specifically prompted to defend itself and its prognosis in response to a series of proposals for state intervention, chiefly linked with the names of Keynes and Lloyd George.

The Treasury position is therefore expounded in a loosely-linked series of documents dating from 1928–9, drafted in the main by Leith-Ross but incorporating arguments derived from Hawtrey. The chief documents comprise:

(i)   Leith-Ross's paper of August 1928 for the Chancellor, criticizing Keynes's proposals published in the *Evening Standard* under the title 'How to organize a wave of prosperity'.[16]

(ii)   The Cabinet Paper CP 53 (29) of February 1929, reaffirming Treasury policy in face of internal dissension within the Conservative Cabinet, notably from the Home Secretary, Sir William Joynson-Hicks, and the Minister of Labour, Sir Arthur Steel-Maitland.[17]

(iii)   Leith-Ross's drafts of a statement of the Treasury View, finally incorporated by Churchill into his Budget speech in April 1929. The background to this statement is illuminated by the contents of a hitherto inaccessible file (T 172/2095) which also highlights the importance of CP 53 (29), above, as the foundation text on the Treasury View.[18]

(iv)   The Treasury Memorandum, published as the final section of the Government's White Paper of May 1929, in criticism of the Liberal proposals on unemployment (that is, Lloyd George's pledge as contained in the manifesto *We Can Conquer Unemployment*, subsequently supported by Keynes and H.D. Henderson in their pamphlet *Can Lloyd George Do It?*)[19]

Though all these documents were addressed to the same problem and manifested essentially the same outlook, there was one respect in which the Treasury shifted ground in the course of the argument. This will become apparent if we examine its response to Keynes's claim (in 'How to organize a wave of prosperity') that 'The fundamental blunder of the Treasury and of the Bank of England has been due, from the beginning, to their belief that if they looked after the deflation of prices the deflation of costs would look after itself'.[20] For this questioned the crucial postulate that wages were in fact flexible, as required by the adjustment mechanism.

When Britain had returned to the Gold Standard, the parity adopted for sterling – the only one considered – was $4.86. There has always been room for controversy over whether this was the right parity, as measured by comparative prices and purchasing power.[21] So far as the consequences of this *démarche* are concerned, however, the point is very simple. If sterling had not been 'overvalued' in the late 1920s, the Bank of England would not have needed to maintain a dear money policy in order to protect it. Yet it became increasingly apparent that this was indeed the position in which the Bank found itself. It was, in the phrase used by its Governor, Montagu Norman, 'under the harrow' in resorting to a high Bank Rate as its only means of preventing a flight from sterling.

According to the 'rules of the game' under the Gold Standard, the authorities would be prompted to intervene whenever there was a serious loss of gold. If the imbalance were due to lack of competitiveness in export prices, this could be remedied by a stiff dose of deflation which would bring down the costs of production and thus correct the disequilibrium at source. Bradbury, as one of the architects of the return to Gold, explained the underlying theory to the Macmillan Committee in 1930:[22]

> The first effect – and this is rather important, because [it is] the normal effect of dear money, what I might call the curative effect towards the reduction of prices – depends to a large extent on its being the short and sharp application of the remedy. . . .The result is a slump in stocks and a rapid fall in prices. That is the normal way in which the gold standard works.

Yet, by the time he gave this account, it was apparent that normal working was in abeyance.

> I have often thought that one of our troubles arises from the fact that we have had, owing to the exchange rate since the War, to apply this dear money consistently over a long period. . . . Its curative power is very largely inhibited unless it is exercised very rapidly.

At what point did the Treasury acknowledge that the stickiness of wages, above all else, stood in the way of a successful adjustment under the Gold Standard? Not in 1928, to judge from Leith-Ross's paper for the Chancellor. He had written to Hawtrey, querying Keynes's claim that wage costs had been stable in the years 1925–8 and adding: 'I shd have thought that the average wage rates showed a substantial decline during the past 4 years.'[23] Hawtrey pointed out to him that the index constructed by the statistician A.L. Bowley bore out Keynes's point; but Leith-Ross's subsequent draft nonetheless read:[24]

> It is, of course, quite true that the reduction of money wages to correspond with the reduction of prices has been the outstanding difficulty since our return to the gold standard and that the Chamberlain-Bradbury Committee seriously under-estimated this difficulty. Political influences have not only operated to mitigate the hardships of industrial depression but have been engaged to a large extent in a deliberate attempt to counteract economic forces by means of subsidies. As a result, the natural resistance of wages to falling prices has been seriously increased, with a corresponding prolongation of economic disturbances. But Mr Keynes exaggerates the extent of this resistance. Apparently he bases his statement that labour costs have not declined during the past 3 years on Professor Bowley's Index of Wages. It only shows how fallacious such indices are.

Leith-Ross's paper cited Ministry of Labour figures against Bowley – showing that the aggregate sums paid out in wages had declined. The paper accordingly identified Britain's main problem not in excessive labour costs but in structural weaknesses in industrial organization which could be remedied by 'a bold industrial concentration policy'.

5

The restoration of the export trade was seen as the fundamental objective, to which all other aims had to be subordinated. This helps explain not only the Treasury's scepticism about schemes for home development but also their cosmopolitan attitude towards capital flows. For they regarded the export of capital as instrumental in stimulating other exports. The Keynes/Lloyd George proposals on public works were seen by the Treasury – not unfairly in the first place – as a means of diverting capital from foreign to home investment. Any such move, the Treasury argued, would entail deleterious consequences. Leith-Ross claimed in 1928 that the level of foreign investment over the previous three years was less than the regular income from past lending; so although the historic capital had not been raided, the income had not, as in the pre-war period, constituted a surplus which could finance further accumulation. (He pointed also to an offsetting increase in British short-term indebtedness). The rationale of foreign investment lay in his further contention that 'what we invest in foreign loans must, sooner or later, be exported; and insofar as it is sunk in development schemes for the Empire, it is probably exported almost at once in the form of capital goods'.[25]

Now there are really two propositions here: one a dogmatic assertion of a necessary effect upon exports (albeit neither immediate nor direct) and the other an immediate and direct pragmatic point about how the close links between the Empire and the mother country actually operated. It is noticeable that in 1929 the Treasury was more easily shifted on the pragmatic than on the dogmatic point. For in February of that year it was faced – in anticipation of the Liberal proposals for home development – with a rival proposal, launched within the Conservative Cabinet, for a scheme of imperial development. It is illuminating to observe how foreign lending was analysed in this context by the Treasury. Here, it might seem, were the very sort of loans – to be 'sunk in development schemes for the Empire' – which the Treasury might regard with special favour. Yet CP 53 (29) declares:[26]

> It should be borne in mind, however, in considering the *immediate* effects of development loans to the Dominions and Colonies upon employment in this country that on the average rather more than one half of the money will be spent on colonial labour, land and materials (thus further turning the exchanges against us), and it is only that portion of the money which is spent on the purchase of British materials which *directly* helps our own industry. The effect of such expenditure in stimulating British industry, even assuming that it is not merely a diversion of resources, is less than is often supposed. It is estimated that a loan of £10 millions for overseas railway development, the expenditure of which would probably take about five years, would only involve an increase of about 1 per cent in annual exports of iron and steel from this country and about 3 per cent in the exports of rolling-stock.

This remarkable disparagement of the very process which the Treasury was otherwise inclined to laud as beneficial probably betokens its determination, for more deep-seated reasons, to resist state expenditure rather than signalling a significant change of view. With the launching of the Liberal plan for home development, overseas loans were once more seen as clearly alternative to state intervention – and their immediate assistance to the domestic economy was suddenly glimpsed anew. Thus the Treasury Memorandum wrote of the historic dependence of British export trades upon foreign loans, as opposed to the more limited impact of domestic schemes:

> The additional work that they might put in hand for bridges, etc., at home would be a poor substitute for the construction contracts of whole railways in foreign countries which they would have to forfeit. Admittedly, in the exceptional economic circumstances of the present time, these arguments must not be over-stressed, but the reactions to which they draw attention should not be overlooked.[27]

In the real world the Treasury was well aware of the immediate dangers of lending abroad on an undue scale and was not always content to leave this to be determined by market forces. Bradbury himself had written in 1924: 'I believe there is a real risk that the success of the policy we recommend may be jeopardised by excessive foreign lending.' And Niemeyer advised Churchill in 1925 that 'we want to go as slow with overseas loans as we can'. Hence the recurrent efforts on the part of the authorities to use moral persuasion to restrain the volume of capital exports. Yet the prevailing attitude of the Treasury knights continued to rest on a series of assumptions neatly explicated by Moggridge: 'that the mechanism involved was classical (i.e. that the loan increased foreign expenditure and reduced domestic expenditure while leaving the level of income unchanged), that if London did not make the loan no one else would, and that the transfer was perfectly effected in such a short period as to rule the financial deterioration out of court'.[28] Thus although the empirical point about the relation between loans and exports was from time to time subject to different emphases, it found more consistent favour and expression when generalized as a theoretical proposition.

CP 53 (29) attributed post-war depression in the export staples to the development of competitors abroad, which implied excess supply, and to the wartime impoverishment of former customers, which implied deficient demand. 'Meanwhile', it argued, 'our own people had grown accustomed to consuming more and saving less than before the war, so that the capital available for investment abroad was limited. It is little wonder, therefore, that our exports have not yet reached the pre-war volume (after adjustment of prices).'[29] The implication here is surely that a higher level of investment abroad, out of a higher level of domestic saving, constituted a crucial means of stimulating British exports. The Treasury's contribution to the Conservative Government's White Paper, published in May 1929, reaffirmed this position. 'On the ordinary view there is an intimate relation between the export of capital and of goods', the Memorandum concluded. 'If the [Liberal] plan were successful in diverting money from investment abroad that change would be accompanied by a great decrease in our exports or increase in imports, either of these things being highly prejudicial to important branches of industry.'[30] Apart from the appeal to history, the Treasury did not elaborate this argument on any of the occasions on which it was advanced.

Presumably it felt no need to do so since the process was implied by the working of the Gold Standard. International outgoings and receipts had to balance. They were substantially balanced by their relative price level (expressed in gold) and compensated or corrected at the margin by transfers of gold itself. These transfers, by augmenting or depleting the gold reserves, prompted central-bank action to inflate or deflate the domestic price level, thus equilibrating the relative prices of exports and imports. This process, once completed, removed the need for the compensation or correction which had instigated it, with a tendency towards perfect equilibrium in the inward and outward flow of goods and services at compatible prices. Foreign investment complicated this picture only to the extent that it represented current exports for which payment (in the form of current imports) was deferred. In this light, therefore, it appeared as a means whereby the country accumulated a stock of wealth abroad for future benefit, by allowing it in the present to maintain an export surplus – indeed foreign loans, by *requiring* an export surplus, could be seen as a major stimulus to exports. This seems to have been the Treasury's understanding of the relationship, at least in the period up to 1929.

6

An alternative model, as postulated by Keynes, is pithily outlined in an article on the German transfer problem:[31]

> Historically, the volume of foreign investment has tended, I think, to adjust itself – at least to a certain extent – to the balance of trade, rather than the other way round, the former being the sensitive and the latter the insensitive factor. In the case of German reparations, on the other hand, we are trying to fix the volume of foreign remittance and compel the balance of trade to adjust itself thereto. Those who see no difficulty in this – like those who saw no difficulty in Great Britain's return to the gold standard – are applying the theory of liquids to what is, if not a solid, at least a sticky mass with strong internal resistances.

On this reading, a given level of transfer across the exchanges – whether German reparations or British investment abroad – might produce its own distortion upon the domestic economy. In order to reduce domestic wages to the level necessary to generate an export surplus, deflationary measures would be necessary. But dear-money orthodoxy – Bradbury's 'short and sharp application of the remedy. . . a rapid fall in prices' – would be defeated by the viscosity of the real-world relationships. The result would be a position of disequilibrium in which all resources were not fully employed.

Keynes's critique of the Treasury in 1929–30 was essentially from this standpoint. His own theory, as expounded in the *Treatise on Money* (1930), did not doubt the tendency towards equilibrium. But he outlined a special case, applicable to Britain, in which the process of adjustment was stuck. This was the thrust of his exposition to the Macmillan Committee, as his listeners did not fail to perceive.[32]

> MACMILLAN: Does it come to this – that because we are not a closed nation the Bank rate cannot achieve the results?
> KEYNES: There is also another reason. It could if we were a *fluid* system. For in that case, when we had a surplus of home investments over savings, the bank rate could always force wages down to a level where exports would be adequate.
> MACMILLAN: It would be the principle of hydraulics.
> KEYNES: Yes; that is the beauty of the Bank rate.

Keynes attributed the *cause* of disequilibrium to excessive or uncompetitive costs, and was even ready to concede, if pressed, that this could be put down to the rigidity of wages. But the *remedy* for it in the real world was, in Keynes's opinion, to be found in two unorthodox proposals (public works and tariffs) which were justified under the special case.[33] The shift in the Treasury position in 1929 was, on second thoughts, to accept the accumulating evidence that Keynes was right about the *cause* and to argue that this implied the simple *remedy* of inverting the process in order to restore flexibility.

Thus in March 1929, following the publication of *We Can Conquer Unemployment*, Leith-Ross again sought clarification from Hawtrey:

> Mr J.M. Keynes says that, despite the general reduction of price levels since 1925, there has been no appreciable reduction during the same period in the rates of wages paid to labour in the United Kingdom. The general table published in the Ministry of Labour Gazette seems to confirm this, but it appears to be so surprising that I should be glad if you would go into it.[34]

When Hawtrey reiterated his opinion of the previous year, that Keynes was correct, and now confirmed that the official statistics told the same story, Leith-Ross was finally persuaded. This appears to mark the point at which the Treasury conceded that the adjustments required for the successful operation of the Gold Standard had simply not been forthcoming.

So long as the Treasury believed that British costs were only marginally out of line with those overseas, this was held to constitute an argument in favour of returning to the Gold Standard. True, it was conceded that the Chamberlain-Bradbury Committee might have underestimated the extent of the discrepancy; and events had shown that 'the adjustment of prices has been a longer and more difficult process than was anticipated', albeit for reasons which were not fully foreseeable. 'But it remains true', CP 53 (29) concluded, 'that the process of adjustment did not impose an impossible strain on the national economy; and that the other factors in favour of reversion to the gold standard were so important as to outweigh the transitional difficulties.' Depreciation of the currency, on this reading, would not have avoided unemployment – which was pre-existing – because although the lower pre-1925 parity had 'no doubt constituted an artificial stimulus to some British industries', it had likewise masked defects of management and equipment; and it needed to be 'remembered that depreciation is a drug, addiction to which must in the end undermine the economic prosperity of any country that indulges in it'. Hence the conclusion: 'Surely it would be unthinkable at this stage, when we have got over the unpleasant jolt necessitated by the reversion to the gold standard, for the Government to treat the question as if it were in any respect an open one.'[35]

Once Leith-Ross had discovered that British wages had by no means overcome the transitional jolt, he merely acted out his own precepts by displaying a smooth flexibility in making the necessary adjustment to his argument:[36]

> The main trouble with our industrial situation at the present time is that our costs of production are not yet on a fully competitive level. This is admitted by all economists, however much they may differ in regard to the remedies. Only last year Mr Keynes wrote that 'the fundamental blunder of the Treasury and the Bank of England has been due to their belief, that if they looked after the deflation of prices, the deflation of costs would look after itself'. If this diagnosis is correct, what we have to do is to reduce costs by improving the organization of our industries, the efficiency of management and the output of labour.

What, then, of unemployment?

> The remedy is easy enough to find. If our workmen were prepared to accept a reduction of 10 per cent in their wages or increase their efficiency by 10 per cent, a large proportion of our present unemployment could be overcome. But in fact organized labour is so attached to the maintenance of the present standard of wages and hours of labour that they would prefer that a million workers should remain in idleness and be maintained permanently out of the Employment Fund, than accept any sacrifice. The result is to throw on to the capital and managerial side of industry a far larger reorganization than would otherwise be necessary: and until labour is prepared to contribute in larger measure to the process of reconstruction, there will inevitably be unemployment.

When this line of analysis was developed in the Treasury Memorandum, the diagnosis was the same: costs of production were the root of the problem and must be made internationally competitive. The prognosis, however, was less brutal. 'There was a time perhaps when reduction of the costs of production was looked upon as largely synonymous with reduction of wages', read the Memorandum as published in May 1929 – looking back all of about six weeks. It now explained that improved organization and efficiency, not to mention 'all that is implied in the term "rationalization"', was what the situation demanded.[37] These changes of emphasis, which may well reflect the difference between a Leith-Ross draft and a Hopkins draft, can be regarded as cosmetic. The point was that, by whatever means, British costs had to become competitive at prices set in gold.

7

It is on public works that Keynes's differences with the Treasury have always attracted most attention, and with good reason. The Treasury View, conceived as a theoretical doctrine or dogma, was the butt of Keynes's criticism in *Can Lloyd George Do It?*, and this perspective is reflected in the subsequent Keynesian literature. Revisionist historians, exploiting the availability of the public records, have shown that administrative and political constraints helped determine the outlook of Whitehall as a whole; but whether the dogmatic Treasury View of 1929 can now safely be dismissed as a myth is another matter.[38] In fact, once CP 53 (29) is revealed as the master text, the evidence in the public records decisively confirms that the formulation of the Treasury View did indeed owe much to precepts of a theoretical character, rather than simply to pragmatic political economy. In particular, the analysis which Hawtrey developed, notably in a learned article published in *Economica* in 1925, exerted a demonstrable influence. It was Hawtrey's rigorous academic specification of the conditions under which 'crowding-out' took place which reinforced the policy advice of Niemeyer and Leith-Ross.[39]

Churchill's Budget speech of April 1929 is the *locus classicus* for the dogmatic promulgation of the Treasury View, just as the Treasury memorandum, published in the Government's White Paper the following month, offers the most authoritative amplification. The Memorandum, it is worth noting, was already in its final draft before Churchill uttered in the House, so there is no need to scrutinize each successively for possible changes in the official line. Both, in fact, substantially derive from the statement in CP 53 (29), where, in four taut paragraphs, Leith-Ross distilled what he took to be Hawtrey's doctrine. The conclusion was that 'a policy of large loans for development would probably be quite nugatory as regards the general employment position, the resources directed by the Government to the employment of extra labour being taken away from the resources of private persons the investment of which would have led to the employment of labour at other points.'[40]

It is an illustration of the difficulty of deriving practical policy from theoretical analysis that the rigour of the Treasury View, which apparently owed so much to Hawtrey, depended on a proviso, the force of which was often subsequently overlooked. Hawtrey repeatedly stated that 'crowding-out' only took place provided there were no expansion of credit. If this condition were relaxed, there was indeed room for new enterprise and for a net gain in employment. Hawtrey, it should be remembered, was arguing specifically against public works as such; and he clinched his case by noting that, once the proviso was relaxed, they became unnecessary, since creating the means to finance them would already have had the requisite expansionary effect. 'To stimulate an expansion of credit is usually only too easy,' Hawtrey argued 'To resort for the purpose to the construction of expensive public works is to burn down the house for the sake of the roast pig.'[41]

In meeting the Liberal arguments for public works, the Treasury summarized the position in a perfectly fair way, categorizing it as 'fundamental that the capital required must be raised without resort to inflation'. The words of the Liberal manifesto itself about inflation – 'It can be entirely ruled out' – were quoted in reaffirmation of this condition. If inflation were ruled out, the Treasury could draw only one inference. 'It seems clear that in these circumstances a very large proportion of any additional Government borrowings can only be procured, without inflation, by diverting money which otherwise would be taken soon by home industry.' This was fully in line with Hawtrey's logic and led to the conclusion: 'The large loans involved, if they are not to involve inflation, must draw on existing capital resources.'[42]

Whether Hawtrey himself had intended to bang, bar and bolt the door against any move to expand credit may, however, be doubted. The notion of manipulating credit in a deflationary situation so as to stimulate the forces of economic expansion is, at any rate, a lurking possibility even in his 1925 statement of the case against public works. It may be noted that Hawtrey himself was not involved in the preparation of the main Treasury drafts dealing with public works in the early months of 1929 because he was on leave for the year at Harvard. It must be possible that he would have sought to hedge the amateur doctrinal declarations of Grigg, Leith-Ross and Churchill himself with proper academic caution. At any rate, Hawtrey's own direct comment on the Liberal plan, written on his return from Harvard in June 1929, developed a suggestion which had always been allowed for in his analysis. For if foreign lending were decreased (whether or not in aid of a public works loan) the immediate effect under the Gold Standard would be to inflate domestic credit. (The extent to which this would be necessary posed an intellectual problem which Hawtrey was to tackle by postulating what might be called a proto-multiplier).[43] Within Hawtrey's schema, therefore, there was a possible pathway to expansion, the desirability of which he may not have normally recommended himself but the existence of which he never attempted to conceal. 'Like a protective tariff, an import of capital is a device for bringing about inflation without depreciation', he wrote in 1925. 'Here is a real tendency to improve employment, and it is remarkable that the advocates of public expenditure as a remedy for unemployment never seem to consider this point.'[44]

The point was that, at a time of depression, one country could improve its employment position, in effect by reflating at home in ways which did not depreciate the gold reserves or the parity of sterling. Though such measures were technically compatible with the Gold Standard, they could be seen as clever dodges which flouted the spirit if not the letter of 'the rules of the game'. Just as it is unsurprising that the authorities frowned upon such gamesmanship, so it is not wholly surprising that Keynes came to be associated with proposals which sought to exploit both of these loopholes.

8

By 1930 professional economic advice was being proffered to the Government through two connected channels. One was the Economic Advisory Council, established by Ramsay MacDonald as Labour Prime Minister, and particularly its committee of economists, set up on Keynes's recommendation in July 1930. 'It may be that economics is not enough of a science to be able to produce useful fruits', he wrote to the Prime Minister. 'But I think it might be given a trial, and that we might assume for a moment, if only as a hypothesis, that it can be treated like any other science, and ask qualified scientists in the subject to say their say.'[45] The membership he suggested comprised, as well as himself, three current or former Cambridge colleagues (Professor A.C. Pigou, D.H. Robertson and H.D. Henderson), the taxation expert Sir Josiah Stamp, Professor Henry Clay of the Bank of England, and Professor Lionel Robbins of the London School of Economics. All were leading figures in their field; all except Robertson and Clay actually served; and all except Robbins also gave evidence to the Macmillan Committee, which was the other channel to have been recently opened.

The Committee on Finance and Industry, under the chairmanship of Lord Macmillan, had been appointed by the Labour Government in October 1929 and it took most of its evidence in the first half of 1930. When Keynes, as a member, gave his 'private evidence' in February and March 1930, it was heard with close attention by the Treasury observer, Leith-Ross – the more so since the forthcoming Treasury evidence was being prepared, under Hopkins's direction, with considerable thoroughness and circumspection. Keynes was not the only academic economist whose advice counted, but it is not just in retrospect that he appears pre-eminent. What Keynes was giving the committee was an intelligent layman's guide to his *Treatise on Money*, published some six months later. It was a work which, unlike the *General Theory*, had a direct and explicit bearing upon current British economic policy; and it was cited by

Keynes to provide the analytical justification for his view both of the causes of the depression and of the appropriate remedies.

Leith-Ross produced an able twelve-page note on Keynes's evidence. He reproduced Keynes's explanation of how Bank Rate should work to equilibrate a favourable balance on current receipts with an adverse balance on the capital account. Moreover, he endorsed the analysis:

> Mr Keynes's diagnosis of our present difficulty, viz. that the normal Bank rate policy has 'jammed' owing to the difficulty of reducing wages is, broadly speaking, admitted. Certainly wages and costs tend to be more stereotyped than they were before the War – probably largely by reason of the existence of the Unemployment Insurance scheme.[46]

On possible remedies – Keynes had outlined seven – Leith-Ross had his own preferences, acknowledging that there might be something in four of them but ruling out the other three (devaluation, tariffs and public works) which were actually those preferred at different times by Keynes. Leith-Ross's criticisms were subsequently encapsulated in a short paper called 'The Assumptions of Mr Keynes', which contested a number of 'theoretic assumptions' before shifting the argument onto another footing:[47]

> The fact is that Keynes, like other economists, lives in a world of abstractions. He speaks of 'Industry', 'Profits', 'Losses,' 'Price level', as if they were realities. In fact, we have no such thing as 'Industry'. What we have is a series of different industries, – some prosperous, some depressed and a number carrying on normally. The position of each has to be examined separately.

This approach, relying much more upon an empirical, multi-causal disaggregation of the problem, became increasingly characteristic of the Treasury henceforward. It was applied in particular to the question of foreign lending, which Keynes was accused of treating 'in too abstract a manner'.[48] Leith-Ross appealed to experience on this point. He argued that the strain on the exchanges arose from paying off capital claims which had arisen from an earlier flight of European capital to London during the post-war era of currency instability. Moreover he cited instances of the restriction of foreign loans leading to a reduction in exports. 'This is the view of the FBI [Federation of British Industries] and it can be shown to be true in special cases, e.g. if Australia ceases to borrow, it certainly entails a reduction of our exports to that country.' Thus Keynes's assumption 'that our foreign loans do not create additional exports' was cautiously qualified though not confidently overturned.[49]

Hopkins's brief for the Macmillan Committee, largely compiled within the Treasury itself, also included a series of notes prepared by the Board of Trade, of which one was devoted to the effects of lending abroad. This began with a short statement of 'the broad theory' that overseas lending had no effect – neither one way nor the other – upon employment 'in the long run', since capital *either* 'employs labour in making the goods that follow it (not necessarily to the same country)', *or*, if invested at home, would employ labour directly. A passage which evidently impressed Hopkins, however, turned to the particular application of this axiom:[50]

> If a country over a long period of years has been in the habit of sending considerable sums overseas, her industries get to be organized on such a relative scale that the necessary additional export of goods follows the money automatically, so to speak. In accordance with their comparative advantages, certain of its industries become dependent on exports or more dependent than they would be otherwise. This being the position, it is evident that, if the export of capital diminished considerably, employment in these industries must suffer. The serious thing is the shock of a sudden change.

Here was an analysis of the beneficial role of foreign lending which, far from being premised upon the assumption of infinite flexibility, was premised upon its opposite. Though providing a more realistic defence of the existing level – and channels – of overseas lending, it could not carry the further implication that an increase in lending would ease the difficulty of the export industries. The case for such remedial measures was largely hypothetical because of the difficulty in identifying such opportunities for productive investment; but here too the analysis pointed to the deficiencies of the Gold Standard adjustment process in effecting the sort of change upon which its successful operation depended.

Advice reaching the Governor of the Bank of England – though too late to reinforce his own evidence to the Macmillan Committee – was along closely similar lines; in particular, a memorandum from Professor Henry Clay of Manchester, who was acquiring a position of considerable influence in the Bank. Clay argued that in 'an economy that was both perfectly fluid and completely self-contained', the balance of investment and consumption could be left to work out itself. Since the existing system was not fluid, however, the process of adjustment led to unemployment. Since it was not self-contained, moreover, it was no use over-loading home demand if there were inadequate productive resources to satisfy it; and it followed that 'the spending that we have to stimulate, if we wish to relieve unemployment, is largely spending by overseas customers'. The fact was 'that unemployment is concentrated in industries which are specialized to export'. Nor, under these conditions, would an increase in imports lead to an increase in exports, as it had in the pre-war world when relative costs were more finely attuned.[51]

To relieve unemployment, therefore, by stimulating the complete spending of income, either on commodities or investments, it is necessary to ensure that the allocation of expenditure will not diverge too much from the allocation to which industry is adjusted. Any sudden or large transfers of means of payment from home to foreign account, or vice versa, or from one class of purchasers to another, is likely to dislocate employment, and cause, not a general increase in employment, but overtime and rapid expansion in one part of the industrial field balanced by increased unemployment in another part.

There is an appealing sense of realism about these comments, which in hindsight appear perceptive in their appreciation of the constraints upon expansion. Clay's first-hand knowledge of the Lancashire cotton industry gave him an insight into the structural problems of the old export staples. This can be viewed, as it has been in some of the recent literature,[52] as a wholesome corrective to the callow optimism of proposals to revitalize 'industry', and turn 'losses' into 'profits', by manipulation of the 'price level' – in short, the assumptions of Mr Keynes. But the pragmatism exemplified by Clay can, by the same token, be seen as a repudiation of the assumptions on which the authorities had relied in brandishing the Gold Standard as the key to British prosperity. The rigidities which, as a matter of demonstrable fact, inhibited the flexible adjustment of the economy were coming to be acknowledged on all sides as integral to the problem; and, although there was still room for more than one view on what was the appropriate response, this was more a matter of finely calibrated judgement rather than doctrinaire polarization of opinion.

9

It is now often taken for granted that on public works there was little difference between the Labour Government of 1929–31 and its Conservative predecessor.[53] Yet the two authoritative statements of the Treasury View on loan-financed capital expenditure had been, first, in Churchill's Budget speech – obviously a partisan statement in a pre-election atmosphere – and, secondly, in the White Paper, published during the General Election itself, and regarded even by *The Times* as 'no more and no less than the Conservative party's statement of its case'.[54] The dogmatic Treasury View of 1929, in short, was used as a plank in the Tory election platform and, like other policy commitments of a partisan character, lapsed upon the change of government. In fact, within six months of taking office, the Labour Government had approved schemes to the value of £48m. – and £110m. within a year. (This compares with the programme of £250m. within two years to which Lloyd George had been pledged.) Admittedly, less than half of these programmes had actually come into operation. Even by June 1931, when the Government had approved schemes worth £186m., those in operation amounted to only £108m. It has been estimated by Roger Middleton that this created jobs for 300,000 men (taking account of indirect and secondary employment).

Now these figures can be read in several ways. Middleton himself cites them as evidence of the inescapable delays involved and of 'the exiguity of the employment generated relative to the magnitude of the unemployment problem' – work for only 10.9 per cent of the total of 2,700,000 reached by June 1931.[55] The point about delay is valid in indicating a real constraint to which inadequate attention had been given. But the relatively small contribution of public works to mitigating the total unemployment figures is, of course, a function of the unprecedented rise in that total. Lloyd George's pledge was, in effect, that it was possible to create 600,000 jobs; and the Labour Government eventually got half way toward this. It is worth asking whether such results would have looked – in the perspective of 1929 – like an unequivocal refutation or a limited vindication of the prospective claims.

A contemporary appraisal is provided by the White Paper on Unemployment, published in December 1930 as the Labour Government's major statement of policy in this field. Its argument was that, although faced with a sudden and exceptional depression in world trade, the Government could claim some success for the twofold policy it had put in hand. This comprised a short-range policy, 'designed to provide immediate employment by pressing forward development work of public utility with the utmost vigour', combined with a long-range policy designed to increase efficiency. The latter included not only encouragement of industrial reorganization and moves towards cheap money, but also interventionist steps to promote exports, to expand electricity supply, to improve housing ('in a general programme of national development'), and to restore agricultural prosperity.[56] Much of this, it should be said, was designed to take the wind out of the sails of proposals canvassed earlier that year by the Liberal Party. Moreover, one section of the White Paper was devoted to 'The Quality of the Population', identifying improvements in welfare and training as an integral part of the Government's long-range economic policy.

Beneficial results were naturally claimed for this policy, notably that it would 'provide employment to the extent of more than 500,000 man years' through 'a programme which compares favourably with that which the Government of any other country has been able to frame to mitigate the unemployment problem resulting from the world depression of trade'.[57] Whether this calculation was over-optimistic is a question that can be left for further econometric investigation. But the claim that public works of an appropriate kind could exert a beneficial impact of this order upon employment marks a sharp difference between this White Paper and that of May 1929 which had scouted such claims as fallacious.

One man at least had reason to regard the 1930 White Paper as having a different filiation altogether – not with the Treasury View of 1929 but with the critique of it in *Can Lloyd George Do It?* For Hubert Henderson was the joint author of both documents. As editor of the Liberal paper, the *Nation*, and a former member of the Cambridge Economics Faculty, he was Keynes's close collaborator in 1929. As a civil servant, following his appointment as joint secretary of the Economic Advisory Council at the beginning of 1930, he then came to work alongside the leading Treasury officials. He and Hopkins – both of them products, as was Phillips too, of Emmanuel College, Cambridge – quickly established a cordial working relationship, and their convergent views are testified in their joint drafting of the White Paper.[58]

To Henderson, the abiding argument for public works was as 'a means of facilitating a large readjustment of the national economy'.[59] It was not an alternative to facing up to the structural problems of the declining staples but an adjunct to the policy of transfer which was necessary. Not only is this emphasis wholly consistent with the argument in *Can Lloyd George Do It?* but Henderson subsequently (1935) reaffirmed his confidence in it: 'There is no doubt, I think, that an environment of prevailingly active trade makes the transfer problem easier to solve.'[60]

The Treasury's objections to public works, of course, had not disappeared overnight, simply because Labour was now in office. But the sweeping claim that they were only capable of displacing, not increasing, employment no longer carried conviction against Keynes's increasing stress upon unused capacity, as developed during and immediately after the election campaign. Hawtrey's analysis had once seemed reassuring to the Treasury because it promised to be watertight; but with Hawtrey himself demonstrating a disconcerting propensity to redefine the premise, it looked as though the argument had, for all practical purposes, sprung a leak. Hopkins seems to have asserted his authority in reformulating policy, especially in presenting the Treasury evidence to the Macmillan Committee along lines which took account of the changed ideological climate.[61]

The Treasury declined to bear the blame for thwarting initiatives designed to create work, which confronted enough obstacles in other quarters. The energy and commitment of ministers in pushing schemes forward was itself questionable, as was the appropriateness of the decision-making structure within government – criticisms mounted by Mosley during the course of his campaign for a more radical approach. What Hopkins stressed were the real administrative difficulties in implementing an effective programme, and the growing worries over confidence. Henderson, with his new responsibilities and new access to inside information, now felt that Keynes had made light of such considerations. Whereas in 1929 Keynes and Henderson were allied as radicals against the Treasury orthodoxy of Hopkins and Leith-Ross, twelve months later Henderson had circumspectly distanced himself from Keynes's alleged irresponsibility, and Hopkins had adroitly freed himself from Leith-Ross's apparent inflexibility. It was the Hopkins–Henderson line on public works which carried the day, with its professed readiness to entertain good schemes tempered by a pragmatic scepticism about achieving dramatic further improvement.

10

The 'knave-proof' model of the economy, it should be remembered, relied heavily upon free trade and upon the self-adjusting mechanism of the Gold Standard to provide a necessary framework of financial discipline. Only when shackled to gold was the domestic economy shackled to the realities of a competitive world market. It is little wonder that those Treasury men who had sat at the feet of Sir John Bradbury in his prime regarded the abandonment of free trade – as he did himself – as an even greater disaster than going off Gold. Bradbury had ruminated along these lines to the Macmillan Committee in the autumn of 1930:[62]

> I am afraid of tampering with Free Trade, and I am afraid of tampering with the gold standard. If I had to choose between tampering with the gold standard as a remedy and Protection, I should be solid for tampering with the gold standard.

As it turned out, and as he had no doubt feared, the one was merely a prelude to the other. Looking back in retirement, Grigg saw that 'our departure from the Gold Standard heralded the beginning of our repellent modern world'. It was the final expulsion from the Garden. 'At the end of it all we could see that the two great stabilizing forces of the nineteenth century had lost their influence – the British Navy and the International Gold Standard worked by and through the Bank of England and the City of London', Grigg concluded in 1947. 'We are now adrift in a universe with no fixed criteria and no automatic regulators or indicators.'[63]

The austere charm of the Gold Standard was as a closed and determinate system. It spoke with the purity of a dead language; it operated with the perfection of calculus; and as such it captivated minds which had been schooled to esteem elegance and rigour. But its appeal was not confined to the Oxford classicists and Cambridge mathematicians who staffed the Treasury. When Keynes expounded its workings to the Macmillan Committee he concluded that 'there is no need to wonder why two generations, both of theorists and of practical men, should have been entranced by it'.[64] Even the romantic autodidact Churchill was not immune, reminiscing in later years about the 'beautiful precision' with which free trade and the Gold Standard had worked 'not in this disastrous century but in the last'.[65]

It was not simply an appraisal of the relevant empirical evidence which had persuaded the authorities of the wisdom of returning to Gold. The object lesson of pre-war British prosperity, of course, weighed in its favour. The arguments about parity could also be joined on both sides, with technical appeals to rival index numbers expressing the relative price levels in Britain and the USA. But the verdict did not ultimately hinge upon the adequacy of such proof. Nor was the unavailability of other possibly useful evidence crucial. The Treasury's sources of information may now seem seriously inadequate but there is little sense that this deficiency was keenly felt at the time, nor that urgent measures were thought necessary to remedy it.

It was, significantly, Keynes who railed against the relative paucity of information about the British economy and the reluctance to make it properly available. 'The secretiveness practised by our business world, from the Bank of England downwards, would be excessive in criminals seeking to evade justice, and is, in fact, a major factor in British inefficiency', he declared in 1926.[66] He was, moreover, responsible for the composition of that part of the Liberal Yellow Book where, cheek by jowl, a chapter pleading for an economic general staff was followed by one on statistics. The Yellow Book denounced 'the deficiency of vital information and the ineffective publication of the information which we have' as a scandalous inhibition upon appropriate remedial action:

> How can the State frame a policy or deal in a rational and scientific manner with the problem, for example, of unemployment, if we do not know the rates of growth and decay in different directions and the actual trends of the industrial system? How can economic science become a true science, capable, perhaps, of benefiting the human lot as much as all the other sciences put together, so long as the economist, unlike other scientists, has to grope for and guess at the relevant data of experience?

The Yellow Book thus disclosed the relation of means to ends: 'The improvement of economic information is necessary for wise intervention or guidance by the State.'[67]

A 'hands-on' approach to the business of economic management might well require a radically improved form of expertise; but the Treasury's motto was 'hands off'. Indeed, the authorities give the impression that they knew all they wanted to know. In 1925 they knew, as Norman put it with self-depreciating humility, that 'the Gold Standard is the best "Governor" that can be devised for a world that is still human, rather than divine'.[68] In the succeeding years, likewise, Niemeyer and Leith-Ross knew in their bones that Keynes was a quack doctor, peddling palliatives which might seem harmless in ministering to the immediate symptoms but were fallacious as a cure; and they turned to Hawtrey for a second opinion to confirm their intuition.

The authorities did not belie their name in upholding established doctrine and declaring it sound. It was a deep inner sense of conviction which led them to cling so fervently to their theory of liquids even when they half suspected that in practice they were confronted with 'a sticky mass with strong internal resistances'. A nineteenth-century positivist concept of 'knowledge', striving for progress through the accretion of new facts, is inadequate here. Perhaps we can now improve upon it and avoid being driven back – much further back – upon a mythopoeic account of how the mandarins, having resisted the temptations of the tree of knowledge, lived to regret eating its fruit. As it was, in the imperfect, indeterminate, fallen epoch that dawned in 1931, they ultimately seized on a synthesis which salvaged potent vestiges of the Eden they had lost.

11

What had been the essential characteristics of 'the historic doctrine of bank rate policy', as explained by Keynes to the Macmillan Committee?[69]

> You see what a very good doctrine it is, because the completely harmonious disposition of the economic forces of the world is preserved merely by the Bank of England changing the Bank rate from time to time in an appropriate way and leaving all the rest to the operation of *laissez faire*. And not only so; the Bank of England is set, in a sense, a very easy task, because movements of gold will always operate as a barometer to tell the Bank of England exactly when a change of bank rate has become necessary, so that the method, assuming that it works according to the way in which it is supposed to work, is as simple as possible. All you have to do is to watch those movements, change the bank rate accordingly and the economic system will then automatically grind out the proper levels of prices and wages at which everyone can be employed, at which business men can get normal profits and which furnishes the most advantageous division of the country's savings between investment at home and investment abroad, all owing to the fact that the Bank rate has this double influence.

The efficacy of this process, if only it were allowed to operate, was not doubted at the time by Keynes – committed to the analysis of his *Treatise on Money* – any more than by Hawtrey. They were therefore unanimous in 1930 in a crucial feature of their policy advice over unemployment. They billed and cooed to one another before the Macmillan Committee in maintaining that cheap money would do the trick. When the more sceptical Clay – streetwise from Manchester – was asked by the Bank for his critique of Keynes's proposals, he seized on this affinity, arguing that[70]

> Mr Keynes's proposed method is open to doubt. His thesis is that the necessary stimulus to investment can be given by lowering the long-term rate of interest. This seems to me akin to Mr Hawtrey's view that you can cure unemployment by keeping the Bank Rate low enough.

On this reading, all the authorities had to do, faced with deflation and depression, was to apply the appropriate monetary policy. According to Keynes, this delightfully simple remedy was barred in the real world because of Britain's obligation under the Gold Standard to bolster the parity of sterling by high interest rates. Hence the expediency of 'second-best' solutions like public works and tariffs under the 'special case' of the *Treatise*. But the special case, of course, was rendered inoperative by Britain's departure from the Gold Standard in 1931 – whereupon Keynes might have been expected to abandon his radical suggestions. In fact, within little more than a year, he was to discover other reasons to justify both tariffs and public works – the theory of effective demand.

The *Treatise* was a theoretical work, of high ambition, which Keynes submitted, among others, to Hawtrey for criticism. The nature of Hawtrey's criticisms, drawn together in a paper which was circulated to the Macmillan Committee in January 1931, were such as to cast considerable doubt upon the validity of the definitions employed and hence upon the theoretical rigour which Keynes claimed. Hawtrey's influence, indeed, was important in shifting Keynes towards the framework of what became the *General Theory*.[71] But Hawtrey himself resisted the allure of the theory of effective demand; instead he remained strikingly consistent both in his own theoretical analysis and in his policy conclusions. His book *The Art of Central Banking* (1932) expounded a theme that was 'practical in that it teaches how to use a power of influencing events'. He maintained that 'there is no less scope for systematic reasoning in the study of means than in the study of causes. The pursuit of wisdom is as scientific as the pursuit of truth.'[72]

The regulation of credit was the essential task, and in a deflationary world this meant an expansion of demand. 'The inflation is desirable', so Hawtrey maintained, in these circumstances. 'Indeed, people who regard the word inflation as necessarily having a bad sense would call this degree of expansion "reflation".'[73] He seems to have been among the first British economists to import this term from Hoover's America, for the obvious reason that it expressed his own conceptions so well. Though prepared to consider budget deficits if cheap money were to fail, Hawtrey still had no time for public works and would have relied, under those circumstances, upon the reduction of taxation in itself to expand demand.

How far did the Treasury likewise come to condone policies of domestic expansion under the new conditions of the 1930s? It can be agreed that the Treasury View no longer stood as a formidable obstacle in the way, as it had in 1929. But this was already true by 1930, after Hopkins's reformulation of policy – admittedly under a Labour Government which professed some sympathy for public works. It was the political colour of the National Government which ruled out interventionist measures after 1931 rather than the influence of the authorities. Indeed, with the end of the Gold Standard, the Bank of England was to become a source of discreet pressure for public works in a way that was perfectly consistent with Clay's longstanding scepticism about the efficacy of cheap money alone. In 1930 he had argued that 'more direct and drastic influences on costs' were necessary as well.[74]

Again [he continued], it is admitted, when the conditions of profitable enterprise exist, and credit has been expanded beyond the point at which industry is fully and profitably employed, so that additional credit merely sends up prices, that restriction of credit or enhancing of its price by the banking system will be an effective brake or check on the boom. What is contended is only that it does not follow, because credit restrictions will check a boom, that credit expansion must create a boom. Taking off the brake is not the same thing as putting on the accelerator. Bank Rate is an excellent brake; but it will not necessarily serve also, by itself, as an accelerator.

Because of this appraisal of the asymmetrical effects of monetary policy, the Bank seems, from as early as 1933, to have been readier than the Treasury to envisage direct intervention to stimulate recovery through public works.[75]

Keynes's new theory of effective demand had taken shape by the end of 1932. It was the basis on which he mounted his renewed pleas for expansion from the beginning of 1933, notably in a series of articles in *The Times* called 'The Means to Prosperity' and a supporting piece in the *New Statesman* called 'The Multiplier'. The Treasury response to these articles, articulated chiefly by Phillips, has been well explained elsewhere, but the role of Henderson deserves special note here. It was he who disabused Phillips of the misconception that Keynes's argument depended on the existence of idle deposits in the banks. Henderson thus understood the force of Keynes's new theory – 'His favourite theme is that the expenditure would serve to create most of the savings requisite to finance the public works' – even if he could not accept it.[76]

The fact that Henderson was to remain sceptical about the multiplier is doubly suggestive. Retrospectively, it surely implies that the concept is not recognizable in *Can Lloyd George Do It?* and cannot properly be imported into the policy arguments of 1929. Prospectively, it shows that the multiplier was not essential to an advocacy of reflationary – or what Henderson called at the time 'frankly inflationary' – measures.[77] For although Henderson did not believe major new public works to be warranted in the situation prevailing in the mid 1930s, he was in favour of 'endeavouring to increase consumption' by higher social spending as an alternative means of administering 'grease for the wheels of transfer' through economic expansion.[78] In fact, a relaxation of Government policy over public works in 1935 waited upon a change of tack by the Chancellor, Neville Chamberlain, as an overtly political – indeed electoral – ploy. The slow tide of economic recovery, meanwhile, was no longer checked by tight credit; and the cheap money policy from 1932 brought Bank Rate down to 2 per cent.

There is more than one way to make sense of these cross-currents. Intellectual support for public works in the 1930s could, for example, be derived from the arguments of Clay, who believed that the structural problems of the economy demanded direct intervention by government, now that the inhibitions of the Gold Standard had been removed. Henderson's line of argument demonstrated that there was scope for fiscal measures to reflate the economy, when appropriate, irrespective of the merits of either public works or the multiplier. Finally, it was Hawtrey who continued to argue that public works in themselves made very little difference and that the logical way to control trade fluctuations was by resorting to cheap money in a slump and applying a credit squeeze when boom conditions developed.

When it came to practical judgement on what to do and when to do it, Phillips was perfectly ready to override Hawtrey's immediate advice; and at this executive level it has to be conceded that the learned man was left immured in his dungeon throughout the 1930s. Yet, surveying Treasury policy in 1937, an observer in the Bank could note wryly, 'whatever they may say about Hawtrey, his theories in fact fill the vacuum left in their minds by the lack of economic theories on this subject of their own.'[79] A further speculation is tempting. For the sort of monetary policy favoured by the Conservatives in the 1950s, in the heyday of the Butskellite consensus, was to leave the Bank of England pulling the levers of inflation and deflation in a manner for which its operation of the Gold Standard might have served as an apprenticeship, albeit that it now responded to a more complex range of signals. It was a modification of the art of central banking – justifiably hailed as 'pure Hawtrey'[80] – for which the appropriate handbook was not necessarily the *General Theory*.

12

This essay has suggested that in the 1920s the Treasury held firmly to the self-acting model of the economy which minimized its own direct role. The Gold Standard was the highest expression of this model. It had been validated by years of experience but it was also underpinned by theoretical axioms about equilibrium. It postulated a process of adjustment, once equilibrium was disturbed, so that another position of equilibrium, with optimal use of all resources, including labour, was quickly established. So long as such adjustments had been, if not wholly painless, then largely invisible, their operation did not give rise to much introspection. It was the actual breakdown of this adjustment process in the 1920s which provoked awkward questions. In the course of answering these, the authorities were forced to explain, and indeed to comprehend, the nature of the process much more thoroughly. These debates served to disclose an assumption of perfect flexibility or fluidity which was of fundamental importance in justifying Treasury policy. This assumption made sense of the high priority accorded to overseas investment and of the principled rejection of public works in 1928–9 (the Treasury View). The model was also of a kind which able administrators, with a traditional education at Oxford or Cambridge, could happily master and defend – a task relished by Niemeyer and Leith-Ross.

The reasons which rendered it indefensible between 1929 and 1931 were diverse. The direct influence of Keynes, albeit more as a publicist than as an academic economist, is demonstrably important. There are signs that the Treasury recognised the force of some of his arguments, especially about the actual state of disequilibrium in which the British economy appeared to be trapped. It may also have become apparent that the dogmatic Treasury View of 1929 rested on a misapprehension about the applicability of Hawtrey's rigorous assumptions to current conditions in Britain. Moreover, both the economic and the political context were changing, and were to change further.

The British economy was plunging deeper into depression under the impact of the world slump, which mocked hopes of an early return to equilibrium through normal trade recovery. Hitherto the lassitude of British exports could be attributed to wage rigidities, with the implication that price flexibility would unlock new markets abroad. But inelastic world demand for British goods *at any price* was the immediate lesson of these years – a further demonstration that the theory of fluids was no longer relevant. In these conditions it is not surprising that a number of economists turned to analysing the problems of disequilibrium, nor that Treasury advice now took full account of the rigidities and imperfections of the economy. Such an approach, too, reflected the more open-minded outlook of the Hopkins–Phillips regime.

In politics, likewise, there were new pressures to which the Treasury had to adapt. True, the Liberal scheme to conquer unemployment, dreamt up by Keynes and Lloyd George, was sidetracked. But the election of a Labour Government should be recognized as marking a significant departure in public works policy. The Treasury adapted to this, in a pragmatic and adroit way, just as it later accepted tariffs as a fact of life under the National Government. Indeed the end of the Gold Standard and the abandonment of free trade shifted policy onto a wholly new footing. For if the self-acting model of the economy no longer exercised its own discipline, some kind of economic regulation was a task which the Treasury, however reluctantly, had to assume itself. Its concessions can be seen as minimal – preserving, so far as possible, the balanced budget convention and operating a cheap money policy at arm's length. But alternative policies were now seriously canvassed – and by other economists as well as Keynes. His distinctive theory of effective demand was not necessarily the touchstone by which such options were judged. The range of technical advice available to government was undoubtedly wider in the 1930s than it had been in the 1920s, and the work of the Economic Advisory Council, though abortive in producing big results, led to a variety of small results, notably through the Committee on Economic Information. In all of this, efforts to achieve a practical consensus on policy naturally took priority over any aspirations for doctrinal conversion, in a way which parallels the later American experience.[81]

It was the Second World War which brought economists into the structure of government on a large scale, and this growth in expertise had some effect in challenging the authority of the old mandarin class. Wilfrid Eady, as Second

Secretary to the Treasury from 1942, had First Class Honours in Classics from Cambridge behind him but evidently felt himself at some disadvantage in discussions with the young professional adviser, James Meade, who records receiving from him 'a most disarming letter saying that he had no training in economics but was trying to master the subject'. As Meade commented in his diary: 'When one looks at it objectively, what a state of affairs it is when the man chiefly responsible for internal and external financial policy has had no technical training. I am sure that in our grandchildren's days this will be considered very odd.'[82]

In a series of recent studies by economic historians, scepticism has been voiced as to whether a genuine 'Keynesian revolution' took place in Treasury policy before the late 1940s – or perhaps even the late 1950s.[83] The best conclusion here may be that the term 'revolution' is itself inappropriate to describe policy changes, which of their nature tend to be incremental, responding tentatively to a range of different pressures. Each historian, moreover, is ultimately at the mercy of his own concept of Keynesianism. Yet some definition is necessary; and one which simply stops at a commitment to counter-cyclical macroeconomic management of overall demand is too indiscriminate. Historians may thus have looked too exclusively to Keynes for the ideas which ultimately filtered into government; and this has led to Keynes being credited/saddled with the praise/blame for shifts in policy of which he was by no means the only begetter. In addition to the sort of 'Curried Keynes' which William Barber suggests was popular in New Deal America,[84] the menu should perhaps also include various anglicized varieties of goulash, fricassee, and ragout, in which the ingredients were chopped, minced, and mixed to suit the customers' tastes.

In recognizing this, however, it is not very illuminating to construct an alternative account in which the influence of ideas, of whatever kind, is systematically discounted as merely instrumental. There are other ways of appraising policy changes and analytical influences here than on a unilinear pro-Keynesian/anti-Keynesian scale; and there is no necessity to plump for either (on the one side) naive Keynesian triumphalism or (on the other) know-nothing administrative reductionism. For it should be acknowledged that the Treasury model of the 1920s had immense strengths – intellectual strengths not least. It was internally consistent; it could be grasped by educated lay minds; its postulates carried the academic authority of economic doctrine; its precepts were those which actually guided 'the authorities' in the real world. As a self-acting model, moreover, it kept most economic issues out of politics except when its own premises (especially free trade) were challenged. This was the knave-proof fiscal constitution. It represented, then, economic knowledge of an analytical kind which made empirical knowledge, if not redundant, then of secondary significance to government.

To some extent it was the purposive accumulation of economic information which called into question the applicability of this model to the real world. More crucially, however, the object lesson of economic depression brutally drove the point home. In the process of adjusting to these unprecedented changes, government may have learnt from economists – but as much about the limitations of pure theory as anything else. The practical wisdom of an administrator like Hopkins was in turn a revelation to an economist like Henderson, and perhaps a salutary lesson to Keynes himself. Who learnt most from whom is a question worth pondering. Much of this learning, moreover, was acquired 'on the job'. The state was called upon to face more choices and came to possess more information in making them. But if we ask in which way government learnt most, the short answer is 'the hard way'. The growth of economic knowledge in a technically more sophisticated sense was largely a product of an era when government had already become inescapably committed to unwonted tasks of economic management, confronting the Treasury with matters about which, left to itself, it had been happy not to know.

Notes

1. I refer to Robert Cuff's distinctions as adapted by the editors in the introduction to Barry Supple and Mary Furner (eds), *The State and Economic Knowledge* (Cambridge, 1990).
2. A populist variant of this account of politics as realized intentions would be to interpret public policy as the people's voice. For this taxonomy see Peter Clarke, 'Political history in the 1980s', in Theodore K. Rabb and Robert I. Rotberg (eds), *The New History* (Princeton, 1982), pp. 45–7.
3. *JMK*, vol. 19, pp. 809, 811 (*Evening Standard*, 19 April 1929).
4. *JMK*, vol. 7, p. 383.
5. See J.Tomlinson, *Problems of British Economic Policy, 1870–1945* (1981); A. Booth and M. Pack, *Employment, Capital and Economic Policy* (Oxford, 1985).
6. *JMK*, vol. 9, p. 125 (*Can Lloyd George Do It?*)
7. The analogous position of the Bank of England is well stated in Henry Clay, *Lord Norman* (1957), p. 167.
8. See the helpful account in G.C. Peden, 'The Treasury as the central department of government, 1919–39', *Public Admin.*, lxi (1983), pp. 371–85; and Roger Middleton, *Towards the Managed Economy* (1985), esp. chs 3 and 5.
9. P.J. Grigg, *Prejudice and Judgment* (1948), p. 182; for the decision to return see D.E. Moggridge, *British Monetary Policy, 1924–31* (Cambridge, 1972), ch. 3.
10. Quoted in Robert Rhodes James, *Churchill: A Study in Failure, 1900–39* (1970), p. 160.
11. See Barry Supple, 'Official economic inquiry and Britain's industrial decline', in Supple and Furner (eds), *The State and Economic Knowledge*, pp. 325–53.
12. For an authoritative account see G.C. Peden, *British Rearmament and the Treasury, 1932–1939* (Edinburgh, 1979), pp. 20–3 and appendix 1, p. 203.
13. See Susan Howson, 'Hawtrey and the real world', in G.C. Harcourt (ed.), *Keynes and His Contemporaries* (1985), pp. 142–88 esp. pp. 176–8, for a well-considered appraisal of Hawtrey's influence, concluding that it was small in the 1930s.
14. *Prejudice and Judgment*, p. 82.
15. See for example *Election Notes for Conservative Speakers and Workers* (National Union of Conservative and Unionist Associations, 1929), pp. 141–2.
16. F. Leith-Ross, memorandum, 9 Aug. 1928, T. 172/2095; first draft, 3 Aug. 1928, also in T. 175/26; all Treasury and Cabinet papers cited from the Public Record Office. 'How to organize a wave of prosperity' is printed in *JMK*, vol. 19, pp. 761–6.

17. CP 53 (29), 'Unemployment', 25 Feb. 1929, CAB 24/202; also in T. 172/2095. For this otherwise unrecorded episode see Peter Clarke, *The Keynesian Revolution in the Making, 1924–36* (Oxford, 1988), pp. 54–62.
18. 'Cure for unemployment memoranda of 1928 and 1929', T. 172/2095, had been kept in the library of the Treasury instead of the archive and was therefore not released to the Public Record Office until the summer of 1986. It forms the documentary spine of my chapter, 'The formulation of the Treasury View, 1925–9', in *Keynesian Revolution in the Making*, pp. 47–69. The fullest draft from it, quoted below, is undated (but Apr. 1929), at fos 215–29.
19. *Memoranda on Certain Proposals relating to Unemployment*, Cmd 3331 (1929).
20. *JMK*, vol. 19, p. 762.
21. For a recent statement of an anti-Keynesian case see K.G.P. Matthews, 'Was sterling overvalued in 1925?', *Econ. Hist. Rev.*, n.s., xxxix (1986), pp. 572–87.
22. Unpublished minutes, 24 Oct. 1930, 3–5; copy in T. 200/5.
23. Leith-Ross to Hawtrey, 1 Aug. 1928, T. 172/2095.
24. Leith-Ross, memorandum, 9 Aug. 1928, T. 172/2095.
25. Ibid.
26. CP 53 (29), par. 12; emphasis in original.
27. Cmd 3331, p. 51.
28. Moggridge *British Monetary Policy*, pp. 205, 207, 217.
29. CP 53 (29), pars 25–6.
30. Cmd 3331, p. 52; cf. Leith-Ross's draft, T. 172/2095, fo. 220.
31. *JMK*, vol. 11, p. 458 ('The German transfer problem', *Econ. Jnl*, March 1929).
32. *JMK*, vol. 20, p. 85 (21 Feb. 1930), emphasis in original.
33. For the clear specification of the 'special case' as the means of reconciling Keynes's views on cheap money with his advocacy of public works at the time of the *Treatise* see D.E. Moggridge and Susan Howson, 'Keynes on monetary policy, 1910–46', *Oxford Econ. Papers*, n.s. xxvi (1974), pp. 226–47, at p. 236. I have extended this analysis, in line with the *Treatise*, to cover tariffs too in *Keynesian Revolution in the Making*, chs 8 and 9.
34. Leith-Ross to Hawtrey, 13 March 1929, T. 175/26.
35. CP 53 (29), pars 22, 28. In this section I am, of course, reporting the Treasury's perceptions; for a sophisticated modern discussion of the real difficulties see R.C.O. Matthews, C.H. Feinstein and J.C. Odling-Smee, *British Economic Growth, 1856–1973* (Oxford, 1982), pp. 314–15, 470–1.
36. Draft for Churchill (April 1929), T. 172/2095, fos 221–2.
37. Cmd 3331, p. 52.
38. Roger Middleton uses the term 'myth' in his essay, 'Treasury policy on unemployment', in Sean Glynn and Alan Booth (eds), *The Road to Full Employment*, (1987), p. 115. This seems an incautious extension of his earlier well-argued points, esp. *Towards the Managed Economy*, ch. 8, building on his article, 'The Treasury in the 1930s: political and administrative constraints to acceptance of the "new" economics', *Oxford Econ. Papers*, n.s., xxxiv (1982), pp. 48–77. The best general account is in G.C. Peden, 'The "Treasury View" on public works and employment in the inter-war period', *Econ. Hist. Rev.*, n.s., xxxvii (1984), pp. 167–81, though in my view this needs some modification, especially in the light of the new evidence in T. 172/2095.
39. R.G. Hawtrey, 'Public expenditure and the demand for labour', *Economica*, v (1925), pp. 38–48. There is thus now documentary support for earlier suggestions about the significance of this article, esp K.J. Hancock, 'Unemployment and the economists in the 1920s', *Economica*, n.s., xxvii (1960), 311, and Susan Howson and Donald Winch, *The Economic Advisory Council* (Cambridge, 1977), p. 27. For the new evidence see Clarke, *Keynesian Revolution in the Making*, pp. 51–4, 62–7.
40. CP 53 (29), par. 7.
41. Hawtrey, 'Public expenditure and the demand for labour', p. 44.
42. Cmd 3331, pp. 45, 50–1, 53.
43. Hawtrey, 'The Liberal Unemployment Plan', 12 June 1929, Hawtrey Papers, HTRY 1/41; also in T. 175/26. For further discussion in relation to the multiplier, see Clarke, *Keynesian Revolution in the Making*, pp. 143–5.

44. Hawtrey, 'Public expenditure and the demand for labour', p. 46.
45. *JMK*, vol. 20, pp. 368–9 (Keynes to MacDonald, 10 July 1930); and see Howson and Winch, *Economic Advisory Council*, pp. 47ff.
46. 'Note on Mr Keynes's exposition to the Committee on Finance and Industry', (n.d. but late Feb. 1930), T. 175/26, fos 164–76.
47. 'The Assumptions of Mr Keynes', revised draft, 28 Mar. 1930, T. 175/26, fo. 181; an earlier draft (in fact, 27 Feb. 1930) is printed as appendix 3 in Thomas Jones, *Whitehall Diary*, ed. Keith Middlemas, 3 vols (Oxford, 1969), vol. 2, pp. 288–9.
48. 'Note on Mr Keynes's exposition', T. 175/26, fo. 171.
49. 'The Assumptions of Mr Keynes', T. 175/26.
50. 'Effects of lending abroad', section 4 of the papers sent by S.J. Chapman to Hopkins, 16 April 1930, T. 200/1.
51. Clay, 'Remedies', enclosed in Clay to Osborne, 18 May 1930, Bank of England archives, S. 44/1 (1).
52. See esp. Mark Casson, *Economics of Unemployment*, (Oxford, 1983) for a sympathetic study of Clay (along with Cannan and Pigou).
53. The challenging insight offered thirty years ago in Robert Skidelsky, *Politicians and the Slump* (1967) has thus become stylized in a potentially misleading way.
54. *The Times*, 13 May 1929.
55. Roger Middleton, 'The Treasury and public investment: a perspective on inter-war economic management', *Public Admin.*, lxi (1983), pp. 351–70, at p. 361. See also S. Howson, 'Slump and unemployment', in R.C. Floud and D.N. McCloskey (eds), *The Economic History of Britain since 1700*, 2 vols (Cambridge, 1981), vol. 2, pp. 265–85, at pp. 279–81.
56. *Statement of the Principal Measures taken by H.M. Government in connection with Unemployment*, Cmd 3746 (1930), pp. 3, 14.
57. Ibid., p. 21.
58. On this see the correspondence/drafts exchanged between them (Dec. 1930) in T. 175/43.
59. H.D. Henderson, 'Do we want public works?' (May 1935) in *The Inter-War Years* (Oxford, 1955), 152.
60. Ibid., p. 159.
61. On Hopkins see G.C. Peden, 'Sir Richard Hopkins and the "Keynesian Revolution" in employment policy', *Econ. Hist. Rev.*, n.s., xxxvi (1983), pp. 281–96. The argument for a crucial shift in perspective is developed in my chapter, 'The reformulation of the Treasury View, 1929–30', *Keynesian Revolution in the Making*, pp. 142–61.
62. Unpublished minutes, 7 Nov. 1930, 29 (T. 200/5).
63. Grigg, *Prejudice and Judgment*, pp. 257, 260.
64. JMK, vol. 20, p. 53 (20 Feb. 1930).
65. Ben Pimlott (ed.), *The Second World War Diary of Hugh Dalton* (1986), p. 578 (7 April 1943).
66. *JMK*, vol. 19, p. 597 (*Nation*, 24 Dec. 1926).
67. *Britain's Industrial Future* (1928), pp. 121–3; for authorship see Roy Harrod, *The Life of John Maynard Keynes*, (1951), p. 393.
68. Norman to Churchill, 7 Feb. 1925, printed in Moggridge, *British Monetary Policy*, p. 272.
69. *JMK*, vol. 20, p. 53 (20 Feb. 1930).
70. Clay, 'Remedies' (18 May 1930), S. 44/1 (1).
71. Clarke, *Keynesian Revolution in the Making*, pp. 236–44.
72. R.G. Hawtrey, *The Art of Central Banking* (1932), p. vi.
73. Ibid., p. 271.
74. Clay, 'Bank Rate, Credit and Employment', 17 May 1930, EID 1/2.
75. R. S. Sayers, *The Bank of England, 1891–1944* (Cambridge, 1976; 1986 edn), pp. 460–3.
76. Henderson to Phillips, 16 March 1933, Henderson Papers, box 10; for a full account of these exchanges see Howson and Winch, *Economic Advisory Council*, pp. 128–30.
77. *JMK*, vol. 20, pp. 164–6 (Henderson to Keynes, 28 Feb. 1933).
78. Henderson, 'Do we want public works?' (May 1935), in *The Inter-War Years*, p. 160.
79. Memorandum for B.G. Catterns (Deputy Governor), 12 Feb. 1937, G1 1/15 (authorship obscure).

80. See George Peden, 'Old dogs and new tricks,' in Supple and Furner (eds), *The State and Economic Knowledge*, p. 229.
81. As reported by Robert Collins, 'The emergence of economic growthmanship in the United States', in Supple and Furner (eds), *The State and Economic Knowledge*, pp. 138–70.
82. James Meade diary, 19 Nov. 1944, Meade Papers 1/3, London School of Economics.
83. See especially Neil Rollings, 'British budgetary policy, 1945–54: a "Keynesian Revolution"?', *Econ. Hist. Rev.*, n.s., xli (1988), pp. 283–98.
84. See William Barber, 'Government as a laboratory for economic learning in the years of the Democratic Roosevelt', in Supple and Furner (eds), *The State and Economic Knowledge*, pp. 103–37, esp. p. 121 for the reference to the influence of Lauchlin Currie in mediating Keynes.

8   The twentieth-century revolution in government: the case of the British Treasury

1

The reference in my title is to a famous article which Oliver MacDonagh published in 1958.[1] It was a spare, uncluttered and elegant essay, as befitted the exposition of a 'model', intended to prompt further refinement. My purpose is not detailed criticism of its propositions; a large and fruitful specialist literature on the nineteenth century pays its own tribute in this respect. Instead I shall take my cue from the Canberra magpie in swooping and snatching at what looks bright and attractive, untroubled by pangs of scholarly conscience in my borrowings: notably of two important and arresting themes which MacDonagh was largely responsible for injecting into the subsequent historiography. First, and rightly in pride of place, is his insight about the autonomous dynamic of the state itself. This was an aspect which had been curiously overlooked – except, of course, in fragmentary and disconnected obiter dicta, which simply illustrates Whitehead's proposition that everything has been said before by someone who did not discover it; whereas it can reasonably be represented as MacDonagh's 'central message'.

Secondly – and more controversially – MacDonagh's scepticism over the role of 'ideas' in this process demands attention. He was concerned with the broad attribution of influence to a single eminent thinker (Bentham), and by analogy I shall take the obvious example of Keynes. It was partly in this connection that MacDonagh met the unlikely charge of fomenting a 'Tory interpretation of history'.[2] It may seem curious that a historian with such a finely-honed literary sensibility should ever have been open to such imputations of anti-intellectualism, belittling the role of men and ideas, and related offences stopping just short of book-burning. To avoid further misconception, let me reiterate what I take to be MacDonagh's point: not that we should stop taking an interest in the writings of Bentham (or Keynes) but that, so far as government is concerned, we are unwise to make sweeping inferences, based on speculation rather than specific evidence, about the practical influence of classic texts.

How profitable is it to apply such notions to the experience of the twentieth century? MacDonagh, of course, was perfectly well aware that the growth of the administrative state was not confined to the period he chose to write about. Yet he did make special claims for it: 'Most historians take it for granted that the function and structure of executive government changed profoundly in the

175

course of the nineteenth century. They would probably agree, moreover, that this change was revolutionary in a sense in which the changes of the seventeenth and eighteenth centuries, or even that of the first half of the twentieth century, were not. . . .'[3] This seems to me unduly dismissive of the relevant sort of changes 'in kind and quantity' which took place between the 1890s and the 1950s, the period I shall chiefly be concerned with. Let me try to justify this.

The ambiguities here can be illustrated by the conflicting subjective impressions or representations of the scope of government which are commonly encountered. Two familiar quotations make the point. One is from Sidney Webb (1890), as quoted by Dicey:[4]

> The practical man, oblivious or contemptuous of any theory of the social organism or general principles of social organisation, has been forced, by the necessities of the time, into an ever-deepening collectivist channel. . . . The individualist town councillor will walk along the municipal pavement, lit by municipal gas, and cleansed by municipal brooms with municipal water, and seeing, by the municipal clock in the municipal market, that he is too early to meet his children coming from the municipal school, hard by the county lunatic asylum and municipal hospital, will use the national telegraph system . . .

– and so on to the councillor's innocent expostulation: 'Self-help, sir, individual self-help, that's what's made our city what it is.' Both Webb and Dicey had a common polemical interest in tendentiously exaggerating the 'collectivist' tendencies of the age (Webb to keep up the spirits of his fellow Fabians, Dicey to make our flesh creep at the ultimate consequences). It is arguable that the councillor was by no means so muddled and that 'collectivism' hardly came into the matter so far as these examples go; he may thus have had a well-conceived grasp of classical economics and its justification of particular kinds of public goods. We should remember that 'individualism' was a theory not of the frequency but of the *grounds* of state intervention.[5]

For a second subjective impression, equally well known and often quoted, contrast A.J.P. Taylor's introduction to his Oxford English History: 'Until August 1914 a sensible, law-abiding Englishmen could pass through life and hardly notice the existence of the state, beyond the post office and the policeman . . . All this was changed by the impact of the Great War.'[6] On this reading, the big story about the growth of the modern state was yet to unfold; and in terms of quantity there is a lot to be said for this view.

Some crude objective pointers are the growth of public spending and the size of the civil service. It is not easy to find fully consistent or comparable statistics for either, but the general trend during the first half of the twentieth century is in each case indisputable. If we take an indexed figure per head for public spending at twenty-year intervals (none of them in wartime), we get the estimates shown in table 8.1, which can also be expressed as a proportion of Gross National Product.[7]

Table 8.1   Indexed figures per head for public spending (1900=100)

		percentage of GNP
1890	53	9
1910	86	13
1930	192	26
1950	349	39

At the beginning of the twentieth century there were about 50,000 non-industrial civil servants, increasing to 70,000 by 1914. After a wartime bulge, numbers fluctuated around 120,000 in the inter-war years. After the Second World War, in which numbers scaled new peaks, a new plateau was reached at around 400,000, touching a maximum of over 550,000 in the mid 1970s.

Starting from a modest base, the Treasury's growth was concentrated into this latter phase. From an overall size of about 350 in 1939, it grew to about 1,500 in the mid 1960s – a fourfold increase in twenty-five years. Allowing for changes in responsibilities, notably the rise and fall of the Civil Service Department, the size of the Treasury itself has stabilized at this level.[8] It is, of course, worthy of study as the top tier of the civil service, setting a pattern for administration. But what makes the case for a distinctively twentieth century revolution in government is its own particular role, which changed in character and scope during this period – from public finance to macroeconomic management. This change was qualitative as well as quantitative, in function and in structure, and it clearly has a resonance well beyond the particular British experience.

In fact the growth of government, in diverse ways, in seeking to manage advanced national economies is now addressed in a burgeoning literature which canvasses various lines of interpretation. This can be seen in Peter Hall's taxonomy of recent approaches:[9]

1. *Functionalist explanations* are postulated, pointing to society's need to resolve brute and inescapable problems, which will remind historians of Kitson Clark's reference to 'blind forces' – subsequently alleged to be one of the hallmarks of the "Tory interpretation'. Although this approach certainly tells us something, it is a characteristic of functionalism to tell us *that* certain things happened but not *how*. Philosophers, one might add, usually find this more intellectually satisfying than historians.

2. *Cultural analysis* is distinguished by pointing to historical differences between societies; these may be claimed to govern their responses to governing and government. This is suggestive – if often soft and slippery.
3. *Public choice* has become a phrase to conjure with in the recent literature (and with no shortage of prentice conjurors especially since James Buchanan's Nobel Prize applauded the work of the Virginia School of public-choice theorists, notably himself and Gordon Tullock).
4. *Group theories* (so-called by Hall) are usually variants on a class interpretation. This raises a pertinent issue – it is always worth asking Lenin's question, 'who whom?' – and it directs attention to the problem of mobilizing coalitions in support of policies.
5. *State-centric theories*. This has become the province of the 'new institutionalism', with the discovery of the state itself as a fruitful subject for study by sociologists, political scientists and economists: the spirit of the endeavour happily captured by the slogan of 'bringing the state back in'.[10]

All of these approaches are capable of shedding a certain amount of light. I propose to say more about public choice, in particular, and I am broadly sympathetic to state-centric theories. But historians can rest assured that I do not propose to present Oliver MacDonagh with some of his own insights hastily gift-wrapped in the trendy trappings of the new institutionalism – which would be rather like a pickpocket trying to sell him his own watch. Instead I shall discuss the case of the Treasury with implicit reference to two themes to which MacDonagh's work alerted historians many years ago: the autonomous dynamic of administration and the supposed influence of a famous doctrine.

2

The Treasury was both the guardian and the prisoner of its own myth. It remained Gladstonian in its austerity and implicit moral rectitude – not sanctimonious but guardedly mistrustful of others' motives, especially, of course, for state expenditure. As one Treasury official, who had served under Sir John Bradbury (Permanent Secretary 1913–19), put it shortly afterwards:

> In a sense there is nearly always a good case for expenditure. Sometimes, perhaps not infrequently, perfectly fatuous proposals are put forward, but more often quite serious proposals for expenditure as to which a good deal can be said for them, particularly if regarded in isolation. But that form of expenditure must be based on considerations of the other side of the account – what other expenditure will it render impossible, and what burden will it throw upon the community? . . . The Treasury thus came to adopt those weapons which are, perhaps, usual with an institution which depends to a great extent on prestige – precedent, formalism, aloofness, and even sometimes obstruction by the process of delay, and sometimes indefinite replies.

This was an insider's view – that of Keynes, and he added: 'behind all that there was a large measure of wisdom'.[11] It was the sort of timeless wisdom later enshrined in a mandarin's opinion before the House of Commons Estimates Committee, that the Treasury 'exists in order to curtail the natural consequences of human nature'.[12] Not only the underlying philosophy but the strategies for making it effective were basically unchanging: preliminary vetting, which a modern Chief Secretary has termed 'wringing the water out of the figures',[13] followed up by remorseless monitoring of authorized expenditure for whatever savings could subsequently be retrieved – described by a Treasury official in 1931 as 'scraping the butter back out of the dog's mouth'.[14]

Moreover, Treasury principles of economy were applied by example as well as exhortation. Between 1862 and 1902 the total civil service vote increased from £7.6m. to £23.6m.; but the 'Upper Establishment' of the Treasury fell from £22,000 to £18,000. (This meanness was over staffing rather than salaries.) There was an Upper Establishment of around 25 in the late nineteenth century – an extraordinarily small number. Even with new responsibilities arising from old age pensions and National Insurance in the Edwardian period, this figure did not rise above 35 before the First World War. A new division was created to cope in 1908, but it was characteristically carved out of the existing personnel.[15]

The logic of 'public choice theory' insists on the solipsism of civil servants themselves as a crucial influence within government. Like other men, bureaucrats are seen as motivated by rational self-interest. No one should doubt that Treasury mandarins were healthily endowed with a survival instinct; but here at least natural selection seemed to favour not Economic Man but his austere cousin Economical Man in a way that qualifies the confident postulates of public-choice theory as stated by Tullock:[16]

> Bureaucrats normally have several private motives. One is, of course, simply not to work too hard. . . . Another is to expand the size of one's own department and in the process of so doing, being willing to go along with the expansion of all the rest. A third is to improve the 'perks' that accompany the particular position.

The Treasury establishment under Bradbury in the early twentieth century stood this motivation upside down – notoriously hard working yet seeking to restrict the growth of their own department – suggesting that we can only employ the public choice model by redefining 'perks' so as to incorporate arcane psychic satisfactions on another plane altogether. Certainly it remains worth asking what they got out of it; but there is also a need for a richer historical reconstitution of motive and ethos, goals and outlook, and of the structure within which they were operative. The social anthropology of Heclo and Wildavsky within the 'Whitehall village' suggests a more fruitful line of approach.[17]

Up to the First World War policy was in the hands of three dozen men, selected by merit through competitive examination from the cream of British graduates. Keynes remarked on the Treasury style:[18]

> Individually, I think you could correctly describe it as very clever, very dry and in a certain sense very cynical; intellectually self-confident and not subject to the whims of people who feel that they are less hidden, and are not quite sure that they know their case. Recruited as it was, particularly in the nineties, from the great universities – and not least from the universities of Scotland – it tended to develop a certain cynical attitude, for the Treasury is not a place where one could attain an unduly exalted idea of human nature.

There was clearly no lack of self-confidence in its own capacity – the sinew and ability was there for aggressive empire-building. Likewise it exhibited no shortage of mistrust of its rivals, which is the classic motive for defensive annexation as a pre-emptive strategy. Moreover, the First World War offered an obvious opportunity for expansion. True, the personnel in the administrative grade had increased to 65 by 1919 and temporarily peaked at about 90 before the post-war cutback. Yet a permanent enlargement of the Treasury role was resisted. In the 1920s it notoriously set its face in the opposite direction, resisting moves for intervention in the economy, especially via public works. Instead, balanced budgets were upheld; the return to the Gold Standard in 1925 was made the prime objective of policy; free trade was defended as long as possible; above all, the Treasury View was promulgated in 1929 – a sweeping doctrine denying the possibility that government spending could raise the overall level of output or employment. These were the principles of sound finance, which were upheld throughout the 1920s in face of high and persistent unemployment. This represented a valiant effort to roll back the frontier of the state to its pre-war line.

There are several possible explanations: economic (that nothing could be done and that market forces produced the best practicable outcome); political (the failure within any party to mount an effective movement for radical changes); electoral (the interests of the 80 per cent of the electorate who were not unemployed); the role of pressure groups (the City of London and international interests). But let us focus on factors concerning the role of the state as such.

Narrow administrative rivalry needs to be taken into account. A road programme on the scale proposed by Lloyd George and Keynes in 1929 – the Liberal manifesto *We Can Conquer Unemployment* was endorsed by Keynes's and Henderson's pamphlet *Can Lloyd George Do It?* – would have involved an unprecedented accretion of power by the Ministry of Transport, for which the Treasury was unprepared. Likewise, public works initiatives could have been used to boost the relative status of the Ministry of Labour which was, in a sense, paid to promote them while the Treasury's professional interest lay in cutting them back. The fact that 'the employment problem . . . is regarded as the affair of the Ministry of Labour' became a mark of self-abnegation on the part of the Ministry, but the potential for it to assert itself more vigorously against the Treasury was surely there.[19]

Moreover, the Treasury was *able* to enforce its will because its pre-eminence within the structure of government had been reinforced at the end of the First World War. Having lost control of spending during the war, it proceeded to exact a terrible vengeance upon spendthrift departments. New procedures were evolved for making ministries accountable; Sir Warren Fisher, Bradbury's successor as Permanent Secretary to the Treasury, was given the title of Head of the Civil Service; a unified structure of appointment and promotion was for the first time imposed upon the civil service – with the Treasury monitoring the system and administering the attendant rewards and punishments. The Treasury, it might be said, aggrandized its own role within the civil service itself without conquering new ground for government in regulating the economy.[20]

So far as its economic role was concerned, the Treasury View represented a coherent and persuasive model, well understood and deeply entrenched. Sound finance was buttressed by moral and ideological axioms. There was a cogent symmetry to its interlocking facets (balanced budgets, the Gold Standard, free trade) which were parts of a self-acting system. Once the principles had been established and institutionalized, its operations were smooth and automatic, with virtually no opportunity for political discretion in distorting market outcome. In Bradbury's famous phrase, which became part of the Treasury's oral tradition, it was 'knave-proof'.[21] Why did this conception inspire such devotion?

First, it entrenched the public service ethic against the vulgar pressures of democratic politics. We should recall that the British electorate was trebled in 1918 with the addition of a large number of women voters and a move to universal male suffrage; granting the 'flapper vote', when equal suffrage inevitably followed in 1928, did little to allay the Treasury's apprehensions. Whatever next? What if a notoriously opportunistic demagogue came along – armed with specious arguments manufactured by an irresponsible Cambridge don who was clearly too clever by half – and promised to conquer unemployment? In this sense the 1929 election simply fulfilled the Treasury's worst fears. Frederick Leith-Ross minuted: 'I am sorry to see that Keynes is renewing the Press propaganda which has done him little good as a politician and considerable harm as an economist.'[22]

Secondly, it could be said that the lack of room for manoeuvre embodied in this system was deceptive because contrived. It enabled the Treasury and the Bank of England to assure the politicians that there was no alternative – but only on their own premises. In fact it left them as 'the authorities' to administer the system without interference. They were like the Calvinist elect whose psychological commitment to choosing a godly life was seemingly unimpaired by a professed belief in predestination.

Thirdly, we should note the *intellectual* appeal of this system to the mandarins. The hydraulic mechanism of the Gold Standard lay at the heart of it, bringing compensating flows of inflation and deflation into play through the pump action of Bank Rate. Once set in motion, it was all a matter of 'automatic adjustments' and displacement effects. The rigour and elegance of this system was beautifully attuned to strong supple minds schooled in the disciplines of classics and mathematics – the subjects in which virtually all the Treasury mandarins had excelled at Oxford and Cambridge. To them, sound finance spoke with the precision of calculus and the purity of a dead language.[23]

The Treasury did not feel it had much to learn from academic economic theory – that was the sort of thing any Wrangler worth his salt could get up in a few weeks (as Keynes himself had in the Michaelmas Term of 1905). This was also the way that Ralph Hawtrey, another Cambridge Wrangler, learnt economics; as such he was tolerated by the Treasury as their house economist, though (as Chancellor 1925–9) Churchill's joke was that Hawtrey's colleagues kept him locked in a dungeon. Nor did they feel the lack of a full range of empirical economic statistics – that was something they happily left in the horny hands of the Board of Trade.

Since the Treasury was well satisfied with this dispensation, their change of role needs to be explained by some exogenous shock, which can readily be found in the intractable pressures of external forces and events. The 1931 crisis was the first of these, when Britain's economic weakness fed a financial crisis and enforced the final departure from the Gold Standard (with tariffs to follow shortly). Next, the Second World War brought obvious dislocation and challenge. It was seen from early days as a problem of mobilizing resources not simply of manipulating wartime finance through loans. This was the context for the 1941 Budget, with its novel framework of national income accounting rather than government revenue and expenditure.

This shift to a macroeconomic perspective is conventionally seen as the beginning of the Keynesian era, and not just by outsiders. No one was better placed for an inside view than Edward Bridges (Permanent Secretary, 1945–56) who wrote in retrospect:[24]

> there have been many occasions on which war has proved a solvent of doubts and
> hesitations and has brought to fruition some change or reform which had lain becalmed
> for many years. Whatever the reason, it was in 1944 that the Coalition Government
> in a White Paper on Employment Policy accepted as one of the primary aims and
> responsibilities of Government in the United Kingdom the maintenance of a high and
> stable level of employment. This White Paper was perhaps the most important single
> landmark on the way to the post-war policy of managing the economy.

Now after the First World War the authorities had attempted to put the clock back to 1914; hence the drive to return to Gold in 1925 and the self-denying ordinance on the Treasury's role and size, all in a final effort to shore up the knave-proof fiscal constitution on Gladstonian lines. This was already seen as a losing battle by 1931. We see a more pragmatic approach in the Treasury in the 1930s under the new leadership of Sir Richard Hopkins (brought from the Board of Inland Revenue). The role of the authorities in managing sterling was by way of a salvage operation. One way or another, extra staff were needed in the top echelon. Treasury reorganization in 1936 allowed for 77 Administrative grade (equivalent to the old Upper Establishment).[25] The big expansion took place from 1940; the permanent effect was to double the numbers in the Administrative grade by the 1960s. The changes were not simply quantitative but qualitative; not just in structure but in function.

3

Should we see here a revolution for which the blueprint was the *General Theory?* Revisionist historians have recently queried earlier claims about a Keynesian revolution in policy-making, with an extreme version maintaining that there was no Keynesian revolution at all.[26] It is certainly true that acceptance of Keynesian ideas was not as swift or complete as was once supposed. Instead this process was halting and patchy and incremental. What did it lead to? It had its apotheosis in 'Butskellism', characterized by Samuel Brittan, one of the most acute observers of the modern Treasury as 'an interesting mixture of planning and freedom, based on the economic teachings of Lord Keynes'.[27] The salient features were thus, in the first place, a policy aimed at the management of demand, with an increasing emphasis on the management of *consumer* demand; and, furthermore, one to be implemented not only through fiscal means but also through *credit* regulation. It is pertinent to ask, therefore, how far these two axioms are laid down in the *General Theory*.

On the first point, it should be noted that Keynes's concept of effective demand was defined as *investment* plus immediately prospective consumption. He had a longstanding record of wishing to regulate investment so as to make full use of resources, and in the *General Theory* he accordingly suggested 'a somewhat comprehensive socialisation of investment'. (The post-war nationalization measures in Britain do not, however, fulfil his criteria of controlling the overall volume of investment, whether public or private – 'it is not the ownership of the instruments of production which it is important for the State to assume.')[28] My point is simply that consumer demand was only one side of Keynes's story – and not the one which he himself chose to emphasize.

Secondly, there is the issue of *how* to regulate. According to the *General Theory*: 'The state will have to exercise a guiding influence on the propensity to consume partly through its scheme of taxation, partly by fixing the rate of interest, and partly, perhaps, in other ways.'[29] Thus a fiscal strategy received clear, if rather cursory, approval (though budget deficits were not explicitly mentioned at all!). Brittan's account is again revealing: 'If Keynesian economics was associated with any one idea among the educated post-war public it was with Budget surpluses and deficits as a way of regulating the economy.'[30] This is undeniably how the policy was enunciated under Cripps, as explained in his Budget speech of 1950: 'Excessive demand produces inflation and inadequate demand results in deflation. The fiscal policy of the Government is the most important single instrument for maintaining that balance.'[31]

What role, then, was assigned to interest rates? Keynes repeatedly stressed the desirability of bringing down the rate to a low *and stable* level (in this sense 'fixing' the rate). His confidence in whether low interest rates were sufficient to stimulate investment waxed and waned. In the early 1930s he agreed with Hawtrey that cheap money would do the trick; his later divergence from Hawtrey was over whether control of credit alone, entailing frequent changes in interest rates, was the right way to regulate the economy. Labour certainly adopted a cheap money policy throughout years 1945–51. But under Butler the Conservatives brought monetary policy into play as well, using changes in Bank Rate as well as fiscal changes in a policy of demand management. This was the policy pejoratively known as stop–go, and a credit squeeze became *the* classic way of stopping.

One conclusion is clear: that this aspect of Butskellism can find no authority in the *General Theory* (nor in Keynes's other writings). Now my main purpose here is not textual exegesis, and I have no wish to replicate the historiographical controversies over how far developments in nineteenth century British government correspond to adumbrations in the writings of Bentham. It surely should come as no great shock to historians that the 'Keynesian revolution' in twentieth-century government showed a highly imperfect fidelity to the texts loosely invoked its support. One reason is that the *General Theory* did not purport to be a handbook on economic policy. Keynes unambiguously said that his aim was to revolutionize economic theory, that it would take another book to apply this to politics, and that 'politics and feelings and passions' were bound to be mixed with his ideas in the course of applying them.

Did a revolution in policy in fact need the *General Theory*? It is arguable that the intellectual synthesis Keynes pulled together in the *Treatise on Money* (1930) would have provided a better basis for winning the immediate argument over state intervention and public works. This implied no challenge to fundamental theory but mounted a strong pragmatic case that real-world imperfections in practice thwarted the process of equilibration – hence the relevance of 'gadgets' as second-best expedients to remedy disequilibrium. Moreover, here Keynes's arguments were congruent with those of A.C. Pigou,

Dennis Robertson, Henry Clay and Hubert Henderson, all of them heavyweight economists who later proved unable to accept the *General Theory*. Keynes is often accused by monetarists (led by Hayek) of writing the *General Theory* as 'a tract for the times' – a legitimation of his immediate policy proposals in the context of the mid 1930s but without real theoretical significance. In fact it is more plausible to argue the opposite: that in this context the *General Theory* was tactically unwise.[32]

Keynes himself is inescapably central to the argument over British economic policy from the 1920s to the 1940s in several roles. He could play the ex-Treasury expert in the Gold Standard discussions. He could act as Liberal publicist and politician in the controversy around *Can Lloyd George Do It?* He appeared as an academic economist when he served on the Macmillan Committee and the Economic Advisory Council. He took his final curtain as 'just Keynes', back in the Treasury again from 1940 until his death in 1946 as adviser to the Chancellor of the Exchequer, international economic statesman and licensed franc-tireur. His direct imprint upon the Treasury in all these roles can be traced clearly. But it is much more difficult to pin down the influence of the *General Theory*.

In terms of intellectual consistency, credit regulation to control the cycle of deflation/reflation was pure Hawtrey (as some old Treasury hands recognized). In his account of Treasury policy in the post-war period, Peden aptly talks of old dogs and new tricks – sometimes they were old tricks too.[33] Although the diminutive Hawtrey was rarely acknowledged as having any practical influence, his insider position in the Treasury itself, albeit in the dungeon, had made his ideas familiar. Having said this, perhaps it would be prudent for me to add that it would, of course, be bizarre to propose Hawtrey's bust for the pedestal in the Treasury pantheon formerly reserved for that of Keynes.

For it is one thing to observe that the nature of Keynes's influence has often been misapprehended by people who have too readily jumped to conclusions: quite another to jump to the opposite conclusion that he had no influence. Let me affirm therefore that I emphatically do not wish to minimize the importance of the *General Theory* (though this constitutes a problem which I am not ready to tackle here). If nothing else, it provided some sort of ideological cover for macroeconomic intervention even when this was implemented through means its author deplored. Moreover, it set the terms of discourse, irreversibly establishing a macroeconomic perspective in the discussion of policy which later doctrines of 'monetarism' to this extent shared. And the *General Theory* provided a persuasive paradigm for a new generation to understand the world – especially for those who considered that the point was to change it. The fact remains that Keynesianism, hardly less than Benthamism, has had an indiscriminate burden of responsibility thrust upon it in explaining the pattern of government growth.

4

The administrative dimension needs to be kept in view. If policy-making can be seen as a learning process, then under Hopkins the Treasury became manifestly ready to learn. The educative force of the 'Keynesian debate' throughout the pre-war decade (1929–39) helped to shift the Treasury towards a more pragmatic view. But this was not simply a one-way process. Hopkins's wealth of administrative experience helped bring the real-world difficulties of administration and legal constraints, politics and the confidence factor, to Keynes's notice. For example, in the Macmillan Committee in 1930 one could say that Keynes won the economic argument (discrediting the Treasury View) but Hopkins won the administrative argument, and that both have a fundamental relevance to policy-making. The Keynes-Hopkins partnership inside the Treasury during the Second World War produced a new synthesis on economic policy. It may be too simple to say that Keynesianism was domesticated and neutered; but was there a 'bastard Keynesianism' after Keynes's death?

Butskellism was essentially an arm's-length approach to the economy. The Attlee Government's 'planning' increasingly turned from physical intervention to macroeconomic control of aggregates through the Budget – symbolized by Cripps's move from the Ministry of Economic Affairs to the Treasury in 1947, taking with him the apparatus of planning as part of his new responsibilities (the Central Economic Planning Staff and the Economic Information Unit).

There is no doubt that the exercise of new functions acquired its own momentum; the introduction of professional expertise exposed new areas of ignorance, not least in the old officials. In particular the Treasury took a new interest in statistics. Indeed in the mid twentieth century this became one of the cornerstones of its power – creating a well-founded suspicion in more than one crisis that the figures were massaged to bludgeon ministers into uncongenial choices. Denis Healey was to attribute this to the Treasury's 'sado-masochism'.[34]

When the Conservatives took over in 1951, Butler's revival of monetary policy (notably the use of Bank Rate changes) to parallel fiscal policy reinforced the macroeconomic strategy. This represented a big contrast with the 1920s and 1930s – except in one crucial respect: 'the authorities' were more firmly in charge than ever. Moreover, the stubborn atavism of style expressed significant continuities. Healey wrote that the Bank of England in the 1970s 'still attempted to maintain the cabbalistic secrecy of its most famous Governor, Montagu Norman, seeing itself as the guardian of mysteries which no ordinary mortal should be allowed to understand'.[35] Within this perspective, subsequent differences between 'fiscal fine tuning' under the Keynesian consensus and 'monetary targetting' under early Thatcherism may look like variations on a theme.

According to David Howell, formerly one of Thatcher's cabinet ministers, the nexus of any government in this country is No. 10 and the Treasury, with the Bank of England as the Treasury's appendage. . . . Under this Government and under the regime that emerged after '79 . . . the nexus between No. 10 and the Treasury is decisive, it overrules, it's everything. The Treasury always know they can win. . . . On the whole, the spirit of the '79 Government . . . has been, 'No, don't bother me with the facts. The Treasury's figures are settled. Good afternoon.'[36]

Of course, from a Treasury viewpoint it looks different, as Sir Leo Pliatzky, a former mandarin, explained:

A lot of people, including some Prime Ministers, don't like the force of circumstances, they don't like the force of reality. They think 'if only I could somehow get a different sort of Treasury.' Okay, why don't they abolish the Treasury instead of trying to set up a counterpoint? Well, they can't because the Treasury stands for reality.[37]

Did Sir Leo have any sense that he was echoing Churchill's defence of Treasury policy in 1925, that it did not 'shackle us to gold' but 'shackle us to realities'?[38]

The tone and manners may have changed since Bradbury's day, when top hats were still de rigueur, but the ready use of christian names may serve as simply a different signal of assumptions about corporate unanimity. While acknowledging that their dominance was rightly based on their high calibre, Bernard Donoughue (as personal adviser to Wilson and Callaghan in the late 1970s) wrote that the Treasury officials could 'be criticized in general for creating a departmental culture of monastic unworldliness. They appear to spend too much of their lives mixing only with other Treasury men. They are often foolishly proud of being untainted or uncorrupted by contact with or practical knowledge of the soiled outside world into whose fiscal and monetary affairs they intervene with devastating effect.'[39]

Keynes suggested in 1921 that the Treasury was 'an institution which came to possess attributes of institutions like a college or City company, or the Church of England'.[40] A vulgar public-choice model, built on the postulate of individualistic maximization, captures little of this abiding idiom and ethos. These men with bulging briefcases on the late train home to the suburbs are not simply after an easy life in which they can feather their own nests. Their wistful quest for fulfilment dwells in a subtly different ambience, hinted at in Bridges' lament that 'we are, unfortunately, lacking in the expressions of corporate life found in a college. We have neither hall nor chapel, neither combination room nor common room'.[41]

Not even a proper washroom! It took the Fulton Report on the Civil Service (1968) to disclose that the Treasury mandarins had to keep their own towels and soap in desk drawers. It is both engaging and rather chilling to find the Treasury's canons of high thinking and plain living still reflected in their personal austerity. It suggests that, for all the revolutionary changes in the Treasury's role that had meanwhile taken place, Sir John Bradbury would still have had a fellow feeling for his successor as Permanent Secretary in the 1980s, Sir Robert Armstrong – a man who, as Australians have special cause to remember, took pride in being economical even with the truth.[42]

Notes

1. Oliver MacDonagh, 'The nineteenth-century revolution in government: a reappraisal', *Historical Journal*, i (1958), pp. 52–67.
2. See in particular Jenifer Hart, 'Nineteenth century social reform: a Tory interpretation of history', *Past and Present*, 31 (July 1965), pp. 39–61.
3. MacDonagh, 'Nineteenth-century revolution', p. 53.
4. A.V. Dicey, *Law and Public Opinion in England* (1905; 1963 edn), p. 287.
5. This is neatly put by Stefan Collini, *Liberalism and Sociology* (Cambridge, 1979), p. 14.
6. A.J.P. Taylor, *English History, 1914–45* (Oxford, 1965), pp. 1–2.
7. Alan T. Peacock and Jack Wiseman, *The Growth of Public Expenditure in the United Kingdom* (Oxford and Princeton, 1961), pp. 164–5.
8. HMSO, *Civil Service Statistics* (1970–). The most recent year available to me was 1987. The establishment of the Civil Service Department caused a drop in Treasury personnel from 1,864 to 964 in 1968–9, and its abolition a rise from 1,006 to 2,582 in 1981–2; the addition of the Civil Service Catering organization brought the amalgamated total to 4,177 and it is this inflated figure which is now customarily cited, e.g. Peter Hennessy, *Whitehall* (1989), p. 394.
9. Peter Hall, *Governing the Economy* (Cambridge, 1986), ch. 1, passim.
10. See Peter B. Evans, Dietrich Rueschemeyer and Theda Skocpol, *Bringing the State Back In* (Cambridge, 1985).
11. *JMK*, vol. 16, pp. 296–307, at p. 297 (lecture on 'The civil service and financial control', 1921).
12. Sir Bruce Fraser, quoted in Hennessy, *Whitehall*, p. 397.
13. Lord Diamond, quoted in Hugh Heclo and Aaron Wildavsky, *The Private Government of Public Money* (2nd edn, 1981), p. 45.
14. B.W. Gilbert, quoted in Eunan O'Halpin, *Head of the Civil Service: A Study of Sir Warren Fisher* (1989), p. 54.
15. See the invaluable study by Henry Roseveare, *The Treasury* (1969), esp. pp. 210–12, 227.
16. Gordon Tullock, 'Public choice', in John Eatwell, Murray Milgate and Peter Newman (eds), *The New Palgrave*, 4 vols (1987), vol. 3, pp. 1040–4, at p. 1043.
17. Heclo and Wildavsky, *Private Government of Public Money*, esp. pp. lxxii, 2.
18. *JMK*, vol. 16, p. 299.
19. See Rodney Lowe, *Adjusting to Democracy* (Oxford, 1986), ch. 6; quotation from Sir Harold Butler, a former official, at p. 191n.
20. K. Burk, 'The Treasury: from impotence to power' in K. Burk (ed.), *War and the State* (1981), pp. 80–107, esp. pp. 96–102; O'Halpin, *Head of the Civil Service*, pp. 24–55.
21. See Roger Middleton, *Towards the Managed Economy* (1985), esp. pp. 31–7, 83–92, for a good appreciation of the coherence of this position.
22. Quoted in Peter Clarke, *The Keynesian Revolution in the Making* (Oxford, 1988), p. 49.
23. This paragraph and the next summarize points I have made more fully in 'The Treasury's analytical model of the British economy between the wars', ch. 7 above.
24. Edward Bridges, *The Treasury* (1966), p. 92.
25. Roseveare, *Treasury*, p. 270; G.C. Peden, *British Rearmament and the Treasury* (Edinburgh, 1979), appendix 1. Peden is the best authority on the career of Hopkins, notably in 'Sir Richard Hopkins and the "Keynesian revolution" in employment policy, 1929–45', *Econ. Hist. Rev.*, xxxvi (1983), pp. 281–96.
26. Jim Tomlinson, 'Why was there never a "Keynesian revolution" in economic policy?', *Economy and Society*, x (1981), pp. 72–87.
27. Samuel Brittan, *The Treasury under the Tories* (Harmondsworth, 1964), p. 162.
28. *JMK*, vol. 7, p. 378.
29. Ibid.

30. Samuel Brittan, *Steering the Economy* (Harmondsworth, 1971), p. 147; this is a radically revised third edition of the work cited above in n. 27.
31. Sir Stafford Cripps, quoted in Bridges, *Treasury*, p. 93.
32. See Clarke, *Keynesian Revolution in the Making*, pp. 167–89, 315–17.
33. G.C. Peden, 'Old dogs and new tricks: the British Treasury and Keynesian economics in the 1940s and 1950s', in Barry Supple and Mary Furner (eds), *The State and Economic Knowledge* (Cambridge and New York, 1990).
34. Denis Healey, *The Time of My Life* (1989), p. 401; cf. Bernard Donoughue, *Prime Minister* (1987), pp. 16, 94, 139.
35. Healey, *Time of My Life*, p. 374.
36. Quoted in Hennessy, *Whitehall*, p. 396.
37. Ibid., p. 397
38. See Martin Gilbert, *Winston S. Churchill*, vol. 5 (1976), p.119.
39. Donoughue, *Prime Minister*, p. 33.
40. *JMK*, vol. 16, p. 299.
41. Quoted in Anthony Sampson, *Anatomy of Britain* (1965), p. 226. All students of the mores of modern Whitehall are indebted to this pioneering work, and its successor, *Anatomy of Britain Today* (1969).
42. [A topical reference in 1989 to Armstrong's defence, in an Australian court, of the disingenuous formulation of official statements in the *Spycatcher* case.]

9 Keynes, Buchanan and the balanced budget doctrine

1

The salience of the name of Keynes in any discussion of public debt and deficits is obvious. He is the prime suspect. It is yet another example of the way that Keynes's own apophthegms about the role of defunct economists and academic scribblers have been seized upon by his latter-day critics as his unique prescient insight – the better to convict him of responsibility for the allegedly deleterious consequences of his own doctrines. When he said that 'soon or late, it is ideas, not vested interests, which are dangerous for good or evil',[1] he was, of course, implicitly claiming that he himself would revolutionize the way the world thought about economics, while ostensibly leaving open a value judgement upon the putative legacy of such a revolution. In the Keynesian golden age after the Second World War, it seemed that his influence could hardly be overestimated or overpraised. If the Gladstonian Treasury ethic of balanced budgets was one casualty of his now successful assault on the previous orthodoxy, this was judged good in that it had apparently ushered in an era of full employment and of historically unexampled economic prosperity.

Two twists have been given to this story in the course of the last generation. The first has been to rewrite the economic history of the 'golden age' allowing Keynesian policies a much less instrumental role in sustaining the level of demand, investment and employment than was at one time supposed. This has had the wholly beneficial effect of replacing a mere assertion about Keynes's impact – *post hoc ergo propter hoc* – with conclusions based upon empirical research. Although this can be seen as an exercise in diminishing Keynes's centrality, it is, of course, hardly anti-Keynesian in itself. Indeed the seminal study here was an article by Robin Matthews, 'Why has Britain had full employment since the war?', published as long ago as 1968; and his subsequent collaborative work with Charles Feinstein and John Odling-Smee fully substantiated the point. In asking 'whether the high average level of demand in the postwar period was attributable to government policy', they found no evidence of a net fiscal stimulus to the economy. 'Net government savings were substantial and positive throughout the postwar period, in contrast to the negligible savings of earlier periods.'[2] Feinstein has recently restated these conclusions in an authoritative synthesis on the economic history of the period since the Second World War. While acknowledging the important indirect (confidence) effects of a government commitment to sustaining full employment through demand management, Feinstein concludes: 'However, the government did not make a more direct contribution to the level of demand by spending more than it was raising in taxation', since such fiscal adjustments as were made 'always took the form of increasing or reducing the size of the government's surplus; at no stage did the budget actually move into deficit'.[3]

The other twist in the story about Keynes and budgets has been no less significant and no less influential – but within a community defined by a common interest in political economy rather than British economic history. I refer, of course, to the development of ideas about public choice, associated particularly with the name of the Nobel laureate, James M. Buchanan. The seminal work here was the book he published in collaboration with Richard E. Wagner, *Democracy in Deficit*, with the telling subtitle, *The Political Legacy of Lord Keynes*. This legacy, it need hardly be added, was replete with ideas dangerous for evil. 'Our specific hypothesis is that the Keynesian theory of economic policy produces inherent biases when applied within the institutions of political democracy', they boldly stated, though promptly and prudently adding the disclaimer that this sweeping claim was actually limited to the United States of America. In fact, the form of their analysis cried out for more general application since it was itself founded on such general claims. One was about the influence of theory upon politics. 'The ideas of the Cambridge academic scribbler did modify, and profoundly, the actions of politicians, and with precisely the sort of time lag that Keynes himself noted in the very last paragraph of his book.'[4] A second claim was about Keynes's own political naivety, with heavy reliance here on Harrod's concept of 'the presuppositions of Harvey Road', to depict a Keynes who was an elitist and rationalist, culpably innocent of the real world of democracy.[5] Hence, crucially, Keynes's blindness towards an asymmetrical appropriation of his doctrines, with a bias towards budget deficits. 'Politicians naturally want to spend and to avoid taxing', they concluded. 'The elimination of the balanced-budget constraint enables politicians to give fuller expression to these quite natural sentiments.'[6]

How far these axioms help illuminate the actual fiscal history of the United States is an interesting question, but one beyond my own competence to explore; it is with their relevance to Britain that I am concerned. Fortunately Buchanan and Wagner have preceded me in reciprocating this concern, since in 1978 they collaborated with John Burton in producing one of the justly influential series of Hobart Papers for the Institute of Economic Affairs, specifically applying their ideas to Britain. In the general restatement of their theory, there was another trip down the well-worn pavements of Harvey Road, leading up to the claim that the Keynesian revolution had removed a crucial constraint on political institutions, altering the character of governmental budgetary policy, since 'little political resistance to budget deficits' was now to be expected, with the result that 'fiscal policy will tend to be applied asymmetrically: deficits will be created frequently, but surpluses will materialise only rarely'.[7]

Burton then took up the cudgels in showing how this had occurred in Great Britain. He produced two tables, 'The pre-Keynesian British budgetary record', covering the century or so up to the Second World War, showing consistent peacetime falls in the National Debt; and 'The Keynesian British budgetary record', with figures showing a budget deficit in every year except two from 1952 to 1976. The contrast between them was left to speak for itself. All that remained to be done was for Burton to link this demonstration of the effect with the explanatory theory, focusing on 'the transmogrification of Britain's fiscal constitution, during World War II, by the Keynesian revolution'. Though it was admittedly only a convention that the budget should be balanced, the point was that all governments had observed it in peacetime. 'The balanced-budget principle played a crucial role in holding the pre-Keynesian fiscal constitution together, and constraining the otherwise inherent biases of that system to over-expenditure and deficit finance. Once the balanced-budget had been bowled over by the Keynesian revolution, those biases were unleashed.'[8] This proposition was reiterated by all three authors in their joint conclusion: 'Once the last vestiges of the Classical norm of the balanced budget were removed, nothing was left to constrain the spending proclivities of politicians, and, indirectly, those of voters themselves.'[9]

The association of Keynesianism, in some chronic and inherent way, with persistent budget deficits naturally became part of the monetarist indictment of the post-war consensus. Conversely, the performance of the British economy in the 1980s was linked with the reversion to an older and more wholesome budgetary doctrine. The entire exposition of Nigel Lawson's 1988 budget was saturated with his own anti-Keynesian presuppositions in this regard. He began by stating that 'the British economy is stronger than at any time since the war', and this because 'for almost nine years now, we have followed the right policies and stuck to them'. In his peroration he repeated that 'in this Budget, I have reaffirmed the prudent policies which have brought us unprecedented economic strength'; he recapitulated his achievements; and he reserved for his final words, in formally commending the Budget to the House, the lapidary claim: 'And I have balanced the Budget.'[10] Moreover, in the body of the statement, Lawson sought approval for his mixture of 'the maintenance of sound money and prudent public finances' by invoking specific historical lessons.

> At one time, it was regarded as the hallmark of good government to maintain a balanced budget; to ensure that, in time of peace, Government spending was fully financed by revenues from taxation, with no need for Government borrowing. Over the years, this simple and beneficent rule was increasingly disregarded. . . . Today I am able to tell the House that in 1987–8, the year now ending, we are set to secure

something previously achieved only on one isolated occasion since the beginning of the 1950s: a balanced budget.[11]

Thus the wheel had apparently come full circle, with thirty locust-ridden years of Keynesian fiscal profligacy ended by a restoration of pre-Keynesian maxims of fiscal prudence – the political legacy of Lord Lawson, one might say. The new twist which public-choice analysis had given to interpreting the course of events since the war thus received its apotheosis in contributing to a reversal of the thrust of policy itself. Plainly Lawson's story derived from, or at least was reinforced by, the analysis to which Buchanan had lent his name. There is the same celebration of the historic balanced-budget doctrine. There is more or less the same appeal to the historical record since the early 1950s, proclaiming that in only one – at most two – years during the Keynesian era had the budget avoided a deficit. So economists and politicians told each other – apparently without ever asking how this tallied with the new economic history of the same period which showed that the government accounts were always in surplus.

Differences of definition are part of the explanation for this inconsistency. Lawson provided an important clue when he put this gloss on what he meant by a balanced budget: 'In other words, henceforth a zero PSBR will be the norm. This provides a clear and simple rule, with a good historical pedigree.'[12] But the historical pedigree of the PSBR in British public accounts goes back barely twenty years. It can hardly have provided the traditional vocabulary of fiscal rectitude. The historic balanced budget doctrine cannot simply be assimilated to modern definitions of deficits, framed by anachronistic concepts like the PSBR.

2

The canons of public finance, as Gladstone left them, centred on one particular set of central government accounts: the Consolidated Fund. The aim was to centralize the channels of both revenue and expenditure, so that the balance of the Consolidated Fund at the Bank of England would automatically reveal the state of the national finances. Once all departments had eventually been dragooned into keeping their own accounts on a standard model, triply vigilant oversight of the whole process by the Treasury, by the Department of Exchequer and Audit, and by the Public Accounts Committee of the House of Commons became a possibility. Under this governance, as one authority on public finance put it, 'the balanced budgetary system gave a complete mirroring of the relation of revenue and expenditure, almost from week to week, certainly by the end of the financial year: on the one side of appropriation against estimate, on the other of disbursement against appropriation. The Consolidated Fund thus became a unique instrument for registering the success of control.'[13]

The centrality of the Consolidated Fund to the structure of government accounts is manifest. It was the technical means by which Gladstone institutionalized the annual budget as a great theatrical exercise in national introspection and reckoning, complete with a long sermon from himself.[14] If the moral notion that the budget ought to be balanced became deeply ingrained, it was understood in terms of the revenue and expenditure of the Consolidated Fund. On the expenditure side, what mattered was expenditure above the famous 'line' in the Exchequer Accounts, dating from the Sinking Fund Act of 1875, broadly excluding capital sums that Parliament had authorized to be met from loans. Self-balancing expenditure of a capital nature was not, in principle, seen as a problem, whatever practical ambiguities arose in applying this principle, for example over the Post Office or the Road Fund; and the treatment of the sinking fund remained the most intractable difficulty, as will be seen.

In the best Gladstonian tradition, therefore, the simple moral imperative of balancing the budget was in practice wrapped in the esoteric conventions of the public accounts. Sir Bernard Mallet, who made a life's work of penetrating these mysteries, quoted a Victorian financial critic's opinion that 'the information in the budget, finance accounts, statistical abstract and special parliamentary returns about Imperial taxation is vitiated by cardinal errors of arrangement and definition, which obscure the subject and mislead public opinion'.[15] In one of his contributions to the Liberal Yellow Book of 1928, Keynes spoke of 'the unintelligibility of the National Accounts, through which no one but a Treasury expert can find his way securely'.[16]

One longstanding problem was the somewhat arbitrary distinction between expenditure 'above the line' and 'below the line'. This broadly distinguished a revenue account from a capital account – but by no means unambiguously, since some capital payments, mainly of a regular rather than a lumpy nature, could be charged above the line, that is, against current revenue. Only an old Treasury hand could be expected to know the difference within this hybrid accounting framework. As Keynes remarked in 1945,

> the present criterion leads to meaningless anomalies. A new G.P.O. is charged 'below', a new Somerset House 'above'. A capital contribution to school buildings is 'above' in the Exchequer Accounts and is paid for out of Revenue, and is 'below' in the Local Authority Accounts and is paid for out of loans. The cost of a road is 'above', of a railway is 'below'. And so on.[17]

Some of these longstanding anomalies reflected the fact that the point of the traditional Exchequer accounts was, self-evidently, *accountability* – a worthy enough rationale in itself but not necessarily helpful in identifying the economic impact of fiscal policy. Hence the tension between the historic conventions and the post-war (Keynesian) conception of the role of the budget. 'A system of accounts, like words, classifies events; and, like language, implies a theory about the world it is used to describe', was how J.C.R. Dow put it. 'National income accounting has in large part been evolved to meet the needs of budgetary policy; and its system of classifications implies a theory of budgetary policy.'[18] Attempts to bring the public accounts within this new rationale are part of the story of the administrative reception of Keynesianism.

A similar problem in making sense of the available figures has caused economic historians to produce their own versions of the historic public accounts, in order to make them consistent with modern series. For example, in their path-breaking work on public expenditure, Alan Peacock and Jack Wiseman explained at one point that their statistics for central government expenditure were 'based on a detailed reclassification of the appropriation accounts' for the period 1890–1919.[19] A central aim of such exercises has been to isolate the impact of government transactions upon the economy and, above all, to strip out capital movements from the current account. Thus in dealing with central government, Feinstein's indispensable guide stated that 'the published accounts have to be reclassified in accordance with the principles of national income accounting'. The figures which he produced became the basis for Susan Howson's table showing the deficit or surplus in central government accounts for the inter-war years.[20] This is, of course, a very useful series, for almost all purposes – the main exception being a consideration of what was believed at the time about the budget balance.

In Roger Middleton's study of this period, building here on the pioneer work of Ursula Hicks, a range of statistics is given, showing the radical differences between the conventionally defined budget balance and his adjusted figures. The net effect can be considerable. For example, a reported small surplus in 1931–2 becomes a deficit of £46 million, or a reported surplus of £29 million in 1937–8 becomes a deficit of £16 million.[21] These adjustments not only make the accounts conform more closely to modern conventions on coverage but also expose the 'fiscal window-dressing' which the Treasury had deliberately introduced and about which, within its own walls, it was cynically candid. One mandarin noted that

> there is no great technical difficulty in producing for a series of years budgets which are balanced at the end of the year to the nearest penny. . . . Perhaps half a dozen financial writers in the country would understand from the published accounts what was happening, but I doubt if any one of the half dozen is capable of making the position clear to the public.[22]

It is pretty obvious that a balanced budget is to some extent a statistical construct, dependent on conventions which change over time and which are neither wholly transparent nor wholly innocent. As Hicks commented at the time: 'The different interpretations of the term "balanced budget", which it is possible to put forth, serve to illustrate the shortcomings of a hybrid account.'[23]

The fact remains that the historic balanced budget convention focused on the current revenue and expenditure of the Consolidated Fund, with the important condition that a surplus here – 'the old sinking fund' – should be applied towards the redemption of the National Debt. The institution of a new sinking fund from 1875 introduced a further complexity since this was a fixed, planned total, not a more or less accidental outcome.[24] The new sinking fund was essentially an *ex ante* figure, relevant to the Budget estimates, whereas the old sinking fund was *ex post*, manifested by the realized surplus at the end of the year. It follows that including the new sinking fund, in its various subsequent guises, in figures which purport to show a realized surplus or deficit merely confuses the issue, as to whether spending was covered by taxes.

Nonetheless, the orthodox contemporary convention, followed by Sir Bernard Mallet, was to include the new sinking fund provision in the realized total for each year. What this succeeds in bringing out is whether the Chancellor had fallen short of fulfilling his stated plan of debt redemption for the year. Obviously a high sinking fund target could produce a deficit in this sense, even though revenue allowed for some debt redemption, albeit at a less ambitious rate than planned. Conversely, budget estimates otherwise headed for deficit, on such a reckoning, could be balanced by manipulating the sinking fund provision. In the 1920s, when Churchill was Chancellor, he notoriously engaged in what the Shadow Chancellor, the Gladstonian purist Philip Snowden, called 'raids' on both the old sinking fund and, analagously, the road fund.[25]

The orthodox version of the balanced budget doctrine reached the height of its rigour in the May Report's recommendations for balancing the budget in 1931. Snowden had conveyed a warning to those members of the Labour cabinet tempted to scale down the sinking-fund provision 'that any attempt of this kind to camouflage the true position would be at once detected, and that it was of paramount importance that the Budget should be balanced in an honest fashion'. But the National Government was in fact able to adopt just this sort of camouflage, without disturbing confidence. The sinking fund, which had been budgeted at £67m. in the last year of the Labour Government, was immediately halved; in 1933–4 provision was slashed to under £8m., and in the last six years before the outbreak of war never exceeded £13m.[26]

This sort of prospective, notional sinking fund never bulked large subsequently, though vestigial sums continued to appear 'above the line' in the Exchequer accounts until their reform under the National Loans Act of 1968. This Act finally took all the Government's borrowing transactions out of the Consolidated Fund, leaving its own revenue and expenditure as a true current account. The net effect of these confusing changes, centring on treatment of the sinking fund, is that the only series which is comparable for the whole of the nineteenth and twentieth centuries is that for the revenue and expenditure of the Consolidated Fund.

By excluding sinking fund provision, of course, the size of any reported surplus up to the Second World War will look larger than it did through the lens of the strong balanced budget doctrine. But this presentation gives a more transparent account both of whether taxes covered spending and of the sums available for debt redemption, which was the whole point of the doctrine in the first place. As the Treasury knight, Sir Herbert Brittain, put it – in a nice mid-twentieth century echo of Ricardo's authority, Hamilton – 'The principle is that the only real Sinking Fund is a surplus of current revenue over current expenditure.'[27] This is exactly what the Consolidated Fund accounts show, with any surplus being applied to the National Loans Fund as debt redemption.

3

If revenue, expenditure (and PSBR, where available) are all expressed as a proportion of current GDP, figures can be produced, as shown in the appendix to this chapter, showing both the pre-Keynesian and the Keynesian budgetary record *on a consistent basis*. It seems sensible to begin this series after the First World War, covering the period when deficits first became a contentious issue.

Mallet's series reports the same pattern as that shown in the appendix, with the one proviso that follows from his treatment of the sinking fund. Instead of simply showing all (*ex post*) debt redemption as a budget surplus, the (*ex ante*) target figure concealed within the new sinking fund provision is classed as 'expenditure'. It was this peculiar definition of expenditure which, on the conventional (Mallet) basis, showed deficits in 1926, 1927, 1930, 1931, 1937 and 1939.[28] There was a deficit in 1933, regardless of the treatment of the sinking fund, as shown in my appendix; but with this exception, it shows a surplus in every year from 1921 to 1939.

Here is a slightly modified story, as compared with what Burton reported in his table, 'The pre-Keynesian budgetary record', which was doubly handicapped in its aim of showing the classic balanced budget in operation. First it did not use the Exchequer accounts but instead took Peacock and Wiseman's figures for total public expenditure, so it did not focus on 'the budget' at all. Secondly, having done this, it was unable to supply a matching figure for revenue. Thus it is impossible to subtract the one from the other, with classical simplicity, to reveal the all-important bottom line – unless some link could be inferred from the reported fluctuations in the National Debt.

For the period following the Second World War, the appendix shows that there was a surplus of revenue over expenditure on the Consolidated Fund in every year from 1948 to 1972, with the possible exception of 1965 (when expenditure was reclassified on a new basis, producing a deficit on the new figures, though a surplus on the old ones). These figures are virtually the same as the conventional surplus 'above the line', in the form reported until the abolition of the line itself in 1968. Though Chancellors from Cripps to Macmillan sometimes hankered after achieving an 'overall surplus', by covering capital expenditure 'below the line' from revenue, this was not, as Macmillan supposed, 'the orthodox financial opinion'.[29]

Only from 1973 did the Consolidated Fund accounts reveal a string of deficits, with a brief swing into surplus for the three years 1988–90, of which the largest surplus was that forecast in Lawson's 1988 Budget statement, and realized in 1989. This surplus amounted to 1.4 per cent of GDP. There had been eighteen years between 1948 and 1972 in which a higher budget surplus than this was realized.

A yawning discrepancy is apparent between these figures and Burton's table on 'the Keynesian budgetary record'. Burton supplied figures under the rubric 'budget deficit', but only by dint of defining it as the Public Sector Borrowing Requirement.[30] Now the modern concept of the PSBR, as used from 1976, may make good sense as a modern definition of a budget deficit, just as Lawson proposed in 1988. Indeed it may be projected backwards, in reconstruction of statistics that aid historical understanding of the effect of government's total impact upon the economy. But the PSBR cannot properly be imported into a historical discussion of the classic balanced budget *doctrine*. This had been framed in quite other terms. Just as it could hardly have acted, before or after Keynes, as a constraint on the growth of the PSBR as such, conversely the new doctrine of the PSBR conceals what the Consolidated Fund accounts were designed to make transparent – the balance between current revenue and expenditure.

Reconciling the two sets of accounts is not difficult, since the Consolidated Fund lies at the heart of central government finance. It does not, however, include the National Insurance Fund, to that extent underrating both tax and expenditure levels as often cited. The balance on the Consolidated Fund goes into the National Loans Fund. The central government borrowing requirement is the net lending of the National Loans Fund *less* any surplus from the Consolidated Fund *plus* the surplus of the National Insurance Fund *plus* departmental balances. The PSBR is simply the total of the central government borrowing requirement plus that of the local authorities and the public corporations. It will be obvious that many of these tributary accounts have a large capital content (especially in the era of privatization) but the true source of central government revenue, as of its current expenditure commitments, remains the Consolidated Fund.

Not only were current spending commitments historically at the root of the problem: they were to remain so. The fact is that the underlying deterioration in the public finances since 1973 was in terms of current expenditure as against revenue, and this is clearly signalled under the traditional conventions, which, for example, show a deficit of over 10 per cent in 1994, historically unparalleled in peacetime. Leaving the ordinary revenue and current expenditure figures concealed within a larger total for the PSBR seems peculiarly perverse since public-choice theory looks for its explanation in the voter-sensitive relationship between taxing and spending.

The problems of the public sector, and of defining it satisfactorily, and of financing its investment, have had little direct bearing on this relationship, as was well appreciated thirty years ago. 'Unfortunately', one well-informed writer commented, 'the Treasury has come to adopt as *the* definition of public spending one which is misleading for many purposes for which it is liable to be used. There are no prizes for guessing that the definition errs on the side of making it seem too high.' Whereas the official definition helped identify how much of the economy was under the control of public authorities, it ignored the fact that 'the question which most people ask when they see a projection of expenditure several years ahead is: What will this mean for taxes?'[31] The balanced budget convention was concerned with this relationship, not with the issue of raising investment for public-sector activities which might equally well have been transferred to the private sector – as, in due course, many of them were to be.

4

The distinction between the government's current spending commitments and the finance of capital investment was crucial to Keynes's own thinking, as will become apparent in the course of examining his own utterances on these issues. In view of the importance which has been attributed to the Keynesian policy of budget deficits, it might be thought that Keynes wrote of little else, or at any rate that what he did write about budget deficits would bulk large in his published writings. Now the consolidated index to the 29 volumes of his Collected Writings itself runs to 373 pages in double columns. Of these, there is one column on budgets, with some fifty lines of entries under various sub-headings, of which those on 'balancing the budget' (6 lines), 'capital, or long-term budget' (4 lines) and 'deficit budgeting' (3 lines) are relevant. There is also a wholly separate entry under 'deficit financing' (2 lines). These two entries explicitly mentioning deficits thus run to five lines between them, or one-tenth of one column out of 746.

Moreover, when these helpful references are followed up, they yield a rather meagre harvest. There is only one reference in the volume covering the 1931 crisis, and that to a letter to the Prime Minister, not advocating a budget deficit but advising MacDonald how to avoid one. Likewise there is one reference in the succeeding volume, this time dating from 1933, and not by Keynes at all but by Hubert Henderson, on the admittedly germane issue of how to define 'loan expenditure'.[32] The vast bulk of the references to deficit budgeting or finance in fact come from the volume dealing with Keynes's role during the Second World War in shaping post-war employment policy, especially through the drafting of the 1944 White Paper which committed government to maintaining a high and stable level of employment. Clearly this phase of his activities, as an active public servant, will merit closer scrutiny in due course.

First, though, what of the theoretical basis for the Keynesian position? In the *General Theory* there are only two direct references to budget deficits. One deals with the effect of a decline of employment (and hence of income) on government, 'which will be liable, willingly or unwillingly, to run into a budgetary deficit or will provide unemployment relief, for example out of borrowed money'.[33] In a book not otherwise known for the modesty of its claims, this seems a rather tentative and cursory way in which to proclaim a revolutionary new doctrine. The other reference is more substantial, comprising two closely-argued pages in chapter 10, which expounds the concept of the multiplier. Here, to be sure, we reach the heart of the theory of effective demand, with the conclusion that at the bottom of a slump public works will pay for themselves, though this effect will diminish as full employment levels are approached. It all turns on the sort of loan expenditure which contemporaries dubbed 'wasteful'. On the contrary: 'Pyramid-building, earthquakes, even wars may serve to increase wealth, if the education of our statesmen on the principles of the classical economics stands in the way of anything better.' There follows a well-known discussion of the conventional preference for wholly wasteful activities – for example, 'the form of digging holes in the ground known as gold-mining' – as compared with only partly wasteful forms, such as building subsidized houses or roads.

The poetry of this fine satirical passage does not elide into the technical prose of public finance. Instead there is an obscure footnote which in fact provides an important clue to Keynes's thinking about deficits: '"loan expenditure" is a convenient expression for the net borrowing of public authorities on all accounts, whether on capital account *or* to meet a budgetary deficit. The one form of loan expenditure operates by increasing *investment* and the other by increasing the propensity to *consume*.'[34] Perhaps this is all that Keynes needed to say in what he repeatedly maintained was a purely theoretical work. The priority in his own mind for increasing investment rather than consumption was to take practical shape in his later proposals for a capital budget. But the clear distinction between such a strategy for stimulating public investment and what he distinguishes, by contrast, as 'a budgetary deficit' is one which rested also on the arcane conventions of the British public accounts.

Keynes's interest in such matters went back some years. He had, of course, been a Treasury official himself during the First World War. In 1924, in his first essay in justifying public works, he had turned his eyes to the sinking fund as a possible source of finance, arguing that he proposed 'not to abolish (or raid) the sinking fund, but to use it'.[35] This suggestion was not immediately pursued. Instead, when he contributed a chapter on 'The Reform of the National Accounts' to the Liberal Yellow Book, Keynes suggested a new and more intelligible framework for the budget. Not only did he propose supplementing the existing, arbitrary cash basis with accounts for income accrued – thus revealing 'the true Surplus or Deficit on the year' – he also broached the idea of a capital account, into which, *inter alia*, the sinking fund would be paid.[36] Apart from this, the Yellow Book said nothing about budgeting for deficits; nor did the argument over public works at the time of the 1929 General Election turn on this issue.

5

There were three major occasions on which Keynes set out his views on balanced budgets: in the 1931 crisis; at the beginning of 1933, with the publication of his policy proposals, best known as *The Means to Prosperity*; and during the Second World War, in the discussions surrounding the 1944 White Paper on Employment Policy.

In 1931 Keynes emerged as an outspoken critic of the approach expounded by the Report of the May Committee. It should be recalled that this had been set up by Snowden, Labour's Chancellor, in order to stiffen his arm in persuading the cabinet of the need for deep expenditure cuts. But when the Report was published, it dramatically raised the stakes. Not only did it include the borrowings of the Unemployment Insurance Scheme, and also the Road Fund, within the ordinary budget: it insisted 'that to produce a properly balanced budget in 1932 including the usual provision for the redemption of debt' – the sinking fund, of course – the total shortfall to be made good, mainly by government cuts, amounted to no less than £120m. (about one-sixth of ordinary expenditure).[37] Keynes's reaction was to propose an altogether different strategy: 'My own policy for the budget, so long as the slump lasts, would be to suspend the Sinking Fund, to continue to borrow for the Unemployment Fund, and to impose a revenue tariff.' He sought to frame the narrower issue of the government's deficit within the larger problem of a spiralling decline in national income and output, which it should be government policy to arrest, but which its own economy measures might deepen. He therefore doubted whether the cuts proposed in themselves could achieve even half their effect in closing the deficit, because of offsets from diminished tax yields and the costs of increased unemployment. 'The net result would necessarily be a substantial increase in the number of unemployed drawing the dole and a decrease in the receipts of taxation as a result of the diminished incomes and profits', he argued. 'Indeed the immediate consequences of the government's reducing its deficit are the exact inverse of the consequences of its financing additional capital works out of loans.'[38]

The butt of Keynes's criticism here, as so often, was the dogmatic Treasury View: the proposition that loan expenditure was incapable of raising national output, only of crowding-out other economic activity. The Treasury View was in this sense a flying buttress supporting the balanced budget doctrine. Accordingly, when the main lines of the May analysis, albeit not all its specific rigours, were accepted by the National Government's Economy Bill in September 1931, Keynes called it 'a triumph for the so-called "Treasury view" in its most extreme form', and commented on its philosophy of retrenchment: 'If the theory which underlies all this is to be accepted, the end will be that no one can be employed, except those happy few who grow their own potatoes, as a result of each of us refusing, for reasons of economy to buy the services of anyone else.'[39] He did not deny that there was a budget problem but argued that it was 'mainly a symptom and consequence of other causes, that economy is in itself liable to aggravate rather than to remove these other causes, and that consequently the budget problem, attacked merely along the lines of economy, is probably insoluble'.[40]

When Keynes returned to this theme in 1933, he did so fortified by the new theory of effective demand which had meanwhile taken shape in his mind. He now roundly asserted that 'you will never balance the Budget through measures which reduce the national income', since it was 'the burden of unemployment and the decline in the national income which are upsetting the Budget'. Hence his watchword: 'Look after the unemployment, and the Budget will look after itself.' Reminded (by a sympathetic interlocutor, Sir Josiah Stamp) that 'views about balanced budgets are a kind of psychological necessity', Keynes tried to make his own perspective clear:

> You are always going back to this question of the Budget. So far as that is concerned, I should say that things like the sinking fund aren't so important in these days as they would be in more prosperous times, and I think that the Chancellor of the Exchequer would be long-sighted if he were to take rather an optimistic view, and give us perhaps in his next Budget rather more relief than is strictly justified by the facts actually in sight. If he does, he will help to bring the facts in sight, which would justify the optimism that he has adopted. But that is not really what I want. It is loan expenditure I am wanting.[41]

In *The Means to Prosperity*, originally a series of articles in *The Times* just before the 1933 Budget, Keynes used the new concept of the multiplier to argue that 'it is a complete mistake to believe that there is a dilemma between schemes for increasing employment and schemes for balancing the budget', suggesting that the contrary was true: 'There is no possibility of balancing the budget except by increasing the national income, which is much the same thing as increasing employment.' Having reiterated his familiar case for public works, he went on to turn it in a new direction: towards tax cuts financed by suspending the sinking fund. 'For the increased spending power of the taxpayer will have precisely the same favourable repercussions as increased spending power due to loan-expenditure; and in some ways this method of increasing expenditure is healthier and better spread throughout the community.' He returned to his suggestion 'that the next budget should be divided into two parts, one of which shall include those items of expenditure which it would be proper to treat as loan-expenditure in present circumstances'.[42] In the run-up to the Budget, Keynes began speaking of 'the second branch of loan expenditure – the relief of taxation out of borrowed money'. What he proposed was a suspension of the sinking fund, a more optimistic estimate of prospective revenue now that employment was recovering, and a degree of government borrowing to be made good in future budgets. 'Whatever the Chancellor dreams, will come true!' Keynes enthused 'We must begin by resuscitating the national income and the national output; and, if we succeed in this, we can be sure that, over a period of time, the yield of the taxes will respond.'[43]

These are Keynes's most explicit pleas for what became known as deficit finance, and they attracted widespread attention. They were duly considered by Neville Chamberlain in his Budget statement a few weeks later, only to be firmly rejected: 'If I were to pretend I could lay out a programme under which what I borrowed this year would be met by a surplus at the end of three years, everyone would soon perceive that I was only resorting to the rather transparent device of making an unbalanced Budget look respectable.' Chamberlain instead appealed to the experience of other countries where he found 'that Budget deficits repeated year after year may be accompanied by a deepening depression and a constantly falling price level'. (The risk was apparently of deflation not inflation.) He claimed that 'at any rate we are free from that fear which besets so many less fortunately placed, the fear that things are going to get worse. We owe our freedom from that fear largely to the fact that we have balanced our Budget.'[44] With this adamantine rebuff of Keynesian heresy, the Treasury held firm to the doctrine of balanced budgets, tempered by fiscal window-dressing, until the Second World War.

It was only in the later stages of the war that Keynes, now a high-ranking Treasury adviser himself, returned to the theme of balanced budgets. By then, under the influence of the New Deal, the terms deficit finance and functional finance had become established – not, however, to Keynes's satisfaction. Instead he adopted a tone of disengaged wariness, partly perhaps for tactical reasons, the better to win over his straitlaced Treasury colleagues, of whose ingrained scepticism about dodges and pretexts for extenuating deficits Keynes was hardly unaware. He now sharpened the distinction between the government's own current expenditure and a 'capital budget' to provide for sufficient national investment. 'I should aim at having a surplus on the ordinary Budget, which would be transferred to the capital Budget, thus gradually replacing dead-weight debt by productive or semi-productive debt', Keynes wrote in 1942, adding that 'I should not aim at attempting to compensate cyclical fluctuations by means of the ordinary Budget. I should leave this duty to the capital budget.'[45]

The concept of a capital budget was given increasingly full exposition. Some of Keynes's arguments were shrewdly conservative, playing down its revolutionary character in favour of its presentational advantages: 'It does not enable anything to be done which could not be done without it by means of the existing technique and in conformity with the existing forms of the Exchequer Accounts.'[46] The effect, therefore, would be to 'leave the regular Budget practically the same as at present. The utmost that might be involved would be a slight tidying up of a few items as between (in technical language) "above" or "below the line" of the Exchequer accounts, and even this would not be really necessary.'[47]

In other defences of the capital budget, speaking among friends who were at least as Keynesian as himself, Keynes showed that it was rather more than a cunningly-disguised stalking horse for deficit finance. To James Meade, who feared that such a division might 'reinforce the orthodoxy of an annual balance for the current budget', Keynes evinced scepticism about 'devices for causing the volume of consumption to fluctuate in preference to devices for varying the volume of investment'. His reasoning is interesting, not least in the light of subsequent criticisms of Keynesianism as both economically and politically myopic.

In the first place, he appealed to a hunch which, with Friedmanite hindsight, it seems fair to call the concept of the stability of the consumption function. Keynes doubted whether

> short-term variations in consumption are in fact practicable. People have established standards of life. Nothing will upset them more than to be subject to pressure constantly to vary them up and down. A remission of taxation on which people could rely for an indefinitely short period might have very limited effects in stimulating their consumption.

In the second place, he exhibited a more robust sense of political economy than is usually credited to the Harvey Road school of naive rationalists, maintaining that 'it is not nearly so easy politically and to the common man to put across the encouragement of consumption in bad times as it is to induce the encouragement of capital expenditure'. Not only was it 'much the easier of the two to put across', but 'the very reason that capital expenditure is capable of paying for itself makes it much better budgetwise and does not involve the progressive increase of budget difficulties, which deficit budgeting for the sake of consumption may bring about or, at any rate, would be accused of bringing about'.[48]

Keynes had, however, included within his capital budget an ingenious plan, devised by Meade, for making social security contributions counter-cyclical. This helped make sense of Keynes's doctrine that it was 'the capital Budget which should fluctuate with the demand for employment', whereas 'the ordinary Budget should be balanced at all times'.[49] The idea of 'unbalancing one way or another the current Budget' stood quite apart, as 'a last resort, only to come into play if the machinery of capital budgeting had broken down'. Keynes was against 'confusing the fundamental idea of the capital budget with the particular, rather desperate expedient of deficit financing'.[50]

Keynes could therefore claim that his proposals for a capital budget were not intended 'to facilitate deficit financing, as I understand this term', as he put it in 1945, within months of his death.

> On the contrary, the purpose is to present a sharp distinction between the policy of collecting in taxes less than the current non-capital expenditure of the state as a means of stimulating *consumption*, and the policy of the Treasury's influencing public capital expenditure as a means of stimulating *investment*. There are times and occasions for each of these policies; but they are essentially different and each, to the extent that it is applied, operates as an *alternative* to the other.[51]

What is interesting is not just what Keynes intended, in his innocence, but which alternative, for thirty years after his own death, a Keynesian Treasury opted for. The answer here is surely that regulation of consumption played a more important part than Keynes might have wished. Indeed it became the means of 'fine-tuning' the economic cycle through fiscal policy. But whatever else it did, or failed to do, this policy did not entail 'collecting in taxes less than the current non-capital expenditure of the state'. Instead it was the 'below-the-line' transactions, ultimately embraced by the PSBR, which came to be used as the Treasury's means of 'influencing public capital expenditure'.

6

The notion of an inherent democratic bias towards self-interested government expenditure is not new. The Utilitarian assumption that voters were motivated by self interest, and that the self interest of a majority who were poor could lead to spoliation of a rich minority, was a staple of nineteenth-century discussions about the consequences of extending the franchise to the working class. Tocqueville argued thus; and John Stuart Mill, the Liberal Robert Lowe and the future Conservative prime minister Lord Salisbury are prominent examples in Britain in the debates which led to the passing of the Second Reform Act in 1867.[52] In a later generation, Bernard Mallet was purely conventional in his reflections: 'in the case of the State, the "utility" derived from expenditure and the "disutility" of obtaining the necessary revenue are necessarily divorced or distributed amongst different persons or classes of persons' and this was 'obviously likely to have very important consequences' in the workings of 'the modern democracy where policy may be ultimately controlled by, and in the interests of, the majority of an electorate consisting mainly of the poorer classes, while revenue is obtained mainly from a minority of wealthier persons'.[53]

The May Committee, reporting to the Government in 1931 on the need for economy, put their analysis within similar assumptions:

> all parties have felt the insistent pressure for promises of 'reforms' as the price of support, such 'reforms' being in fact mostly of the nature of privileges or benefits for particular classes at the cost of the general taxpayer. . . . At election times those desiring increased expenditure on particular objects are usually far better organized, far more active and vocal than those who favour the vague and uninspiring course of strict economy. . . .[54]

Thus the appetite for this sort of expenditure, notably on social programmes or other handouts supposedly favoured by a clamorous democratic electorate, and fed by the appeasement of self-serving politicians, was what some contemporaries feared. Such hypotheses about the working of the political system, which have subsequently constituted the agenda for the public-choice explanation of the democratic deficit, may seem plausible enough in the abstract. But when they are tested against the empirical evidence of British political history, these axioms fail to account for the dominant features of the landscape in this 'Conservative century'. Where is the explanation of the stern resistance which socialism has encountered, or for the protracted fallibility of the Labour Party? How does one explain the fact that the two major capitalist slumps of the twentieth century led to prolonged periods of government by the political right?

The real story is a good deal more complex. In particular it needs to be understood how and why and when Keynesianism acquired ideological purchase. There is no intuitive ground for simply asserting or assuming that it was bound to prevail, for good or evil. Keynes himself obviously thought that his ideas were common sense. But, faced with stubborn scepticism in the 1930s, he was forced to ask: 'Why should this method of approach appear to so many people to be novel and odd and paradoxical?'[55] Ten years later he was still warning James Meade that 'These ideas are too young and tender to be put to the strain which your present line of thought would require'.[56] In the high noon of post-war Keynesianism, the young Samuel Brittan was facing the same barrier of incomprehension in explaining that 'finding the money' was not the real problem in financing public sector investment. 'So far from being generally accepted as obvious common sense, the doctrines of Keynes run contrary to the way in which people have been taught to think about good housekeeping from childhood onwards. . . . '[57] And by 1980 Thatcherites had grasped the significance of this point in turning the tables on the new economics in good populist style. 'Monetarism, after all, is really rather obvious', wrote Nigel Lawson: '. . . It is Keynesianism, which seems to stand everything on its head, which is the difficult and esoteric doctrine.'[58]

Actually existing Keynesianism in post-war Britain clearly diverged in important respects from the ideas of the historical Keynes. On budget deficits, however, the policy followed for nearly thirty years seems broadly consistent with his own precepts. The record, moreover, was not that of chronic deficits, which could then be explained by the supposition that government spending had now escaped the constraint of a balanced budget. Measured by the historic standard, there is simply no problem to explain, since, throughout: the 'tax-and-spend' era, the spending was covered by the taxes. If it is true that expensive welfare commitments were undertaken, it is also true that these were affordable at full employment and output, just as Beveridge had long ago insisted. If it is true that budget deficits failed to provide an easy escape from the difficulties subsequently encountered by the British economy, it is also true that they could hardly have been a longstanding cause of those difficulties.

If it was only in the 1970s that deficits opened up, it seems sensible to look first for an explanation in the developments of that period, before resorting to more universal theories which simultaneously explain too much and too little. One starting point in understanding what happened is the fact that from 1971 to 1974, while nominal GDP grew by 50 per cent and expenditure from the Consolidated Fund by 42 per cent, its revenue only increased by 15 per cent – hence the fall in revenue, as shown in the appendix, of no less than 8 per cent of GDP over only three years. Of course, this took place against a background of concurrently rising inflation (which to some extent masked, reflected and generated this change) and rising unemployment, with its associated rise in payments by government to the unemployed. Keynes's dictum – 'Look after the unemployment, and the Budget will look after itself' – thus points to a more significant aspect of this particular historical relationship in Great Britain than does the rival hypothesis of the democratic deficit.

Notes

1. *JMK*, vol. 7, p. 384. I am grateful to Eugenio Biagini, Donald Moggridge, Barry Supple, John Thompson and Maria Tippett, as well as participants at the Gresham Conference chaired by Sir Samuel Brittan, and one highly placed correspondent, for their comments on an earlier draft.
2. R.C.O. Matthews, C.H. Feinstein and J.C. Odling-Smee, *British Economic Growth, 1856–1973* (Oxford, 1982), p. 310; cf. R.C.O. Matthews, 'Why has Britain had full employment since the war?', *Econ. Jnl*, lxxxii (1982), pp. 195–204.
3. Charles Feinstein, 'Success and failure: Britain's economic growth since 1948', in Roderick Floud and Donald McCloskey (eds), *The Economic History of Britain since 1700*, 2nd edn, 3 vols (Cambridge, 1994), vol. 3, p. 107. See also the useful survey by T.J. Hatton and K. Alec Chrystal, 'The budget and fiscal policy', in N.F.R. Crafts and N.W.C. Woodward (eds), *The British Economy since 1945* (Oxford, 1991), esp. pp. 74–5 on the post-war position in the public sector as a whole.
4. James M. Buchanan and Richard E. Wagner, *Democracy in Deficit: The Political Legacy of Lord Keynes* (New York and London, 1977) pp. x, 37; cf. *JMK*, vol. 7, pp. 383–4: 'there are not many who are influenced by new theories after they are twenty-five or thirty years of age'.
5. Buchanan and Wagner, *Democracy in Deficit*, pp. 7, 78ff. On the 'presuppositions of Harvey Road', see Roy Harrod, *The Life of John Maynard Keynes* (1951), pp. 192–3.

6. Buchanan and Wagner, *Democracy in Deficit*, p. 183.
7. James M. Buchanan, Richard E. Wagner and John Burton, *The Consequences of Mr Keynes* (Institute of Economic Affairs, 1978), p. 18 (by Buchanan and Wagner).
8. Ibid., pp. 36, 47; tables I and II at pp. 32, 34; cf. pp. 41, 44, 57 (by Burton).
9. Ibid., p. 79.
10. Nigel Lawson, budget statement, 15 March 1988, House of Commons Debates, vol. 129 (1987–8) cols 993, 1013.
11. Ibid., cols 995–6.
12. Ibid.
13. Ursula K. Hicks, *British Public Finances: Their Structure and Development, 1880–1952* (Oxford, 1954), pp. 147–8.
14. See the invaluable studies by H.C.G. Matthew, *Gladstone, 1809–1874* (Oxford, 1988), pp. 112ff; and Eugenio Biagini, *Liberty, Retrenchment and Reform* (Cambridge, 1992), pp. 103ff.
15. Bernard Mallet, *British Budgets, 1887–8 to 1912–13* (1913), p. 411.
16. *Britain's Industrial Future* (1928); for authorship see *JMK*, 19, p. 731.
17. *JMK*, vol. 27, pp. 406–7 (Memorandum by Keynes for the National Debt Enquiry, 21 June 1945); cf Herbert Brittain, *The British Budgetary System* (1959), pp. 42–3 for a defence of such practices.
18. J.C.R. Dow, *The Management of the British Economy, 1945–60* (Cambridge, 1964; 1970 edn), p. 183; cf. Alec Cairncross and Nina Watts, *The Economic Section, 1939–61* (1989), pp. 233–5.
19. Alan T. Peacock and Jack Wiseman, *The Growth of Public Expenditure in the United Kingdom* (1961; 1994 reprint), p. 162.
20. C.H. Feinstein, *National Income. Expenditure and Output of the United Kingdom, 1855–1965* (Cambridge, 1972), p. 66; cf. the explanation of his general objective on p. 1; Susan Howson, *Domestic Monetary Management in Britain, 1919–38* (Cambridge, 1975), table 4A, p. 155.
21. Roger Middleton, *Towards the Managed Economy: Keynes, the Treasury and the Fiscal Policy debate of the 1930s* (1985), pp. 80–1; cf. Ursula K. Hicks, *The Finance of British Government, 1920–1936* (Oxford, 1938; new imp. 1970), table I, p. 289, for alternative accounts of the balance of the budget.
22. Sir F. Phillips, 1936, quoted in Middleton, *Towards the Managed Economy*, p. 82.
23. Hicks, *Finance of British Government, 1920–1936*, p. 286.
24. Bernard Mallet and C. Oswald George, *British Budgets: Third Series, 1921–2 to 1932–3* (Macmillan, 1933), pp. 526–7; Brittain, *The British Budgetary System*, pp. 201–4.
25. Bernard Mallet and C. Oswald George, *Bntish Budgets: Second Series, 1913–14 to 1920–21* (Macmillan, 1929), pp. 166–9, 194–5; Mary Short, 'The politics of personal taxation: budget-making in Britain, 1917–31', Cambridge PhD thesis (1985), pp. 208ff.
26. Middleton, *Towards the Managed Economy* pp. 100, 194.
27. Brittain, *British Budgetary System*, p. 201. Compare Robert Hamilton in the 1818 edition of his classic text: 'The excess of revenue above expenditure is the only real sinking fund by which the public debt can be discharged.' I rely here on Donald Winch, 'The political economy of public finance in the "long" eighteenth century', originally a paper to the same Gresham conference as mine, and first published as RUSEL Working Paper No. 26 (University of Exeter, 1996), p. 23 n. 56.
28. Mallet and George, *British Budgets: Third Series*, pp. 556–7; cf Mallet and George, *British Budgets: Second Series*, pp. 390–1; Bernard Mallet, *British Budgets, 1887–8 to 1912–13* (Macmillan, 1913), pp. 476–7; Middleton, *Towards the Managed Economy*, p. 81
29. Cairncross and Watts, *Economic Section*, p. 276; cf. pp. 249–50, 261–2, 283, and the table showing the surplus above the line, 1945–60, p. 237. There is a useful discussion of the different definitions of a deficit in Jim Tomlinson, *British Macroeconomic Policy since 1940* (1985), pp. 107ff.
30. Meanwhile no further reference was made to the National Debt. While this omission has something to be said for it, the opportunity was missed to disclose that by the 1970s, having steadily fallen for thirty years, the Debt had reached its lowest level as a proportion of GDP since the outbreak of the First World War. See Buchanan, Wagner and Burton, *Economic Consequences*, tables I and II, pp. 32, 34.
31. Samuel Brittan, *The Treasury under the Tories* (Penguin, 1964), pp. 93–4.

32. *JMK*, vol. 20, pp. 589ff; *JMK*, vol. 21, p. 167.
33. *JMK*, vol. 7, p. 98.
34. *JMK*, vol. 7, pp. 128–9 and n. (my emphasis).
35. *JMK*, vol. 19, p. 225 (*Nation and Athenaeum*, 7 June 1924).
36. *Britain's Industrial Future*, pp. 422–3.
37. Committee on National Expenditure, Report, Cmd 3920 (1931), par. 30; cf. summary, par. 564.
38. *JMK*, vol. 21, pp. 143, 145 (*New Statesman*, 15 Aug. 1931).
39. *JMK*, vol. 9, p. 147.
40. *JMK*, vol. 9, p. 240 (*Evening Standard*, 10 Sept. 1931).
41. *JMK*, vol. 21, pp. 149–50, 153 (*Listener*, 11 Jan. 1933).
42. *JMK*, vol. 9, pp. 347–8 and n. ('The Means to Prosperity', English edn, from *The Times*, March 1933).
43. *JMK*, vol. 21, pp. 183–4 ('The Means to Prosperity: Mr Keynes's reply to criticism', (*The Times*, 5 April 1933).
44. B.E.V. Sabine, *British Budgets in Peace and War, 1932–45* (Allen and Unwin, 1970), pp. 15–16.
45. To Hopkins and others, 'Budgetary Policy', 15 May 1942, *JMK*, vol. 27, pp. 277–8. There is a cogent account of these wartime discussions in D.E. Moggridge, *Maynard Keynes: An Economist's Biography* (1992), pp. 709–17; and see Jim Tomlinson, *Employment Policy: The Crucial Years 1939–55* (Oxford, 1987), pp. 49–59, 108ff; Cairncross and Watts, *Economic Section*, pp. 76–87, and Alan Booth, *British Economic Policy, 1931–49: Was There a Keynesian Revolution?* (1989), pp. 51ff.
46. *JMK*, vol. 27, p. 405 (Memorandum by Keynes for the National Debt Enquiry, 21 June 1945).
47. *JMK*, vol. 27, p. 368 (Note by Keynes, 14 Feb. 1944).
48. *JMK*, vol. 27, pp. 319–20 (Meade to Keynes, 19 April 1943; Keynes to Meade, 25 April 1943).
49. *JMK*, vol. 27, pp. 224–5 (Keynes to Hopkins, 20 July 1942.)
50. *JMK*, vol. 27, pp. 353–4 (Keynes to Sir Wilfrid Eady, 10 June 1943).
51. Keynes's emphasis: *JMK*, vol. 27, p. 406 (Memorandum by Keynes for the National Debt Enquiry, 21 June 1945.) My analysis thus substantially confirms the (neglected) account by J.A. Kriegel, 'Budget deficits, stabilisation policy and liquidity preference: Keynes's post-war policy proposals', in Fausto Vicarelli (ed.), *Keynes's Relevance Today* (1985), pp. 28–50.
52. See Alan Peacock, *Public Choice Analysis in Historical Perspective* (Cambridge, 1992), pp. 44ff, for an interesting discussion of Tocqueville.
53. Mallet and George, *British Budgets: Second Series*, pp. 383–4.
54. Cmd 3920 (1931), par. 22; cf. par. 574; and see the suggestive discussion of budgetary orthodoxy in Middleton, *Towards the Managed Economy*, pp. 83–92.
55. *JMK*, vol. 9, pp. 349–50 ('The Means to Prosperity', 1933).
56. *JMK*, vol. 27, p. 320 (Keynes to Meade, 25 April 1943).
57. Brittan, *The Treasury under the Tories*, p. 93.
58. Nigel Lawson, *The New Conservatism*, Centre for Policy Studies (1980), p. 18.

Appendix

Consolidated Fund as a proportion of GDP
Budget figures to April/GDP for previous calendar year

Year ending March	1. Revenue	2. Expenditure	3. Balance	4. PSBR (sign reversed) (Clarke)	5. (Burton)
1920	24.2	30.0	−5.9		
1921 (old)	23.8	20.0	3.8		
(new)	25.4	21.2	4.2		
1922	23.8	22.6	1.2		
1923	22.1	19.7	2.4		
1924	21.3	19.1	2.2		
1925	20.0	18.8	1.2		
1926	19.3	18.4	0.9		
1927	20.4	19.8	0.6		
1928	20.4	18.7	1.7		
1929	20.1	18.3	1.8		
1930	19.2	18.4	0.8		
1931	20.3	19.3	1.0		
1932	21.8	21.0	0.8		
1933	21.8	22.0	−0.2		
1934	21.4	20.4	1.0		
1935	20.1	19.6	0.5		
1936	20.4	19.7	0.7		
1937	20.6	20.4	0.2		
1938	20.2	19.3	0.9		
1939	20.2	20.2	0.0		
1947	41.3	47.8	−6.5		
1948	43.1	36.0	7.1		
1949	40.5	32.2	8.3		
1950	37.6	32.3	5.3		
1951	36.6	30.1	6.5		
1952	36.6	33.4	3.2		
1953	33.7	32.8	0.9		−5.6
1954	31.0	30.1	0.9		−4.0
1955	31.7	28.7	3.0		−2.4
1956	30.5	28.0	2.5		−2.8

Year ending March	1. Revenue	2. Expenditure	3. Balance	4. PSBR (sign reversed) (Clarke)	5. (Burton)
1957	29.9	28.1	1.8		−3.1
1958	29.3	26.9	2.4		−2.6
1959	28.9	26.9	2.0		−2.5
1960	28.2	26.3	1.9		−2.7
1961	28.0	27.2	0.8		−3.1
1962	27.2	25.4	1.8		−2.9
1963	26.6	25.1	1.5		−2.2
1964	25.3	24.9	0.4		−3.2
1965 (old)	26.2	24.7	1.5		−3.4
(new)		27.0	−0.8		
1966	27.5	26.8	0.7	−3.9	−3.9
1967	30.7	28.5	2.2	−2.9	−2.9
1968 (old)	33.6	32.6	1.0	−5.3	−5.4
(new)	31.8	30.8	1.0		
1969	35.1	30.5	4.6	−3.4	−3.4
1970	38.1	32.0	6.1	1.1	1.2
1971	36.0	32.0	4.0	0.0	0.0
1972	33.8	31.0	2.8	−2.8	−2.8
1973	30.7	31.6	−0.9	−3.6	−4.0
1974	28.0	30.6	−2.6	−6.7*	−6.6
1975	31.2	35.4	−4.2	−10.5	−8.6
1976	30.8	37.7	−6.9	−10.8	−11.4
1977	29.7	34.7	−5.0	−7.3	−8.8
1978	30.1	34.1	−4.0	−4.2	
1979	29.0	34.6	−5.6	−6.2	
1980	31.7	35.6	−3.9	−5.8	
1981	33.2	38.2	−5.0	−6.3	
1982	35.2	38.9	−3.7	−3.9	
1983	35.0	38.1	−3.1	−3.8	
1984	33.8	37.3	−3.5	−3.7	
1985	35.0	37.6	−2.6	−3.6	
1986	34.5	35.8	−1.3	−1.8	
1987	33.9	33.5	−1.6	−1.1	
1988	34.1	33.4	0.7	1.0	
1989	33.3	31.9	1.4	3.6	
1990	32.8	32.0	0.8	1.8	

Year ending March	1. Revenue	2. Expenditure	3. Balance	4. 5. PSBR (sign reversed)	
				(Clarke)	(Burton)
1991	33.9	34.3	−0.4	0.1	
1992	34.6	37.1	−2.5	−2.8	
1993	33.5	40.3	−6.8	−6.3	
1994	31.1	41.4	−10.3	−8.3	
1995	33.0	40.2	−7.2	−6.2	

Note   * Series for calendar years to 1973; financial years 1974 on.

Sources: Cols 1–3: up to 1980 calculated from B.R. Mitchell, *British Historical Statistics* (Cambridge, 1988), tables 3 and 4, pp. 581–93 (public expenditure and revenue); table 5, pp. 831–5 (GDP at factor cost); *Annual Abstract of Statistics*, tables 16.4 and 14.1 continue these series post-1980.

Col. 4: see *Annual Abstract* (1985–), tables 16.1 and 16.5 for the PSBR for the financial year, with statistics back to 1973–4; the PSBR is given for the calendar year, *Annual Abstract* (1977–), with statistics back to 1965; previously table 353 supplied only the central government borrowing requirement, and only for the calendar year. In the recent series see also tables 3.5 and 3.11 for the National Insurance Fund, and the annual *Blue Book*, tables 7.1 and 7.2.

Col. 5: PSBR calculations for calendar years 1953–77 reproduced from Buchanan, Wagner and Burton, *Economic Consequences*, table II, p. 34 (given there as for calendar years 1952–76).

10   The Keynesian consensus and its enemies: the argument over macroeconomic policy in Britain since the Second World War

1

Until the Second World War, no government professed to have a macroeconomic policy. The concept simply did not exist. To be sure, governments had long been held responsible, in a general way, for the health of the economy and it is obvious that 'hard times' hurt the party in power. This helped to bring the heavens down on the Conservative Government in the General Election of 1880, serving as the electoral meteorology behind the rain-dance performed with such ostentation by Gladstone in his Midlothian campaign. Conversely, an uncovenanted upturn in the export trade apparently vindicated the free trade case in the 1906 General Election and made Joseph Chamberlain's prescient warnings about manufacturing decline look like empty scaremongering. The arguments over the Gold Standard in the 1920s were, to our eyes, unmistakeably about macroeconomic issues; and in this sense the advocates of sound money, with their theory of a self-equilibrating system that was therefore 'knave-proof', were simply blinded by their own ideology to the actual consequences of what they were doing – Keynes's point, of course, in his public criticism of the return to Gold in 1925. Indeed this controversial decision inaugurated, under the prompting of continuing unemployment, a continuing debate – concerned in many different ways with the economic role of the state – which was macroeconomic *avant la lettre*.[1]

It seems that we owe the actual term to P. De Wolff in an article published in 1941 in the *Economic Journal* (of which Keynes was still editor). De Wolff built upon an earlier differentiation between micro-dynamic and macro-dynamic analysis and, according to *The New Palgrave*, was 'quite clear about the distinction between micro- and macroeconomics', one being valid 'for a single person or family', the other 'for a large group of persons or families'.[2] But while this is pointing in the right direction, it fails to capture the essential definition of macroeconomics as the study of the system as a whole, not simply of one sector, however great in magnitude, nor of any sub-set of economic agents, however numerous.

This distinction is in fact made much better by Keynes himself, who inescapably bulks large in any discussion of macroeconomic policy. So far as I am aware he never used the expression macroeconomics (or microeconomics) in any of his writings, though he must surely have become aware of its growing

213

usage in the five years before his death. Look in the index of his collected writings and there is only a hop, skip and a jump from Macmillan Committee ('*see* Finance and Industry') to Magicians ('Newton the last of the'). Yet, like M. Jourdain, Keynes's prose was unimpaired by his lack of the right word for it. Book Two of the *General Theory*, concerned with 'Definitions and Ideas', leads up to a clinching assertion, in its final sentence, of 'the vital difference between the theory of the economic behaviour of the aggregate and the theory of the behaviour of the individual unit'.[3]

Indeed in the preface to the French edition Keynes tried to pretend that this was why he had termed it 'a *general* theory. I mean by this that I am chiefly concerned with the behaviour of the economic system as a whole, – with aggregate incomes, aggregate profits, aggregate output, aggregate employment, aggregate investment, aggregate saving rather than with the incomes, profits, output, employment, investment and saving of particular industries, firms or individuals.'[4] It was this determination to seize on the aggregate dimension – not just as an analytical issue but also as a policy tool – which makes the early history of macroeconomic policy in Britain so largely synonymous with the history of Keynesianism.

Keynesian macroeconomic theory may have been devised at the bottom of the slump, but it was symmetrical in its policy implications, as its author explicitly affirmed. 'The best we can hope to achieve is to use those kinds of investment which it is relatively easy to plan as a make-weight, bringing them in so as to preserve as much stability of aggregate investment as we can manage at the right and appropriate level', he wrote in 1937, at the peak of British economic recovery. 'Just as it was advisable for the Government to incur debt during the slump', he argued, 'so for the same reasons it is now advisable that they should incline to the opposite policy.'[5] The irony in the administrative reception of Keynesianism is that it was 'the opposite policy' which prevailed during the 1940s. For it is now clear that the concepts of the *General Theory* were first operationalized within the administrative community in a way which spoke to the macroeconomic issue raised by the Second World War: how to control inflation.

For present purposes, it is not the administrative but the ideological impact of Keynesianism which is the focus – meaning by ideological the social or political purchase of Keynes's ideas, or ideas attributed to him, in a particular historical argument. Since we are concerned with 'actually existing Keynesianism', it should come as no surprise to discover that ideological distortions of Keynes's original intentions were a price that had to be paid for the influence of the doctrine.[6] What I have to say here bears less upon the policy-making process, on which there is now a fine scholarly literature, than upon the justifying rhetoric in which the central ideas were couched.

I shall take a number of representative texts in the political discussion of Keynesianism and macro-economic policy over a period of forty years, and quote them, sometimes extensively, in order to capture and illustrate strategies of argument, rather than to assess their objective validity. It will become clear that this discourse cannot simply be characterized as a conflict between progressive and conservative positions. Indeed, if the rhetoric which helped justify the post-war consensus arguably held its own nemesis, through being pitched in an over-confident and triumphalist register, such characteristics were often echoed, or even amplified, in the anti-Keynesian rhetoric which ultimately displaced it. Progressive illusions, imputing boundless competence to projects for reform, may have a timeless element, as may a conservative wisdom, tempering enthusiasm with wholesome pragmatism. The story of the rise and fall of Keynesianism in post-war Britain, however, hardly suggests that one side had a monopoly on the illusions and the other on the wisdom.

2

The ideological impact of Keynesianism makes a more straightforward, less ironical, story than that of its administrative reception. The enemy here was clearly unemployment rather than inflation. It was unemployment, rhetorically termed Idleness, which had a star billing in the Beveridge Report as one of 'five giants on the road of reconstruction', along with Want, Disease, Ignorance and Squalor.[7] Beveridge reached for no elevated soubriquet to characterize inflation, which retained its lower-case pygmy status throughout his Report. Conversely, Want could not be slain without first dealing with Idleness. Progressive reforms marched together in a happy example of mutual support – what Hirschman identifies as synergy.[8] Beveridge needed to banish mass unemployment in order to make his grand vision of social insurance viable. Hence the third assumption of the Beveridge Plan, that full employment would be maintained. True, the actuarial premise here was for an overall level of unemployment up to 8.5 per cent, which was soon to seem an unacceptably high rather than a desirably low figure. What was required, the Report explained, was 'not the abolition of all unemployment, but the abolition of mass unemployment and of unemployment prolonged year after year for the same individual'.[9]

Beveridge adduced five reasons for this contention. One was that cash payments, while suitable for tiding workers over, would, in the longer term, have a demoralizing effect. Another was that it became impossible to test unemployment by an offer of work if there were no work to offer. The availability of work, moreover, actively drew in people who would otherwise lapse into debility. These three reasons were concerned with the working of a social insurance scheme, showing its administrative interdependence with a buoyant labour market. 'Fourth, and most important', Beveridge continued, 'income security which is all that can be given by social insurance is so inadequate a provision for human happiness that to put it forward by itself as a sole or principal measure of reconstruction hardly seems worth doing.' Participation in productive employment, he suggested, was a great end in itself; the ethic of work thus provided a higher symbiosis between reforms which tackled the linked evils of unemployment and poverty. Finally, Beveridge pointed to the heavy cost of his Plan, warning that 'if to the necessary cost waste is added, it may become insupportable'. For unemployment simultaneously increased claims while depleting available resources.[10]

Beveridge himself soon became converted to the practicability of reducing unemployment below 3 per cent. It was this more ambitious target which defined 'full employment' in the debates of 1944, as against 'the maintenance of a high and stable level of employment after the war' which was what the Coalition Government's White Paper more prudently promised.[11] Either way, it was unemployment which was at the centre of the arguments.

The White Paper began by clearly identifying mass unemployment as a macroeconomic problem, for which the government now accepted responsibility. True, many caveats followed. Nigel Lawson, as Chancellor of the Exchequer more than forty years on, mischievously strung some of them together in an address to economists. Not only (so he found in paragraph 56) would it be 'a disaster if the intention of the Government to maintain total expenditure were interpreted as exonerating the citizen from the duty of fending for himself', but he was able to seize upon the remarkable comment in paragraph 74 that 'None of the main proposals contained in this Paper involves deliberate planning for a deficit in the National Budget in years of sub-normal trade activity'.[12] The provenance of the document is thus evident, as a compromise achieved through committee work. Hence paragraph 66 upholds the 'notion of pressing forward quickly with public expenditure when incomes were falling and the outlook was dark' despite the 'strong resistance from persons who are accustomed, with good reason, to conduct their private affairs according to the very opposite principle'.[13] Yet this counter-cyclical fiscal doctrine is promptly undercut by the apparently inconsistent paragraph 74, in which Lawson took comfort.

The fact is that everything else in the White Paper is by way of qualification to its central claim. Lawson knew this perfectly well in 1987, just as Keynes did in 1944 when he wrote that it was 'the general line and purpose of policy' that mattered at this stage. 'The object of the White Paper', he affirmed, 'is to choose the pattern of our future policy.'[14] This it did, most prominently in the foreword: 'A country will not suffer from mass unemployment so long as the total demand for its goods and services is maintained at a high level.'[15] That this claim was founded on a Keynesian multiplier analysis was later made explicit.[16]

The policy to be followed included not only strictly Keynesian measures for the counter-cyclical regulation of public investment but also parallel measures, chiefly due to Meade, for controlling swings in consumption expenditure by varying the rates of social insurance contributions. 'The ideal to be aimed at is some corrective influence which would come into play automatically – on the analogy of a thermostatic control – in accordance with rules determined in advance and well understood by the public.'[17] The analogy chosen here may seem banal and commonplace to us but must have inspired mixed feelings in the chilly British homes of an era of open fires and fuel rationing.

The general tone of the White Paper, however, is authentically that of the 1940s and did not, despite claims by some subsequent historians, hold out easy promises of a 'New Jerusalem'.

> It cannot be expected that the public, after years of wartime restrictions, will find these proposals altogether palatable; and the Government have no intention of maintaining wartime restrictions for restriction's sake. But they are resolved that, so long as supplies are abnormally short, the most urgent needs shall be met first. Without some of the existing controls this could not be achieved; prices would rise and the limited supplies would go, not to those whose need was greatest, but to those able to pay the highest price. The Government are confident that the public will continue to give, for as long as is necessary, the same wholehearted support to the policy of 'fair shares' that it has given in war-time.[18]

This kind of language made an obvious appeal to the political left. This was congruent with the way that the case for macroeconomic regulation of the economy was commonly meshed into a debate about planning, the buzz-word of the 1940s. It was under this guise that Keynesianism was assimilated to conventional arguments for socialism. When John Parker was commissioned by Penguin to put the Labour case in a book published in 1947, he struck this chord in the chapter called 'A Planned Economy':

> At the back of the minds of all those who have been through the two wars is the fear of a fresh slump and of widespread unemployment. The effect of Lord Keynes' teaching and of wartime experience has been the creation of a very widespread belief in Britain that unemployment can be practically prevented by the full development of a planned economy. Booms and slumps, it is hoped, can be ironed out if a deliberate attempt is made to do so.[19]

The fact is that planning had become an essentially contested term, a Humpty-Dumpty word which was invested with glosses appropriate to the arguments in which it was currently imbricated. 'Am I a planner?' asked James Meade in 1948.

> If a planner necessarily believes in a quantitative programme of output, employment and sales for particular industries, occupations and markets and the exercise of such direct controls by the State as are necessary to carry this out, I am certainly no planner. If an anti-planner necessarily denies that the State should so influence the

workings of the price mechanism that certain major objectives of full employment, stability, equity, freedom and the like are achieved, then I am a planner.[20]

This was consistent with Meade's advocacy since 1945, as head of the economic section, of the combined use of both planning and the price mechanism: a distinction between liberal (macroeconomic) and socialist (microeconomic) planning with which Sir Alec Cairncross has made us familiar.[21]

One obvious feature of the claims for post-war macroeconomic management is the claim to novelty. This even bursts through the staid prose of the White Paper: 'The Government are prepared to accept in future the responsibility for taking action at the earliest possible stage to arrest a threatened slump. This involves a new approach and a new responsibility for the State.'[22] Here was an explicit contrast with the old belief that trade depression automatically brought its own corrective. 'In these matters', it was proclaimed, 'we shall be pioneers.'[23]

3

The peroration to the White Paper sets its economic aspirations within a political framework: 'The Government believe that, once the war has been won, we can make a fresh approach, with better chances of success than ever before, to the task of maintaining a high and stable level of employment without sacrificing the essential liberties of a free society.'[24] So far, so uplifting. The implicit objection here, of course, was that mounted in its classic form by F.A. Hayek's *Road to Serfdom*. As Hirschman has shown, Hayek's critique of the welfare state can be seen as an example of the argument that such a proposal, far from achieving the best, would actually *jeopardize* the good.[25] As such it is essentially political, asserting the incompatibility of regulation with liberty. The sort of planning associated with full-employment policies was equally his target: indeed more so, since he seized on the essentially macroeconomic nature of the project to bring out its danger.

> Many separate plans do not make a planned whole – in fact, as the planners ought to be the first to admit they may be worse than no plan. But the democratic legislature will long hesitate to relinquish the decisions on really vital issues, and so long as it does so it makes it impossible for anyone else to provide the comprehensive plan. Yet agreement that planning is necessary, together with the inability of democratic assemblies to produce a plan, will evoke stronger and stronger demands that the government or some single individual should be given powers to act on their own responsibility. The belief is becoming more and more widespread that, if things are to get done, the responsible authorities must be freed from the fetters of democratic procedure.[26]

This gave the special reason – though of course there were many others – 'why "liberal socialism" as most people in the Western world imagine it is purely theoretical, while the practice of socialism is everywhere totalitarian'.[27] The support of the Labour Party for planning was not wholly surprising, but Hayek hinted at the futility as well as the jeopardy which lay in train: 'It is one of the saddest spectacles of our time to see a great democratic movement support a policy which must lead to the destruction of democracy and which meanwhile can benefit only a minority of the masses who support it.'[28] Such arguments entered into post-war Conservative propaganda, albeit often in a watered-down form.[29]

If Hayek's political argument against Keynesianism was much the same as his argument against the welfare state, and was unsurprisingly directed against broadly the same opponents, it should likewise be unsurprising that this famous economist also mounted a specifically economic argument. In its weak form this rested on the futility of trying to buck the markets; in its strong form, which should not be overlooked, it pointed to perverse effects. Hayek contested Keynes head-on, asserting a dichotomous view of the available economic strategies. 'Both competition and central direction become poor and inefficient tools if they are incomplete; they are alternative principles used to solve the same problem, and a mixture of the two means that neither will really work and that the result will be worse than if either system had been consistently relied upon.'[30]

Keynes took issue with this view, in the course of an otherwise highly emollient private response to Hayek: 'I should say that what we want is not no planning, or even less planning, indeed I should say that we almost certainly want more.'[31] He remained wholly unmoved by Hayek's fundamental economic contention that this sort of planning was dysfunctional, whereas for Hayek a nightmare scenario was already foretold: 'if we are determined not to allow unemployment at any price, and are not willing to use coercion, we shall be driven to all sorts of desperate expedients, none of which can bring any lasting relief and all of which will seriously interfere with the most productive use of our resources.' The prospect was of 'an inflationary expansion on such a scale that the disturbances, hardships, and injustices caused would be much greater than those to be cured'.[32]

What is plainly disclosed, of course, as these spiralling counter-effects progressively cancel the early gains, is an economic situation worse than the problems which these naive expedients were designed to remedy in the first place:

There will always be a possible maximum of employment in the short run which can be achieved by giving all people employment where they happen to be and which can be achieved by monetary expansion. But not only can this maximum be maintained solely by progressive inflationary expansion and with the effect of holding up those redistributions of labour between industries made necessary by the changed circumstances, and which so long as workmen are free to choose their jobs will always come about only with some delays and thereby cause some unemployment: to aim always at the maximum of employment achievable by monetary means is a policy which is certain in the end to defeat its own purpose. It tends to lower the productivity of labour and thereby constantly increases the proportion of the working population which can be kept employed at present wages only by artificial means.[33]

Here is a different case from the political argument with which the polemical author of *The Road to Serfdom* is generally identified: a case, however, which is easily assimilated with the rest of the oeuvre of the great apostle of economic liberalism. Hayek's distinctive doctrinaire approach has often been contrasted with the abhorrence of rationalism which is to be found in writers like Oakeshott. Yet there is another face to Hayek's argument which is far more conservative than liberal in its justification of 'men's submission to the impersonal forces of the market' – the more so when this was justified by an appeal to such forces as superstition. Such a commendation of conservative instincts appealed to a deeper rationale than vulgar rationalism. 'It may indeed be the case that infinitely more intelligence on the part of everybody would be needed than anybody now possesses, if we were even merely to maintain our present complex civilisation without anybody having to do things of which he does not comprehend the necessity', Hayek enjoined. 'The refusal to yield to forces which we neither understand nor can recognise as the conscious decisions of an intelligent being is the product of an incomplete and therefore erroneous rationalism.'[34]

4

It was Keynes not Hayek who captured the ear of the opinion-forming elite in post-war Britain. In particular the canonical status of the *General Theory* was now assured, as much by vague invocation as by specific citation. The White Paper went as far as was decent in making this plain:

> the Government recognise that they are entering a field where theory can be applied to practical issues with confidence and certainty only as experience accumulates and experiment extends over untried ground. Not long ago, the ideas embodied in the present proposals were unfamiliar to the general public and the subject of controversy among economists. To-day, the conception of an expansionist economy and the broad principles governing its growth are widely accepted by men of affairs as well as by technical experts in all the great industrial countries.[35]

In the two post-war books commissioned by Penguin from Labour and Conservative spokesmen, giving their cases access to a mass paperback market, there are differences of emphasis, as one would expect. Thus Quintin Hogg's account is imbued with caution:

> Unemployment can temporarily be mitigated, and perhaps eliminated in a country, notwithstanding its international character, by government action which artificially increases demand in any way. This, however, means to some extent adopting a closed economy which, internationally speaking, is anti-social, and may involve the assumption of dictatorial powers. Moreover, unless the demand is carefully selected

this palliative cannot last long. It cannot in any event last indefinitely unless ultimately world conditions improve.[36]

Conversely, in John Parker's account there was a residual flavour of socialist scepticism about relying on market mechanisms – 'since it must be remembered that in one sense labour is always being "directed" by the demands of consumers' – to achieve what Cripps was now terming 'democratic' planning, as distinct from the 'totalitarian' kind.[37]

Yet Hogg's and Parker's accounts of the 1930s are on broadly similar lines. A wrong-headed approach, it was held, had been adopted in meeting the 1931 crisis; but this could be extenuated and excused in the absence of a fully articulated Keynesian agenda. According to Quintin Hogg, it was not really a partisan matter – 'The Labour Government are not to be blamed for not following this course' – and instead he cited the Keynesian claim, 'with which I, as a Conservative, agree, that given low rates of interest, high wages, and adequate social security (for this is what redistribution means) this terrible scourge can again be relegated to the category of minor nuisances and we shall be free to face the real problem of civilisation – the lifting of humanity out of the primeval slime.'[38]

Writing in the *New Fabian Essays*, five years later, John Strachey appealed to the post-war experience of both Britain and the USA to show how a democratic government could raise the standard of life – provided it had not only the will but also the expertise. 'The government of the left when installed must know how to give effect to the push of the democratic forces', he wrote, mindful of the historical contrast with Léon Blum in France and Ramsay MacDonald in Britain. 'The techniques for making an economic system work at full power – granted one has the will to do so – were in fact only worked out in the nineteen-thirties. The elucidations of the late Lord Keynes have in this respect played a genuine historical role.'[39]

What were these much-lauded techniques? Keynes himself had a longstanding record of wishing to regulate investment so as to make full use of resources, and in the *General Theory* he accordingly suggested 'a somewhat comprehensive socialisation of investment'. The post-war nationalization measures in Britain, however, hardly fulfilled his criteria of controlling the overall volume of investment, whether public or private – 'it is not the ownership of the instruments of production which it is important for the State to assume.'[40] Nonetheless, Labour appealed to a synergy between its nationalisation programme and a full-employment policy, under the elastic rubric of planning. They had seen the future – and it worked. Thus, looking back on the record of the Attlee Government in 1952, Austen Albu could claim that, insofar as the rationale for the nationalization programme had lain here, it had achieved its objective: 'The dominating motive in 1945 of planning for full employment has been satisfied with only one-fifth of industry nationalised, and there is a growing view that, in so far as internal conditions are concerned, this can be continued.'[41]

In regulating the level of effective demand Keynes's instincts were always to concentrate on investment. Practically all that the *General Theory* said about consumption was: 'The State will have to exercise a guiding influence on the propensity to consume partly through its scheme of taxation, partly by fixing the rate of interest, and partly, perhaps, in other ways.'[42] Under the Labour Government, there was a commitment to macroeconomic management of the level of demand through fiscal policy, supplemented by the use of direct controls to keep inflationary pressure in check. This is how Sir Stafford Cripps explained the matter in his Budget speech of 1950: 'Excessive demand produces inflation and inadequate demand results in deflation. The fiscal policy of the Government is the most important single instrument for maintaining that balance.'[43]

By contrast, the use of monetary policy as an economic regulator smacked of the bad old deflationary days of the Gold Standard, and was abjured by Labour. In taking this line Dalton could initially claim both theoretical and practical endorsement from Keynes. Keynes repeatedly stressed the desirability of bringing down the rate to a low *and stable* level (in this sense 'fixing' the rate). Keynes's often-quoted notion of bringing about 'the euthanasia of the rentier'[44] made a natural appeal to Labour supporters, not least Dalton himself. But although the Bank of England's discount rate remained fixed at the level of only 2 per cent until the Labour Government lost office at the end of 1951, it is now clear that Gaitskell as Chancellor was ready in principle to use monetary policy in support of budgetary policy – a case which his revisionist supporter Crosland was to elaborate in *The Future of Socialism* (1956).[45]

5

It was in the *New Fabian Essays* (1952) that Crosland broached his fairly complacent assessment of the post-capitalist nature of contemporary Britain:

> The trend of employment is towards a high level, and a recurrence of chronic mass unemployment is most unlikely. The Keynesian techniques are now well understood, and there is no reason to fear a repetition of the New Deal experience of a government with the will to spend its way out of a recession, but frustrated in doing so by faulty knowledge. The political pressure for full employment is stronger than ever before; the experience of the inter-war years bit so deeply into the political psychology of the nation that full employment, if threatened, would always constitute the dominant issue at any election, and no right-wing party could now survive a year in office if it permitted the figures of unemployment which were previously quite normal.[46]

Such confidence – hubris is another word – had not grown overnight. At the end of the war there had been a general expectation that the post-1945 experience would parallel that of post-1918: a couple of years' inflationary boom, with a slump around the corner. This fear was implicit in the 1944 White Paper. It was a prospect which, as John Parker reported, 'most British socialists believe to be inevitable, although they are not agreed on the date when the slump is likely to arrive, nor what course it is likely to follow'.[47] True, Dalton's Budget speech in April 1947 said that inflation rather than deflation was now the immediate danger. Yet Meade, writing in 1948, when inflation was already at the front of his own mind, prefaced his arguments with the comment: 'We are all agreed that measures must be taken to stimulate total monetary demand and to prevent it from falling below the level necessary to sustain a high output and high employment when the time next comes – as sooner or later it assuredly will come – when a deficient total demand threatens to engulf us in a major depression.'[48]

It was only from 1951 that a wholly different assumption about the nature of the economic problem supplied a new context for all these arguments. This occurred initially in the context of a rearmament programme which injected a huge boost of demand into the economy; as a proportion of GNP, defence spending rose by 3.5 per cent in three years while the budget surplus was cut by nearly 5 per cent between 1951 and 1954.[49] Little wonder that economists – *a fortiori* the Keynesian revisionists represented in *New Fabian Essays* – stopped worrying about a slump. Even so, Strachey still qualified his judgement that, in most major respects, 'our economy is exhibiting behaviour quite different from that which it exhibited during the whole of the inter-war period' with the proviso that 'it may be argued that it is as yet too early to claim that we have succeeded in eliminating trade depressions'.[50] But although it may have been judged premature to dismiss any possibility of a slump, *fear* of a slump had nonetheless disappeared because the weapons now existed to fight it – even if there should prove to be insufficient cleverness in anticipating and obviating it. The old-fashioned capitalist misery had been abolished, perhaps capitalism too. 'It is now quite clear that capitalism has not the strength to resist the process of metamorphosis into a qualitatively different kind of society' was how Crosland put it, and a further conclusion naturally followed: 'Such an economy is far more likely to give rise to chronic inflation than chronic deflation.'[51]

Out of the frying pan into the fire? Not a bit of it! Strachey peremptorily refused to admit that 'the unmistakable fact that a full employment economy generates powerful inflationary forces is a fatal defect: it is a bias in the new system which must be identified and vigorously counteracted. But granted that it is done, there is nothing fatal about it.'[52] If the great locomotive of economic expansion had exceeded expectations about the horsepower it was capable of sustaining, this was simply a condition to which its suitably skilled driver would have to adapt: 'The habitual posture of the Chancellor of the Exchequer in a full employment economy will be that of a man pulling and hauling with might and main at the brake levers of the economy. It will not be a very popular or comfortable posture. But what of it? It is his job!'[53]

The steam-Keynesianism of the Labour revisionists was superseded by a fittingly privatized image from the impresario of Conservative Keynesianism in the 1950s, Harold Macmillan: 'The real truth is that both a brake and an accelerator are essential for a motor car; their use is a matter of judgement but their purpose must remain essentially the same – to go forward safely; or, in economic terms, expansion in a balanced economy.'[54] The main difference in demand management under the Conservatives was the reinforcement of fiscal fine tuning with a monetary policy that now used interest-rate changes to the same ends. Here was the optimistic vision of progress in controlling and regulating the macroeconomic forces which could maintain full employment while keeping inflation in check. Stop-go, of course, was one name for this kind of economic policy; and 'Butskellism' for the political consensus which underpinned it. Samuel Brittan offered this summary in 1964:

> It was an interesting mixture of planning and freedom, based on the economic teachings of Lord Keynes. Planning during this period was concerned with one global total – the amount the nation was spending on goods and services – the 'level of demand' in economists' language. If production sagged, or unemployment looked like creeping up, extra purchasing power was pumped into the system through the Budget, the banks, or the hire-purchase houses. If employment was a bit too full or the pound came under strain, demand was withdrawn through these same channels.[55]

The crucial constraint was an implicit trade-off between unemployment and inflation, which was formalized in the well-known 'Phillips curve' in 1958.[56] If there was a consensus on macroeconomic policy at this time, as I believe there was, it was about this constraint on the available political options, not about whether to opt for lower unemployment at the risk of higher inflation or vice versa – issues on which Labour and Conservatives naturally differed.

6

It was the very existence of this constraining framework which was to be the butt of the so-called monetarist counter-attack. According to Friedman's famous homily on monetarism in 1967, 'there is always a temporary trade-off between inflation and unemployment; there is no permanent trade-off. The temporary trade-off comes not from inflation per se, but from unanticipated inflation, which generally means, from a rising rate of inflation.'[57] The futility of such tinkering is the obvious message, and, as Hirschman has observed, one nicely calculated to provoke maximum exasperation and asperity.[58] Yet it should not be overlooked that the charge of futility levelled against Keynesian policies has often been supplemented – possibly in an otiose way – by the further claim that such policies produce not merely self-cancelling but actually perverse effects. Thus Friedman accused the monetary authorities of 'a propensity to overreact' which meant that 'they feel impelled to step on the brake, or the accelerator, as the case may be, too hard'.[59] Macmillan's motor-car was thus subject to disastrously erratic regulation, as at least one of its passengers (Sir Keith Joseph) ruefully testified in retrospect:

> The effect of over-reacting to temporary recession has been to push up inflation to ever higher levels, not to help the unemployed, but to increase their numbers. Thus excessive injections of money, undertaken by intelligent and enlightened men with good intentions, have wrought great havoc in our economy and society. The benefits have been largely temporary - and in any case cruelly reversed in the inevitable 'stop' that follows, but the evil has lived on.[60]

It is tempting to think of the monetarist critique as a mirror-image of the post-war consensus which it subverted: as a rival panacea asserted with the same cocksure triumphalism of which Keynesians had been guilty a generation previously. A glance at how monetarism was sold, and thereby subjected to its own process of ideological debasement, would hardly dispel such an impression. The keen mind of Nigel Lawson, for example, was not inhibited by undue intellectual humility. When he disclosed his thoughts about the role of macro- and microeconomic policy in his Mais lecture in 1984, he claimed that

> the proper role of each is precisely the opposite of that assigned to it by the conventional post-War wisdom. It is the conquest of inflation, and not the pursuit of growth and employment, which is or should be the objective of macroeconomic policy. And it is the creation of conditions conducive to growth and employment, and not the suppression of price rises, which is or should be the objective of microeconomic policy.[61]

If Keynes had left macroeconomic policy standing on its head, Lawson's world-historical role was evidently to turn it the right way up again.

The radical doctrines of the left may thus be mirrored by the radical doctrines of the right; but perhaps they are more tellingly countered by a sober appeal to the intractable realities of an imperfect world. In this sense Friedman's most effective thrust was surely the general caveat which he entered about our inherent fallibility in action, because of inherent flaws in our information:

> We simply do not know enough to be able to recognise minor disturbances when they occur or to be able to predict either what their effects will be with any precision or what monetary policy is required to offset their effects. We do not know enough to be able to achieve stated objectives by delicate, or even fairly coarse, changes in the mix of monetary and fiscal policy.[62]

The futility of pitting our puny wits against the complex battery of information marshalled by the sophisticated signals of the free market was an insight which Friedman could well have learnt at Hayek's knee. It proved to be the more prescient part of an economic case against macroeconomic planning, whereas Hayek's political diatribe against the spectre of serfdom, however understandable at the time, later seemed alarmist. The rhetoric of reaction was in this sense better served by arguments which struck an affinity with an authentically conservative temperament, founded on scepticism about projects for the improvement of the human condition. The polemics of progress, conversely, ultimately rang hollow in claiming too much for the macroeconomic competence of post-war government, ignoring at their peril the salutary cautions buried in the 1944 White Paper. I have already quoted its claim that 'we shall be pioneers'. This was immediately tempered with the injunction: 'We must determine, therefore, to learn from experience; to invent and improve the instruments of our new policy as we move forward to its goal. And it would be no less foolish to ignore, than to be dismayed by, the certainty that unsuspected obstacles will emerge in practice.'[63]

Notes

1. I have dealt with this debate in *The Keynesian Revolution in the Making, 1924–36* (Oxford, 1988) and 'The Treasury's analytical model of the British economy between the wars', in Barry Supple and Mary Furner (eds), *The State and Economic Knowledge* (Cambridge, 1990), pp. 171–207, [reprinted as ch. 7 in this volume]. I am grateful to Stefan Collini, John Thompson and Maria Tippett, as well as to members of the Sheffield conference of April 1994, for their criticism of an earlier draft.
2. Citations from the entry by Hal R. Varian, *The New Palgrave*, ed. John Eatwell, Murray Milgate and Peter Newman (1987), *sub* 'microeconomics'.
3. *JMK*, vol. 7, p. 85.
4. *JMK*, vol. 7, p. xxxii.
5. *JMK*, vol. 21, pp. 387, 390 ('How to avoid a slump', Jan. 1937).
6. For an expansion of the points in this and the previous paragraph see 'The historical Keynes and the history of Keynesianism', ch. 1 above. In both that and the present essay I lean on the fine studies of policy-making by Alec Cairncross, *Years of Recovery: British Economic Policy, 1945–51* (1985); Alan Booth, *British Economic Policy, 1931–49: Was There a Keynesian Revolution?* (1989); Susan Howson, *British Monetary Policy, 1945–51* (Oxford, 1993)
7. *Social Insurance and Allied Services: Report by Sir William Beveridge*, Cmd 6404 (Nov. 1942), par. 8.
8. Cf. Albert. Hirschman, *The Rhetoric of Reaction* (1991), p. 151.
9. Cmd 6404, par. 441.
10. Cmd 6404, par. 440.
11. *Employment Policy*, Cmd 6527 (May 1944), foreword.
12. See Nigel Lawson's introduction to Walter Eltis and Peter Sinclair (eds), *Keynes and Economic Policy* (1988), pp. xv–xvi; also quotations from pars 49 and 77.
13. Cmd 6527, par. 66.
14. *JMK*, vol. 27, pp. 377–9 (Keynes to Sir Alan Barlow, 15 June 1944).
15. Cmd 6527, foreword.
16. Cmd 6527, par. 40.
17. Cmd 6527, par. 68.
18. Cmd 6527, par. 17. Correlli Barnett has tendentiously glossed this episode as a triumph for the 'glib confidence' of 'New Jerusalemism'; see *The Audit of War* (1986), pp. 257–63.

19. John Parker, *Labour Marches On* (Penguin, 1947), p. 55.
20. James Edward Meade, *Planning and the Price Mechanism: The Liberal-Socialist Solution* (1948), p. v.
21. Cairncross, *Years of Recovery*, pp. 308–9.
22. Cmd 6527, par. 41.
23. Cmd 6527, par. 80.
24. Cmd 6527, par. 87.
25. Hirschman, *Rhetoric of Reaction*, pp. 110ff.
26. F.A. Hayek, *The Road to Serfdom* (1944), p. 50.
27. Hayek, *Road to Serfdom*, pp. 151–2.
28. Hayek, *Road to Serfdom*, p. 148.
29. See Quintin Hogg, *The Case for Conservatism* (Penguin, 1947), pp. 220–1.
30. Hayek, *Road to Serfdom*, p. 31.
31. *JMK*, vol. 27, pp. 386–7 (Keynes to Hayek, 28 June 1944).
32. Hayek, *Road to Serfdom*, p. 154.
33. Hayek, *Road to Serfdom*, p. 154.
34. Hayek, *Road to Serfdom*, pp. 151–2.
35. Cmd 6527, par. 80.
36. Hogg, *Case for Conservatism*, pp. 220–1.
37. Parker, *Labour Marches On*, p. 56.
38. Hogg, *Case for Conservatism*, pp. 219, 223–4.
39. John Strachey, 'Tasks and achievements of British Labour', in R.H.S. Crossman (ed.), *New Fabian Essays* (1952; new edn 1970), pp. 189–90.
40. *JMK*, vol. 7, p. 378.
41. Austen Albu, 'The organisation of industry', in Crossman (ed.), *New Fabian Essays*, p. 127.
42. *JMK*, vol. 7, p. 378.
43. Sir Stafford Cripps, quoted in Edward Bridges, *The Treasury* (1966), p. 93.
44. *JMK*, vol. 7, p. 376.
45. See pp. 409–14 and the authoritative treatment in Howson, *British Monetary Policy*, pp. 291–2, 305–7.
46. C.A.R. Crosland, 'The transition from capitalism', in Crossman (ed.), *New Fabian Essays*, pp. 39–40.
47. Parker, *Labour Marches On*, p. 56; cf. Howson, *British Monetary Policy*, pp. 25, 50, 120, 146–7.
48. James Meade, *Planning and the Price Mechanism* (1948), p. 12.; cf. Howson, *British Monetary Policy*, p. 163.
49. I have substantiated this point in 'The historical Keynes and the history of Keynesianism', ch. 1 above.
50. Strachey, 'Tasks and achievements of British Labour', in Crossman (ed.), *New Fabian Essays*, p. 185.
51. Crosland, 'The transition from capitalism', in Crossman (ed.), *New Fabian Essays*, pp. 38, 41.
52. Strachey, 'Tasks and achievements of British Labour', in Crossman (ed.), *New Fabian Essays*, p. 196.
53. Ibid., p. 197.
54. Harold Macmillan, 'The Middle Way – 20 Years After' (1958), in H. Macmillan, *The Middle Way* (new edn, 1966), p. xxv.
55. Samuel Brittan, *The Treasury under the Tories* (Penguin, 1964), p. 162.
56. A.W. Phillips, 'The relation between unemployment and the rate of change of money wages in the United Kingdom, 1861–1957', *Economica*, xxv (1958).
57. Milton Friedman, 'The role of monetary policy' (1967), in *The Optimum Quantity of Money* (1969), p. 104.
58. Hirschman, *Rhetoric of Reaction*, pp. 45, 74.
59. Friedman, *Optimum Quantity of Money*, p. 109.
60. Sir Keith Joseph, speech at Preston, *The Times*, 6 Sept. 1974.
61. Nigel Lawson, *The View from No. 11. Memoirs of a Tory Radical* (1992), pp. 414–15.
62. Friedman, *Optimum Quantity of Money*, p. 107.
63. Cmd 6527, par. 80.

Index